THE CEO BOOK

Navigate the Twelve Habits of
Highly Successful CEOs

JOHN HALE

www.halecg.com

Copyright © 2024 by John Hale. All rights reserved.

Published by Hale Consulting Group
15 Manning Street
South Brisbane 4101 Australia
www.halecg.com

This book or any portion thereof may not be reproduced or used in any manner without the author's express written permission.

Limit of Liability/Disclaimer of Warranty: While the publisher and author have used their best efforts in preparing this book, they make no representations or warranties regarding the accuracy or completeness of the contents of this book and expressly disclaim any implied warranties of merchantability or fitness for a particular purpose. No warranty may be created or extended by sales representatives or written sales materials. The publisher and author are not acting as advisors in this book.

This book and the content provided herein are simply for educational purposes and do not in any way take the place of business advice from a professional advisor, be that strategic, financial, legal or otherwise. The information and strategies contained herein may not be suitable for your situation. This book includes non-factual models and metaphors from the author's life, narratives, and ideas adapted from many sources.

All efforts have been made to ensure that the content provided in this book is inspiring and helpful for readers. However, this book only partially treats the subjects contained within it. The author assumes no liability for losses or damages due to the information provided. You are responsible for your own choices, actions and results.

Illustrations: Silvia Roos and Megan Taylor
Book Design: Jana Rade

FIRST EDITION
Paperback: ISBN 978-0-6486590-6-8
E-Book: ISBN 978-0-6486590-7-5

 A catalogue record for this book is available from the National Library of Australia

For Sean and David

*I love your passion for life
and everything you do.*

ALSO BY THE AUTHOR

The Strategy Book

The Strategy Note

The Strategic Accountant

CONTENTS

PREFACE	1
INTRODUCTION	3
SECTION ONE - CARE FOR YOUR PEOPLE	11
HABIT ONE - BUILD GENUINE SAFETY	13
CARE FOR PEOPLE	16
MAINTAIN TRUST	22
EMBRACE CONFLICT	27
HABIT TWO - ENERGISE MIDDLE MANAGERS	37
EMPOWER WOMEN'S VOICES	41
HIRE SMARTER PEOPLE	45
CHOOSE YOUR COMPANIONS	50
HABIT THREE - FOSTER DEEP EMPATHY	61
MODEL PRESENCE	71
COACH WITH EMPATHY	75
LEAD WITH CARE	78
HABIT FOUR - ELIMINATE POOR PERFORMERS	89
HIRE ALL STARS	94
INSTIL VALUED BEHAVIOURS	99
QUESTION YOUR COLLEAGUES	103

SECTION TWO - KNOW WHICH WAY TO GO — 117

HABIT FIVE - ANTICIPATE FUTURE TRENDS — 119
- SCAN THE HORIZON — 124
- NAME THE TRENDS — 133
- SHAPE THE FUTURE — 138

HABIT SIX - ESTABLISH SHARED PURPOSE — 145
- COMMUNICATE YOUR VISION — 149
- LEAD BY EXAMPLE — 152
- PROMOTE CONFIDENCE — 159

HABIT SEVEN - KEEP COMPETITORS CLOSE — 169
- ANALYSE THE COMPETITION — 172
- KNOW YOURSELF — 175
- MASTER COMBAT — 180

HABIT EIGHT - ENHANCE PERSONAL EFFECTIVENESS — 195
- PRIORITISE SELF-CARE — 202
- BALANCE WORK-LIFE — 209
- CULTIVATE SUPPORT NETWORKS — 212

SECTION THREE - ALIGN AND ALLOCATE RESOURCES — 221

HABIT NINE - EXPLAIN STRATEGY CLEARLY — 223
- COMMUNICATE CLEARLY — 226
- MANAGE CRISIS SITUATIONS — 229
- BE MEDIA SAVVY — 236

HABIT TEN - GOVERN RESOURCES PORTFOLIO — 247
- PROTECT YOUR INTELLIGENCE — 250
- MAKE SMART DECISIONS — 255
- GROW DIGITAL WINGS — 261

HABIT ELEVEN - MENTOR DIRECT REPORTS   273

    LEAD WITH VULNERABILITY   284
    ENCOURAGE CRITICAL THINKING   285
    REVIEW AFTER ACTION   289

HABIT TWELVE - MAXIMISE BOARD COMMITMENT   297

    BUILD OUTSTANDING BOARDS   300
    KNOW YOUR STAKEHOLDERS   304
    TACKLE DIFFICULT ASSIGNMENTS   314

CONCLUSION

    DANCING WITH WOLVES   328
    TWELVE CONSEQUENTIAL HABITS   330
    WISDOM FROM FRIENDS   333

APPENDIX ONE - ZHĀGĒN DE XIÀ DĀNTIÁN   341

APPENDIX TWO - THE ACE QUIZ   343

APPENDIX THREE - COST OF CAPITAL   349

APPENDIX FOUR - CEO QUIZ   355

APPENDIX FIVE - SCORE CEO QUIZ   369

APPENDIX SIX - CYBER RESILIENCE   371

APPENDIX SEVEN - CREATIVITY   377

INDEX OF ILLUSTRATIONS	383
GLOSSARY OF TERMS	387
BIBLIOGRAPHY	415
ACKNOWLEDGEMENTS	427
ABOUT THE AUTHOR	429

PREFACE

Stars pierced the night as we walked.

I asked, "Which way is North?"

Without resorting to his phone, Valentino raised his hand, dropping an imaginary vertical line midway between Orion's Belt and Sirius to the South Pole.

Valentino embodies what every CEO must cultivate - the ability to navigate.

"That's North!" he declared, gesturing in the opposite direction.

"Bravo!" I echoed.

I wrote this book for Valentino.

Why?

Whether he realises it or not, Valentino would be a passionate and caring CEO.

You may also be a passionate and caring leader. In this case, this book is for you too.

The success habits in this book have been gathered from diverse realms, including corporate, military and government. Take on the habits that serve your context and set aside those that do not.

Not all habits are universally applicable.

You may enjoy this book by reading it from beginning to end, or you may prefer to move ahead to a particular habit that is useful now.

Either strategy is fine.

This book has ample space for jotting down ideas, completing activities and doodling. Writing in this book will help to deepen your understanding and enhance your retention.

As the author of this book, I offer my insights and gratitude. I thank the mentors and clients who have shaped my understanding of leadership and the colleagues who have challenged my perspective.

To muses like Valentino, who unwittingly inspired the words that follow, I honour you.

INTRODUCTION

Rowan, a kind and measured soul, had just returned from a skiing holiday in Colorado.

With a smile as warm as the sun's embrace, he greeted me at La Belle Époque, a local café. La Belle Époque was a beautiful era in France, marked by prosperity and significant technological progress. As a retired CEO, Rowan had presided over a beautiful era at his advanced satellite communications company - a wild time with evolving industry standards.

For Rowan, survival meant navigating the complexities of competitive markets, product design and high-tech manufacturing. His one-hundred-strong team of engineers and managers achieved prosperity and significant technological progress. Under Rowan's leadership, his firm contributed one hundred million dollars to the Australian economy.

I discussed my plan for this book with Rowan. After reading the table of contents, Rowan felt that I had successfully captured the CEO's role. However, he mentioned that context dramatically influences what is required. He shared that letting people go had been the most challenging aspect of his role. Rowan reflected, 'I was too kind. At times, I needed a bit more mongrel.'

Rowan then recounted three primary functions that guided him for two decades:

1. Gaining employee buy-in.
2. Having a clear vision.
3. Ensuring alignment among all parts of the business.

After lunch, Rowan revealed his recent health scare. The beautiful era of Rowan's professional life put the shadow side of being a CEO in stark relief. This shadow health and well-being side is one I know well from working as a CEO Coach for over thirty years. Something my fellow CEO Coach, Dolores also appreciates.

Dolores helps CEOs confront their shadow, emphasising that ego management and self-care are pivotal. Self-awareness permits CEOs to wield their power with integrity. Self-care fosters greater compassion, which aids CEOs in assembling mutually accountable and ambitious teams with a distinct purpose.

Expanded awareness helps CEOs navigate volatility, uncertainty, complexity and ambiguity (VUCA), and increasingly chaotic contexts characterised by brittleness, anxiety, nonlinearity and incomprehensibility (BANI). We will examine how CEOs can approach VUCA and BANI in Habit Five.

My friend Graham has been the CEO of his global travel agency since its inception 45 years ago. He is the most humble, healthy and considerate CEO I have met. He exemplifies the ego management, self-care and expanded awareness Dolores promotes.

INTRODUCTION

Graham finished the most recent London Marathon in under six hours. He is adept at forming mutually accountable and ambitious teams and diligently fosters clarity amidst uncertainty. At the time of writing, he is steering a two-hundred-million-dollar global acquisition and investor roadshow to secure his company's future earnings and success. Graham inspired me to complete my first marathon.

So, what are Graham's secrets for prosperity?

Graham asserts that having the right leaders and team members accounts for approximately sixty to seventy per cent of a CEO's success.[1] Being persistent and patient is equally important, as most businesses take ten to fifteen years to achieve moderate success. Graham remains inquisitive and expansive in his thinking, which encompasses listening to and learning from smart people before forming his own opinions.

For Dolores, her work with CEOs is an ongoing journey of learning. My exchanges with Dolores explore the essence of leadership and its impact on humanity. Our dialogue often distils into questions about love. We continually prompt one another with, "What would love do in this situation?" - a guiding principle in our engagements with CEOs.

In a recent meeting with Dolores, I demonstrated how she might use a probability tree to help a CEO make an irreversible and consequential decision. We will explore the importance of these decisions in Habit Twelve. Dolores then asked me how I use the Enneagram in my practice. I explained that I utilise the Enneagram to help CEOs better understand themselves and others. The Enneagram is outside the scope of this book. However, Robert Bruce's new book, 'The Way of the Enneagram'[12] is something I often gift to my clients.

Before becoming an Enneagram teacher, Robert was an investment banker and strategy consultant. When asked, Robert named three key CEO responsibilities:

1. Care for your people.
2. Have ongoing strategic conversations to create the future.
3. Constantly raise your consciousness and your organisation's consciousness.

Dolores introduced me to Nicole, the CEO of a start-up in California dedicated to empowering CEOs and organisations to lead with authenticity and love.[3] When chatting with Nicole about my ideas for this book, Nicole conveyed her three secrets for being a successful CEO.

1. Have Faith - the kind of faith that moves mountains and makes the invisible real.
2. Embody Integrity - align your human faculties, thoughts, feelings and actions.
3. Be of Service - use your power to empower others.

Nicole reminded me that we are spiritual beings having uniquely human experiences and that some of us are called upon to play the CEO role. Nicole suggests that the CEO role does not define us. We refine it through our authenticity and giving.

So, what habits will you need to be successful?

INTRODUCTION

As Rowan suggested, the habits you will need depend on the context.

Graham and Robert suggest that having the right team and caring for them is vital. Patience and perseverance are required. Remaining curious and engaging in regular dialogues about the future helps CEOs identify the best path forward. Dolores and Nicole believe consciousness, integrity and compassion enable CEOs to align their internal and firmwide resources while maintaining faith in the face of uncertainty.

My answer is like that of my friends. To be successful, CEOs must:

1. Care for their people.
2. Know which way to go.
3. Align and allocate resources.

When I allocated time to find some accessible and shining examples of leadership, it was easy. There are millions of successful leaders all over the world. To illustrate the success habits of CEOs, I selected twelve recognised and successful but not always universally admired leaders.

The twelve habits are sorted into three sections.

The first four habits will assist you in **caring for your people**.

In Habit One, we encounter the most successful coach in the history of basketball, Gregg Popovich, who *builds genuine safety* for his players. In Habit Two, we meet Estée Lauder, who birthed an entire industry by empowering women and *energising middle managers*. In Habit Three, we learn how Satya Nadella, CEO of Microsoft, united a divided culture by *fostering deep empathy*. In Habit Four, we meet Netflix's Founder and CEO, Reed Hastings, who ensures the highest talent level by *eliminating poor performers*. Something Rowan struggled to do.

The next four habits help you to **know which way to go**.

In Habit Five, we meet Mohammed bin Salman (MBS), the Crown Prince of Saudi Arabia, who shows us how to *anticipate trends* and embrace the future. In Habit Six, we learn from Elon Musk, the King of Big Hairy Audacious Goals (BHAGs), about the power of *establishing a shared purpose*. Then, in Habit Seven, I divulge why *keeping competitors close* is crucial through the story of YouTube CEO Susan Wojcicki. In Habit Eight, we meet Katrina Lake, CEO of Stitch Fix, who shows us why CEOs need to *enhance their personal effectiveness*.

The last four habits will help you **align and allocate resources.**

In Habit Nine, we imagine life as Apple CEO Tim Cook, who *explains strategy clearly* and installs policies that ensure everyone works towards the same objectives. In Habit Ten, we encounter Ken Frazier, CEO of Merck & Co, who is skilled at *governing the resources portfolio*: people, social capital, assets, finance, IP and technology. In Habit Eleven, I introduce you to Navy Seal Commander Dave 'Coop' Cooper, who helped his fellow SEALS shed light and save lives by *mentoring direct reports*. Lastly, in Habit Twelve, PepsiCo CEO Indra Nooyi shows us how to *maximise board commitment* by engaging diverse boards, knowing her industry and tackling difficult assignments.

Are you ready?

INTRODUCTION

In our first habit, we lay the groundwork of safety and constructive conflict with Coach Pop to build a spirit of teamwork - Esprit de corps.

SECTION ONE
CARE FOR YOUR PEOPLE

Habit One - Build Genuine Safety

Habit Two - Energise Middle Managers

Habit Three - Foster Deep Empathy

Habit Four - Eliminate Poor Performers

HABIT ONE
BUILD GENUINE SAFETY

GREGG POPOVICH
SAN ANTONIO SPURS

Care For People
Maintain Trust
Embrace Conflict

The moment Pop calls for a timeout, I feel a surge of anticipation.

The AT&T Centre, usually filled with cheers and chants, falls into a hush. I lean forward, my eyes glued to the Jumbotron above, which displays the huddle.

The silence breaks as stuntman Michael Costello, dressed as Coyote, skips across the court and shoots tightly wrapped Spurs t-shirts into the crowd with an air cannon.

Back in the huddle, Pop is sketching out a play. His players safely encircled around him, sharing their ideas.

I'm struck by the shifting atmosphere - from the crowd's buzz to the concentrated player intimacy - which is a testament to Pop's generosity and leadership.

I'm not just a spectator. I feel like part of the team, connected by a deeper resolve.

There's a palpable sense of unity and purpose in the huddle.

As the timeout ends, Pop offers,

"It's not about any one person. You've got to get over yourself and realise that it takes a group to get this done."

I am hopeful. I feel secure, ready to witness the San Antonio Spurs rally and respond, assured of the winning pivot they are about to make.

HABIT ONE: BUILD GENUINE SAFETY

A safe culture is one in which people feel comfortable speaking up, expressing their ideas and taking risks without fear of retribution.[4] They feel physically and emotionally safe and are treated with respect and dignity.[5]

Please read that last sentence again.

They feel physically and emotionally safe and are treated with respect and dignity.

When cultures are safe, strategic conversations are easy and people learn faster.[6] When people feel unsafe, 'culture eats strategy for breakfast.'[7]

The average tenure for an NBA coach is 2.4 years, the lowest average tenure among all professional sports. After 30 years as Head Coach of the Spurs, Gregg Popovich's longevity and success are the result of three things: caring for people, maintaining trust and actively embracing conflict.

The optimal term for a public company CEO is 12 years.[8] However, the average CEO tenure is closer to 6 years, which keeps shrinking.[9] Boards and CEOs should take a leaf out of Popovich's book.

CARE FOR PEOPLE

To care for people, CEOs need to be more like coaches, treating people issues or the 'soft stuff' as the hard piece of the puzzle.[10] Paradoxically, the easy parts are often the so-called hard issues like finding capital, managing cash flow and strategy formulation. People issues can be hard work.

Intellectually, a CEO needs to understand Theory X and Theory Y[11] as it applies to their people.

Theory X assumes that employees are frequently lazy, avoid responsibility and are indifferent to organisational goals. Theory X contends that employees prefer to be directed by others. As a result, leaders must actively manage employees and allocate resources. Such employees need close supervision and motivation via rewards and punishments.[12]

With Theory X, an Authoritative Leadership style is required. Authoritative Leaders provide direction and have a clear vision of what success looks like. They give team members regular constructive feedback as they work towards delivering on the strategy.

Theory Y assumes that employees are self-motivated, seek responsibility, and look for creative ways to help deliver on the strategy. It contends that employees prefer to direct themselves. As a result, leaders must partner creatively with employees in allocating work and resources. Such employees find meaning in their work and enjoy the rewards that follow.

HABIT ONE: BUILD GENUINE SAFETY

With Theory Y, work supervision is not required, and threats of punishment add little extra motivation. Theory Y suggests that a Participatory Leadership style is needed in most instances. Participatory Leaders ensure team members work together on problems, challenges and issues. Sometimes, team members vote on various options they have created together.

Popovich's coaching style demonstrates elements of both Theory X and Theory Y.

On the one hand, Popovich is known for his strict and demanding coaching approach. He has high expectations for his players and holds them accountable for their performance.[13] This could reflect a Theory X approach, as Popovich's expectations and accountability measures could be seen as a form of control and supervision.

At the same time, Popovich is known for his ability to connect with his players and his willingness to give them the freedom to make decisions and take risks on the court.[14] This could reflect a Theory Y approach, as his supportive and empowering leadership style fosters self-motivation and self-direction in his players.

Overall, Pop's coaching style illustrates the complexity of motivation and how different approaches can be used to stay effective in shifting situations.

Applying a Participatory Leadership style to a Theory X employee or an Authoritative Leadership style to a Theory Y employee can waste time and energy, especially if the organisational culture is unsafe and employees are not cared for.

Pop's care for his players is legendary. He prioritises the health of his players, often sitting out even marginally tired players to ensure that they are solid and well-rested for the next game.[15]

Pop actively avoids recruiting selfish, lazy and 'precious' All-Star players. At San Antonio, the team is the star and the players are selfless. When speaking about the Spurs, Lakers' All-Star LeBron James says, "Guys move, cut, pass, you've got a shot, you take it. But it is all for the team and never about the individual."[16]

Pop understands that talent can win games, but teamwork and intelligence win championships. In their 45-season history, the Spurs have made the playoffs 38 times and won six NBA titles. Pop coached the team to five of those titles.

What is Pop's secret?

Courtside, Pop is an old-school and unapologetic Authoritarian Leader. He has been described as having a demanding and strict approach to coaching.[17] Pop is famous for his blunt style and volcanic courtside outbursts:

"For fuck's sake. I can't make every decision for you."

"I don't have 14 timeouts. You guys have got to get together and talk!"

"Next guy who misses a free throw will buy me a new car!"

Pop is also a Participatory Leader.

HABIT ONE: BUILD GENUINE SAFETY

Pop is known for his ability to involve his players in the decision-making process and to give them the freedom to make decisions on the court.[18]

Off the court, Pop looks less like a court marshalling general and more like a friendly uncle at a BBQ.[19] When he can, Pop shifts and moves in close - so close that his nose nearly touches his players. He takes a genuine interest in the culture of his players' countries, partners, and kids. Pop chats to his players in several languages, as there are often players from seven or more countries on the team.

Pop connects with each player after games. He is often seen smiling, with his face set in a lopsided and toothy grin, and he says, "Love you, brother." He often gives each player a heartfelt bear hug before moving on to the next player.[20]

The Spurs assistant coach, Chip England, conveys that Pop is unlike most coaches, "A lot of coaches can yell or be nice. Pop does both. He delivers two things together: he will tell you the truth with no BS, and then he'll love you to death."

The Spurs eat together as often as they play basketball. There are team dinners. There are smaller group dinners with just a handful of players. And coaches' dinners happen on the road before a game. Pop plans all the dinners, picking the wines and restaurants.[21]

Most evenings, Pop invites everyone to reflect.

"What did you think of today's game?"

"What would you have done in that situation?"

Pop prefers the Optimal Zone in Figure 1.1. This is the sweet spot where he can deploy a Participatory Leadership style with self-directed and responsible team players (Theory Y). Pop avoids Theory X by ensuring Spurs Scouts never recruit selfish or lazy NBA All-Stars.

Figure 1.1 Leadership Theory Matrix

HABIT ONE: BUILD GENUINE SAFETY

Pop's scouting template includes a tick box marked "Not a Spur." A tick in that box means that the Spurs will never recruit that player, regardless of talent.

The Spurs' culture is legendary for its care. Spurs players feel safe, and their teamwork and winning record are the envy of the NBA.

Deep down, each Spurs' team member knows that Pop believes in them. Yet, even when the Spurs are playing perfectly together, Pop will always find room for improvement!

Candid and frank dialogue is needed. When CEOs and their people care personally for each other, both parties can directly challenge the other.

If leaders challenge but do not care, people experience their leaders as oppressive and aggressive.[22]

If leaders care but do not challenge, people will keep their thoughts hidden.

If leaders do not care or challenge, people may behave insincerely and manipulate their situation, degrading trust.

MAINTAIN TRUST

Trust can be earned in one of two ways: affectively, through relationships, or task-based, through knowledge of a situation.

Pop's basketball intelligence quotient (IQ) and knowledge earn him task-based trust with his team.

Pop's emotional intelligence (EQ) and affection for his players and coaches earn him relationship-based trust. He has a legendary reputation for building strong and supportive relationships with his players. He is always willing to listen to their concerns and offer guidance and support.

Ettore Messina, a Spurs assistant coach, reveals:

"Players, management, coaches, doctors and physiotherapists – Pop cares about all of them. And that makes everyone proud to be a part of the organisation. This is family first, basketball club second."

Pop knows his players are imprinted in various ways by each other, their families, cultures and countries of origin.

Pop appreciates that trust rules vary by country and culture.

Earning trust may take years in countries such as Japan, China, India and Saudi Arabia. Relationship-based trust is valued. Trust is based on the quality of the relationship. Business is emotional, heartfelt and protected within closed networks.[23]

HABIT ONE: BUILD GENUINE SAFETY

Trust can be earned in a single task-driven meeting in countries like the USA, UK, Australia and Germany.[24] Task-based trust is valued. Trust is driven by the intellectual match between parties and the logic of doing business together. The task itself transcends the relationship. In many Western countries, business is business, a frank and open meeting of minds.

Figure 1.2 Global Leadership Approaches

At one point, Pop's top ten players were from ten different cultures:[25]

As shown on the right-hand side of Figure 1.2., some players came from cultures that relied on relationship-based trust:

Manu Ginóbili - Argentina
Tim Duncan - Virgin Islands
Patty Mills - Aboriginal and Torres Strait Islander[26]
Tiago Splitter - Brazil
Marco Belinelli - Italy
Boris Diaw - France

Other players came from cultures that relied on task-based trust:

Tony Parker - Belgium
Aron Baynes - Australia
Cory Joseph - Canada
Danny Green - USA

As Pop earns both relationship and task-based trust, all players respect him.

Interestingly, most players preferred Pop's Participatory Leadership style partly due to their cultures of origin. These same players found his fiery, Authoritative Leadership style challenging, and they often joked about living in fear of Pop when their game fell short.

Exceptions to the above were Boris Diaw of France and Marco Belinelli of Italy, who did not appear to take Pop's volcanic outbursts and criticism personally. Pop's Authoritative Leadership style was a better match for these players.

HABIT ONE: BUILD GENUINE SAFETY

Pop's task-driven Logical Solutions may not have worked so well with the players from Argentina, the Virgin Islands and Brazil, who prefer Friendly Alliances or those from France and Italy, who like the safety of sharing in Closed Networks.

Over time, the players likely softened Pop's old-school Authoritative Leadership style. Eventually, even leaders become like the people they spend time with.

Like Pop, the best CEOs build and maintain trust with employees and stakeholders by paying close attention to their people's cultural origins. They also schedule the right mix of task-based and relationship-based meetings and activities and demonstrate a mix of Participatory and Authoritative Leadership.

Pop sets clear expectations and measures results. Successful CEOs do the same.

Pop measures percentages like points, rebounds, assists, steals and blocked shots. He also values free throw percentages. For example, a free throw percentage of close to 90% is not an unreasonable expectation for an NBA player.

At times, employees complain that their CEOs and managers have unreasonable expectations. However, when leaders clarify why they give feedback, employees can become more trusting and perform better.

Offering context with feedback is critical. Coming up with sets of performance expectations or key performance indicators (KPIs) and sending them out independently will do little for people's underlying trust.

Trust must be earned.

Psychologists from Stanford, Yale and Columbia Universities studying cycles of trust and mistrust came up with the phrase 'Magical Feedback.'[27] This is a straightforward phrase that gives no information about how to improve and delivers a powerful cultural signal.

An example of a magical feedback phrase is,

"I'm giving you these comments because I have very high expectations, and I know that you can reach them."[28][29]

These nineteen words make an individual feel:

1. They are part of the group.
2. The group is special and has high standards.
3. The manager believes they can reach those standards.

On their own, these three statements have limited impact. Together, they are magical.

Pop's coaching embodies magical feedback.[30]

For Pop and the Spurs, every dinner, every elbow touch, every hug and every impromptu conversation reinforces the narrative: You are part of this group. This group is special. I believe you can meet our high standards.[31]

The Spurs do not succeed because they have the most talented players. They succeed because Pop is skilled at maintaining task-based trust and relationship-based trust. He delivers critical and, at times, negative feedback within a culture of safety and healthy conflict.

EMBRACE CONFLICT

We must remain centred to embrace conflict successfully.

Wise CEOs embrace conflict once their people feel safe and trust each other.

Spurs assistant coach Ettore Messina compares Pop's leadership style to that of a wise teacher or sage:

"What's interesting is that he always pushes his coaching staff to argue with him. Sometimes, Pop reminds me of one of those Greek sophists who tried to find the truth through arguments. Pop encourages discussion and a variety of opinions, seeing them as a means to improve as a unit."[32]

Pop understands the value of conflict and will taunt players who stay quiet for too long. Figure 1.3. illustrates five ways to embrace conflict.[33]

THE CEO BOOK

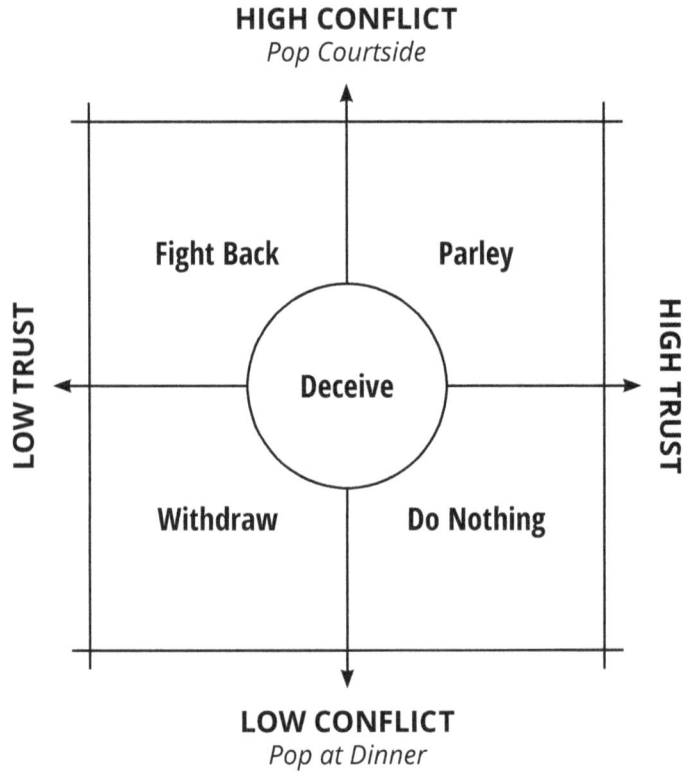

Figure 1.3 Conflict-Trust Moves[33]

Fight Back - Fighting back is often an unwise and overused tactic. It should be a last resort when no other options are available, or a serious issue is at stake. Fighting back is common in relationships where trust has been eroded, and conflict is increasing.

Withdraw - Withdrawal is a wise choice when no other options are available, and an escape path is open. It is a default stance when trust has been eroded, and conflict is low.

HABIT ONE: BUILD GENUINE SAFETY

Parley - Parley is a wise choice from the losing position of a zero-sum game. When the levels of trust and conflict are high, parleying is preferred to fighting back. Negotiating a win-win outcome for both parties should be the preferred option.

Deceive - When the time and place are wrong, deception or surprise buys time. Here, inventing stories that contain 'a grain of truth' buys time until a better strategy becomes available. Deception is a common tactic when both trust and the nature of conflict are difficult to determine.

Do Nothing - Doing nothing also buys time and allows one to observe things. It is a wise choice when 'what is really going on' is unclear. Doing nothing can be easier in high-trust relationships where the level of conflict is low.

When Pop yelled at his players, 'Next guy who misses a free throw is going to buy me a new car!' Spurs' Centre Tim Duncan, who enjoys a high-trust relationship with Pop, stayed centred and replied, 'What colour do you want?'[34]

With his vulnerability, Duncan, whose free throw percentage is below 70%, took some heat from the moment to regain Pop's trust in the team.

Duncan helped Pop and the team move on so they could refocus on the game.

Staying centred and focused amid conflict can be magical.

When we are centred, we join the other party in the conflict and agree or empathise with their right to feel whatever they feel. Even if their stance in the dispute may be wrong, one does not argue with the fact that they are angry or upset. Instead of questioning or denying another's feelings, we respect their entitlement to feel how they feel.

Once we move to their side of the conflict, we can help lead the conversation in new ways.

Duncan's ability to remain centred amid Pop's volcanic outbursts allowed him to respectfully parley and humorously lead Pop to re-balance the conversation in favour of the game plan.

Remaining balanced during conflict comes down to centering. Martial artists have spent thousands of years studying the art of balance. Instead of using knives and swords, they meet life and conflicts in a relaxed but alert manner.

We cannot face an advancing sword-wielding opponent while hysterically off balance any more than we can face an angry meeting of union reps when our centre of gravity is off balance or somewhere above our right eyebrow!

To practice being centred, see Appendix One - Zhāgēn de Xià Dāntián.

Successful CEOs know that their practice of embracing conflict is critical. Centring yourself and managing your emotional state in the face of conflict is a powerful skill.

HABIT ONE: BUILD GENUINE SAFETY

Once we learn to live from our centre, we can respond to conflict from moment to moment. At times, we can withdraw or do nothing. Sometimes, we can use tactical deception to buy time or fight back because the issue is mission-critical. In other cases, we can choose to parley.

Coach Pop shows us how to build genuine safety and manifest a culture of respect and care. In the Spurs' nurturing family-like environment, people, irrespective of race or nationality, feel secure and are driven to excel. Pop mirrors the broader responsibility of every CEO to create a magical workplace where trusting employees thrive and conflict is harnessed as a constructive force.

In the next habit, we will hear a magical rags-to-riches story and learn about the importance of energising middle managers.

Please find a pen and jot down a few notes from this habit. This book has plenty of blank pages to record your ideas and thoughts.

Once you have made a few notes, move to Activity One.

ACTIVITY ONE

1.1 Creating safety for employees is a foundational principle.

    Q1. Do your employees feel nurtured, challenged and safe? Why?
    Q2. On the blank pages opposite, critique your firm's employee induction and onboarding processes.
    Q3. Are they working well?
    Q4. How could they be changed to build genuine safety and a sense of belonging?

1.2 There should be clear policies and procedures with open communication to build genuine safety. This can be achieved through open-door policies, anonymous suggestion boxes and regular feedback sessions. Increasing levels of diversity and inclusion can also help.

Employee health and work-life balance are vital to building a safe culture. Counselling services, employee assistance programs, and educational resources can support employees struggling with physical or mental health issues.

    Q1. Do you have anonymous suggestion boxes that are monitored?
    Q2. Do you offer counselling services for your people?

1.3 Review your use of both leadership styles to gain trust:

   Q1. Which stakeholders and situations work best with Authoritative Leadership?
   Q2. Which stakeholders and situations work best with Participatory Leadership?

1.4 On the opposite blank pages, jot down your ideas on using the Magical Feedback sentence with your various stakeholder groups.

"I'm giving you these comments because I have very high expectations, and I know that you can reach them."

1.5 Decide if you work in a low, medium or high conflict environment and whether the overall atmosphere of trust is low, medium or high.

   Q1. On the opposite blank pages, note how you currently embrace conflict.
   Q2. Which of the five approaches to conflict could help you to be more successful in conflict situations?

Fight back? Withdraw? Parley? Deceive? or Do nothing?

The safety of the people shall be the highest law.

Cicero

HABIT TWO
ENERGISE MIDDLE MANAGERS

Adapted from
CC BY-SA 4.0 DEED

ESTÉE LAUDER
ESTÉE LAUDER COMPANIES

Empower Women's Voices
Hire Smarter People
Choose Your Companions

The Grand Opening of the Frost Brothers' Department Store in San Antonio was set to be a special day.

The store's middle managers saw the arrival of a chaotic and shabbily dressed woman as an affront.

That same day, Estée Lauder's roadshow, which promoted her earliest products to retail outlets, reached San Antonio.

Lauder enjoyed travelling and wore a friendly and engaging smile. She believed in the power of beauty to transform lives.

As the shabbily dressed woman approached the counter, Lauder was poised to assist her.

A middle manager tapped Lauder's shoulder and whispered,

"Not her, Mrs. Lauder. Don't waste your time. She's not going to buy anything. I live around here. I know her type."[35]

Undeterred, Lauder transformed the woman's appearance, using various skincare products. The woman was so pleased that she purchased two of each product Lauder had used on her face.

Estée Lauder's insight into the significance of beauty for women inspired the middle manager, who had initially dismissed the woman as a non-purchaser. Thanks to Lauder's leadership, the middle manager realised that one should never underestimate a customer's desire for beauty or freedom.

HABIT TWO: ENERGISE MIDDLE MANAGERS

Leaders tolerate chaos and innovate. Managers value order and administer things.[36] By energising middle managers, they become more like leaders.

Energised middle managers are the sinew that binds a CEO to the heartbeat of the frontline.

Historically, middle management was the highest point any woman or person of colour could aspire to.[37] Yet some leaders still refuse to hire people smarter than themselves, avoiding the creative and intellectual firepower their firm needs to keep innovating.

This insecurity means smart women and people of colour are often overlooked for leadership roles. This can be further compounded by the 'Peter Principle,' where loyal managers of average success rise through a firm's hierarchy via promotions and inadequate training until they reach a level of incompetence.[38]

Much of Lauder's childhood was spent trying to make ends meet. Like her eight siblings, she was forced to work in the family hardware store, where she got her first taste of business. Yet, freedom and beauty for Lauder were idealised as a child. Her childhood dream was to become a beautiful actress with her name in lights, attracting flowers and handsome men.[39]

In her late teens, Lauder helped her uncle, Dr. John Schotz, with his business, which sold beauty products such as creams, rouge and fragrances. Her uncle also taught her how to wash her face and perform facial massages. After graduating high school, she focused exclusively on her uncle's cosmetics business.

Lauder launched her perfume empire in 1945 by introducing her first fragrance, Youth-Dew, a bath oil that doubled as a perfume.

Instead of using French perfume drops behind each ear, women began using Youth-Dew by the bottle in their bath water. In her first year, Lauder sold 50,000 bottles; by 1984, that figure had risen to 150 million.

Lauder's eldest son, Leonard, was born in 1933. At 13, Leonard helped his mother establish her brand in the family's kitchen. When Leonard graduated from university, he sought freedom by serving with distinction, in the US Navy.

By age twenty-five, Leonard came home with an ability to energise officers and an appreciation for the high standards of conduct required at sea. These were lessons he could apply to leading a business. Leonard returned to help his mother and rose through the ranks to become President of The Estée Lauder Companies from 1972 to 1995.

Leonard was appointed CEO from 1982 to 1999 and Chairman from 1995 to 2009. In his five decades of leadership at Estée Lauder, Leonard transformed the business from a brand with eight products in one country into a multi-brand, global icon.

As a former CEO, Leonard admits none of his success would have been possible without his mother's habit of 'energising the middle.' The

HABIT TWO: ENERGISE MIDDLE MANAGERS

Estée Lauder Company energises middle managers by empowering women's voices, hiring smart people and deliberately choosing the company they keep.[40]

EMPOWER WOMEN'S VOICES

Giving women and traditional minorities an equal voice is a crucial way to create a diverse and inclusive workplace.

Enlightened CEOs understand that giving women an equal voice is excellent for business. A 2019 study of 1069 leading firms across 35 countries and 24 industries revealed that giving women's voices equal importance resulted in higher productivity and greater profitability.[41]

Yet, context is important. In highly gender-inclusive and high human development countries like the Netherlands, Sweden and Norway, giving women an equal voice results in a 7% increase in a firm's market value.[42]

However, such outcomes only held in contexts where gender inclusivity was acceptable and normal. So, the benefits of giving women an equal voice only made a positive difference if a woman's voice was deemed valuable. In countries and companies where women have an equal voice, there are important societal-level health, empowerment and labour market dynamics at play.

Dimensions	Health		Empowerment		Labour Market	
Indicators	Maternal mortality ratio	Adolescent birth rate	Female and male population with at least secondary education	Female and male shares of parliamentary seats	Female and male labour force participation rates	
Dimension Index	Female reproductive health index		Female empowerment health index	Female labour market index	Male empowerment health index	Male labour market index
			Female gender index		Male gender index	
				Gender Inequality Index (GII)		

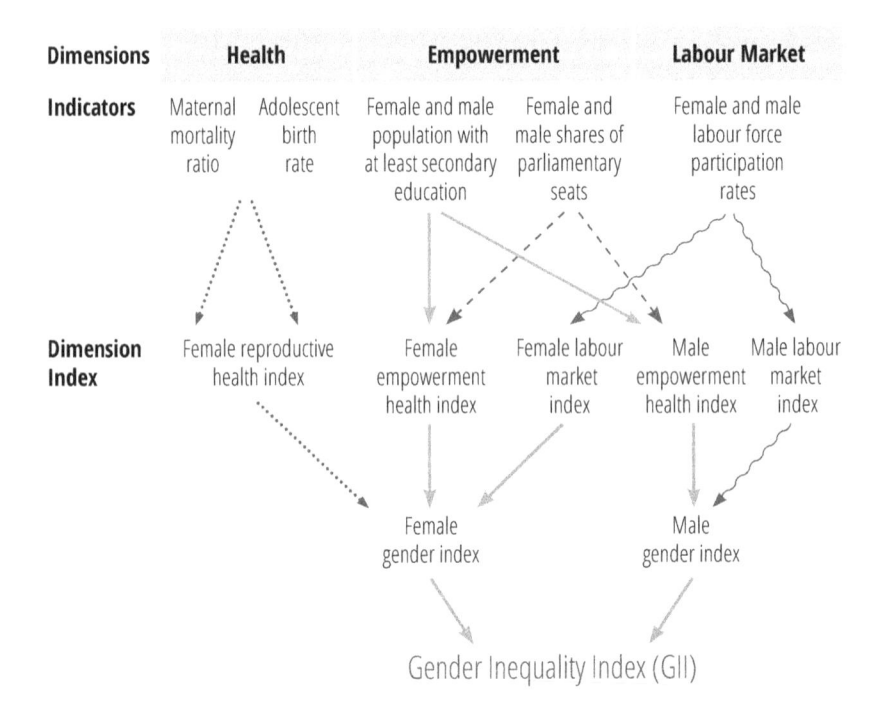

Figure 2.1 United Nations Gender Inequality Index

In low human development countries with low gender-inclusive scores, such as Yemen, Nigeria and Pakistan, a woman's voice is not valued as necessary. Hence, allowing women to speak has no impact on company performance.

While many countries have regulatory support via obligatory laws that give women an equal voice, these countries still need normalised cultural acceptance to ensure women's ideas are valued. Laws and underlying societal and company-specific norms can be at odds. The United Nations Gender Inequality Index (GII) paints a critical picture.

HABIT TWO: ENERGISE MIDDLE MANAGERS

The GII, depicted in Figure 2.1, is based on three primary dimensions:

1. Reproductive Health is measured by maternal mortality ratio and adolescent birth rates.
2. Empowerment is assessed through the proportion of parliamentary seats occupied by females and the proportion of adult females and males aged 25 years and older with at least some secondary education.
3. Economic Status is evaluated through the labour market participation rate of female and male populations aged 15 years and older.

For example, Sweden is ranked number four globally for gender equality, behind Denmark, Norway and Switzerland. Sweden has a GII of 0.013, which is the result of 62% of women in the population with jobs, 92% of women with a secondary education, 47% of seats in parliament being held by women, 0.3% of adolescent girls becoming mothers and 0.004% infant deaths at birth.[43]

In stark contrast, Yemen, ranked 170 out of 193 countries for gender equality, has a GII of 0.82. It is the result of 6% of women with jobs, 22% of women with a secondary education, 1% of seats in parliament being held by women, 55% of adolescent girls becoming mothers and 0.2% infant deaths at birth.[44]

When an organisation is gender equal and genuinely diverse, it attracts more talent. The global job website Glassdoor found that 67% of job seekers consider workforce diversity when evaluating an offer, particularly for talented female candidates.

Indeed, countries and firms that give women, people of colour and LGBTQIA+ people an equal voice and value that voice will benefit from inclusion sooner than their competitors.[45]

Leonard Lauder has repeatedly voiced the following advice:

"Never make an important decision without a woman at the table."

Lauder explains:

"Growing up with a mother like Estée Lauder, how could I not respect and seek out smart, tough women? Strong women have made some of the best decisions for this company. Today, this is what's called 'mirroring the market'."[46][47]

This is good advice.

In many consumer markets, advice from numerous sources reveals that women are the ultimate purchase decision-makers. Even when a man makes a purchase, he will often be guided by his wife, partner or a female friend.

It is comforting to see that in countries where women are gaining an equal voice, unplanned pregnancies, genital mutilation, domestic violence, familial homicide and carbon dioxide emissions per capita are trending lower.[48][49][50]

When women have an equal voice, average life expectancy, education, internet access, mobile phone ownership, average incomes, paid maternity leave and the incidence of women in senior and middle management positions rise faster than in less equal societies.[51]

HIRE SMARTER PEOPLE

Hiring people smarter than you is an effective leadership practice that both Leonard Lauder and Steve Jobs, co-founder of Apple, understood and embraced.

Leonard Lauder recognised the importance of hiring smart people and deliberately reviewing who to keep and who to let go of. By hiring and promoting smart women, Estée Lauder was able to tap into a range of perspectives and ideas that drove its innovation and success.

Steve Jobs also understood the importance of hiring people who were smarter than him. In an interview with the New York Times, he explained "It doesn't make any difference how smart you are, what really matters is how you get along with people." He believed that by hiring managers who were smarter than him, he could learn from them and draw upon their expertise to drive the success of Apple.

Some less-than-stellar CEOs settle for dependable but less-than-stellar middle managers with similar skill sets to themselves.

Successful CEOs think differently. For them, having smart people is essential. CEOs may sometimes feel intimidated at the prospect of leading highly intelligent people. The ability to be humble helps. CEOs can practice getting out of their own way and inviting those more intelligent than them into meetings.

It can feel risky to become the least intelligent person in the room.

Care is needed.

A super-smart person is often not a good team player and may lack humility.

In Pop's words, this player is "Not a Spur."

Some of your super-smart players may be challenging to work with and work for. When people are too smart for their own good and the company's good, they must go.

HABIT TWO: ENERGISE MIDDLE MANAGERS

Figure 2.2 Dunning-Kruger Effect

However, before letting them go, it can be helpful to plot smart-alec employees on The Dunning Kruger model in Figure 2.2, which maps a person's evolving confidence and competence.

New hires typically move in stages from conscious incompetence to unconscious competence. Something Steve Jobs understood. Like Pop, a sense of belonging was what Jobs most looked for in a recruit:

"Recruiting is hard. It is just finding the needles in the haystack. New hires must be smart. But the real issue for me is, will they fall in love with Apple?"[52]

After hiring more than 5000 people, Jobs explained:

"You can't know enough in a one-hour hiring interview. So, in the end, it is ultimately based on your gut instinct. How do I feel about this person? What are they like when they're challenged? Why are they here? I ask everybody: 'Why are you here?' The answers themselves are not what you're looking for. It is the meta-data."

A similar belief around hiring played an enormous role in the careful growth of Estée Lauder. Estée and her son Leonard built a company with some of the brightest and dedicated people in the world.

Whenever Leonard Lauder had to fire someone, he would think back to his Navy days and say:

"Everyone has worth. The fact that we have not been able to take advantage of your skills is not your fault. It is our fault."[53]

This reverse fault approach proved a harmonious way to farewell people from Estée Lauder. Leonard Lauder also advocates not hiring your best friends or former classmates. Friendship is friendship, but business is business. Only hire people that you can fire. Firing a true friend can be the most painful experience in the world.

HABIT TWO: ENERGISE MIDDLE MANAGERS

The Navy gave Leonard many experiences that helped him become a successful CEO. At sea, ships operate 24/7. Leonard understood that others take over when in-charge officers and sailors are asleep or off-shift. Leonard was never threatened by officers or middle managers smarter than him. He would welcome them and embrace them. You may be a company's CEO, but you cannot do everything. You cannot be there to direct all the time.

Leonard saw value in hiring reliable 'betas' or what he called surrogate leaders:

"You must hire surrogates - thoughtful, responsible people who enhance your knowledge, extend your reach and pump up your performance. They don't have to be like you - in fact, the last thing you want is a team of mini-mes. Difference - whether it is a different background, different ethnicity, different age, or different gender - it is a source of strength. As a man leading a beauty company that markets primarily to women, I can't emphasise that strongly enough."[54]

Research by Gallup reveals that the number of bosses people should have is one.[55] Matrix structures can mean that lots of workers report to multiple masters. According to Gallup, two-thirds of employees in the US occasionally or consistently work in different teams.[56] Matrix approaches have benefits, but clarity is not one of them.

Those who work in a matrix are less likely to know what is expected of them and more likely to spend their day bogged down in meetings. Leaders in matrix structures will do well to make employees feel like they have one boss, even when they do not.

Leonard never hired employees to look around for him. He always had his ear to the ground. He listened. He looked. And he never said 'never' or 'always' about anything.[57]

Nothing was off-limits.

Estée Lauder and her son loved creating new things, taking calculated risks and choosing the company they kept.

CHOOSE YOUR COMPANIONS

CEOs should consciously choose their companions.

As a young girl, Estée Lauder instinctively knew that you are known and judged by the company you keep.

Lauder was acutely aware of her lack of status, which stemmed from a painful childhood of trying to make ends meet. Her childhood dream was to become a beautiful actress with her name in lights, attracting flowers and handsome men. Lauder eventually got the flowers, a wonderful man in husband Joseph, and her name in department stores all over the world.

Despite being born in Queens, NY, Lauder's favourite story was that she was raised by her Viennese mother in fashionable Flushing, Long

Island, in a luxurious home with horse stables, a chauffeured car and an Italian nurse. Eventually, Lauder's claims of descent from European aristocracy were discredited in an unauthorised biography, *Estée Lauder: Beyond the Magic*.[58]

Nevertheless, from a strategic standpoint, Lauder understood that one's distribution defines them. She worked hard at making a luxurious impression early on, landing Saks Fifth Avenue as her fifth distributor. Lauder aimed to launch first at the top of the market and stay there. Lauder energised her people to take the high road, even when others took the low road or took shots at her.

Estée Lauder always maintained her premium identity. She turned her back on the extra sales volumes that could be gleaned by selling in a distribution channel that did not match the price point and lifestyle experience she demanded for her brand. She wanted to sell her products in high-end specialty stores because of the prestige they gave her.

The endorsements of well-known stores like Saks Fifth Avenue, Neiman Marcus and Harrods were critical for Estée Lauder. She worked hard to get her firm into the luxury segment and stayed there. She constructed her entire strategy and energised middle managers around the understanding that you are judged by the company you keep.

Critically, you are known as much by where you do not sell as by where you do sell.

Enlightened CEOs do not dilute brands and follow the siren song of mass distribution. If they are in the luxury segment, they stay in the luxury segment.

Lauder encouraged her son Leonard to do the same regarding segmentation. Leonard explains:

"If you launch at the top segment of the market, you have two options: up or down. If you launch into the heart of the market, there's always someone who will sell cheaper than you; you'll have no choice but to follow them in a race to the bottom. Launch first, launch strong, and stay strong."[59]

As cheaper brands appeared and grabbed early market share, Estée Lauder quickly acquired those brands and took them up-market. Estée Lauder bought competitors like M.A.C. and Bobbi Brown early on before their discounted presence could hurt the market.

This was and still is a principal strategy of Estée Lauder. Estée Lauder acquires or creates a new brand, and all their brands keep their own names, and these brands still compete with each other. So, M.A.C. is still M.A.C. even if it is part of the Estée Lauder Companies.

Estée Lauder Companies constantly acquire the competition and protect the price point and value of the entire beauty and skincare industry, as their impressive Portfolio Map in Figure 2.3 reveals.

Regarding competition, Estée Lauder chooses the company they keep - themselves!

HABIT TWO: ENERGISE MIDDLE MANAGERS

Estée Lauder is like the beverage company Coca-Cola. Coca-Cola has created or acquired over 200 brands - from sodas to waters, coffees to teas, juices to kombuchas, and a growing list of flavoured alcoholic beverages - in more than 200+ countries and territories.

Premium Price Point

Classic Lifestyle — LA MER, JO MALONE, DARPHIN, ESTĒE LAUDER, PRESCRIPTIVES, CLINIQUE, aramis | *Progressive Lifestyle* — Kilian, TOM FORD, AVEDA, BOBBI BROWN, ORIGINS, Too Faced, smashbox, MAC

Entry Price Point

Figure 2.3 Estée Lauder Portfolio Map

Leonard Lauder's son, William, joined the Estée Lauder brand soon after he graduated with an economics degree from Wharton Business School in 1983. William understood the importance of hiring the right people to drive an organisation's success. In interviews with CNBC and Bloomberg, William emphasised the importance of building a team of diverse and talented individuals aligned with the company's values and mission.[60]

William oversaw the introduction of nine of the company's specialty brands, including Aveda, M.A.C., Prescriptives, and Bobbi Brown. He also managed joint ventures with Chanel and Clarins. William served as CEO from 2004 to 2009, when Fabrizio Freda succeeded him.

To set Freda up for success, William Lauder told Freda on his first day as CEO, "Don't give me any solutions right away. Just listen, understand - and then create."[61]

Today, Freda's big challenge, like millions of CEOs, is helping their businesses succeed in the era of tech disruption. At a time when volatility, uncertainty, complexity, and ambiguity are predictably unpredictable, Freda is energising his youthful and gender-inclusive middle management to determine Estée Lauder's future direction.

In doing so, Freda is repeating the behaviours of Estée, Leonard and William Lauder:

1. Give Women an Equal Voice
2. Hire People Smarter Than You
3. Choose the Company You Keep

In recent years, Freda has invited Estée Lauder's best and brightest middle managers to become reverse mentors.

Freda energised the Gen-Y Millennials (digital natives born between 1981 and 1996) from Estée Lauder's middle managers to lead global strategic conversations around new markets, products and shopping on smartphones.

HABIT TWO: ENERGISE MIDDLE MANAGERS

One key benefit of reverse mentoring is that it helps to bridge the gap between different generations and levels of experience within an organisation. It allows younger employees to share their unique perspectives and ideas with more senior colleagues while allowing each generation to learn from their counterparts. This reversal fosters a dynamic and innovative organisational culture.

This intergenerational organisation-wide approach was the subject of an inspiring 2022 YouTube interview with Fabrizio Freda on Estée Lauder's Global Reverse Mentoring Program.

Once more, a youthful, regenerative and beautiful cycle creates the future at Estée Lauder. Today, some of these energised middle managers are the same age as Leonard Lauder when he took responsibility for creating the company's first R&D Lab for his mother.

The Lauders were experts at energising middle managers and empowering women. They recruited intellectually superior talent and always chose their companions.

In the next habit, we will meet a leader who chose empathy as his companion at a time when a cartoonist drew his company's organisational chart with warring gangs pointing guns at one another.

Now might be an excellent time to take a short break and energise yourself. When you come back, jot down a few notes from this habit.

Then, move on to Activity Two.

HABIT TWO: ENERGISE MIDDLE MANAGERS

ACTIVITY TWO

2.1   Giving women an equal voice that is valued can result in higher productivity and greater profitability.

   Q1. What is the percentage of the minority gender in your firm?
   Q2. Is this percentage replicated in your middle management and senior leadership teams?
   Q3. Why not?

2.2   Download the Gender Inequality Index (GII) dataset on the United Nations Development Programme website or explore the website's interactive GII graphing tool. Enter the countries your businesses operate in to determine the country-based cultural acceptance levels for women having an equal and valued voice.

   Q1. What changes in your firm's policies, procedures and daily rituals will give women an equal, valued voice and change cultural norms?

2.3   Hiring talented, responsible middle managers who enhance your knowledge, extend your reach, and boost your performance makes a difference, especially if they have a different background, ethnicity, age, or gender.

   Q1. What can you do to raise the talent of your middle managers?
   Q2. Do you agree with the statements:

(i) "You are judged by the company you keep." Why?

(ii) "Your distribution defines you." Why?

2.4 Estée Lauder CEO, Fabrizio Freda energises middle managers to determine the future directions of Estée Lauder with his Global Reverse Mentoring Program. Freda established internal advisory boards of middle managers, empowered to educate and reverse-mentor the Board, C-Suite and executive branches.

Freda targets his firm's Gen-Y Millennials to lead global strategic conversations about new markets, products, brands, and the use of smartphones, social media, and AI.

Q1. How will your firm energise its middle managers?
Q2. Could you establish a reverse mentoring programme?

HABIT TWO: ENERGISE MIDDLE MANAGERS

Leadership is a series of behaviours rather than a role for heroes.

Margaret Wheatley

HABIT THREE

FOSTER DEEP EMPATHY

SATYA NADELLA
MICROSOFT CORPORATION

Model Presence
Coach With Empathy
Lead With Care

In 2016, my friend Tom innocently asked:

"Why aren't you using Office?"

"Why should I?" I inquired, dismissing his question as misguided loyalty.

My judgment was a mirror of my stubborn loyalty to the Apple ecosystem.

A decade earlier, I had traded my cumbersome laptop for a shiny MacBook Pro and the seamless experience of Apple's complimentary Pages, Numbers and Keynote apps.

By 2014, a wind of transformation blew through Microsoft's corridors under Satya Nadella's stewardship.

The era of greed and ego under Gates and Ballmer was over.

A new CEO was on deck.

The landscape shifted so notably that my scepticism began to wane.

Thanks to Tom, I saw Office 365 as a product and a portal to a world where work and collaboration reached new frontiers.

Office 365 was available for a mere $70. It was about more than just having the latest Word, PowerPoint or Excel version. I could access my work from anywhere with One Drive cloud storage, manage my emails and calendar through a premium Outlook service, and collaborate with colleagues via Teams.

HABIT THREE: FOSTER DEEP EMPATHY

These features, continuous updates and advanced security to protect against cyber threats were all part of the package.

What beckoned me wasn't merely the lure of a good deal - the cost of two dozen coffees for a year's subscription. It was the realisation that Microsoft had evolved.

Nadella's vision seemed clear: reinvent Microsoft as a customer-centric and innovative company.

By empathically putting the needs of employees and customers first, Nadella helped Microsoft rise to number one in market capitalisation for the first time since the 1999 Dotcom Bubble.

Nadella was born and raised in India. He received his electrical engineering degree from the Manipal Institute of Technology before earning a master's in computing and an MBA from the University of Chicago. Nadella applied to join Microsoft in 1992 because he wanted to work for a company with a mission to change the world.

Ironically, Nadella's lack of empathy nearly cost him the chance to join Microsoft. In his early professional years before joining Microsoft, Nadella admits that he had not yet mastered the art of placing himself in another's shoes.

After a full day of job interviews at Microsoft with various engineering leaders who tested his grit and intelligence, Nadella met Richard Tait, an up-and-coming manager. Tait did not give Nadella an engineering problem or coding scenario.

Tait asked Nadella a straightforward question:

"Imagine you see a baby lying in the street, and the baby is crying. What do you do?"[62]

"You call 911," Nadella replied without much thought.

Tait walked Nadella out of his office, put his arm around him and said,

"You need some empathy, man. If a baby is laying on the street crying, pick up the baby."[63]

Nadella began to realise the importance of empathy.

Tait was a kind man and gave Nadella the job anyway, but Tait's words remained with Nadella forever and guided his path to Microsoft CEO.

In recent years, Microsoft's Founder and former CEO, Bill Gates wrote:

"I've known Satya Nadella for more than twenty years. I got to know him in the mid-nineties when I was CEO of Microsoft, and he was working on our server software, which was just taking off at the time. We took a long-term approach to building the business, which had two benefits: It gave the company another growth engine, and it fostered many of the new leaders who run Microsoft today, including Satya.

Later, I worked intensely with Satya when he moved over to run our efforts to build a world-class search engine. We had fallen behind Google, and our original search team had moved on. Satya was part

HABIT THREE: FOSTER DEEP EMPATHY

of the group that came in to turn things around. He was humble, forward-looking and pragmatic. He raised smart questions about our strategy. And he worked well with hard-core engineers.

So, it was no surprise that, once Satya became Microsoft's CEO, he immediately put his mark on the company. Satya has charted a course to make the most of the opportunities created by technology while also facing up to the hard questions."[64] [65]

At the time Nadella became CEO, Microsoft was falling behind. Innovation had been replaced by bureaucracy. Internal politics had replaced teamwork. In these troubled times, a cartoonist drew Microsoft's organisational chart with warring gangs pointing guns at one another.

This cartoon bothered Nadella immensely.

Nadella wanted to lead a firm where people trusted one another. As the new CEO, Nadella understood that his job was to refresh Microsoft's culture so that one hundred thousand employees could better shape the firm's future.

Today, Nadella wants his employees to say, 'Microsoft works for me,' not 'I work for Microsoft.'

To achieve this, Nadella champions a framework called Model Coach Care (MCC).

The framework's first part, Model, implies that leaders must model what they want from their people. This part recognises the unconscious ways we mimic one another. In other words, as a leader, your people are more likely to behave like you than do what you say.

The second part, Coach, means leaders must be great coaches and help their people perform at their best.

The third part, Care, is the fundamental currency, especially when teams increasingly work virtually and in different time zones. Care means placing yourself in the shoes of the people you lead and manage and helping them succeed.

A formative event that helped seed the MCC framework occurred in 1996 when Nadella's son Zain was born prematurely by emergency caesarean section due to utero asphyxiation, which caused severe cerebral palsy. Nadella's son would require a wheelchair and rely on a carer for the rest of his life.

At that time, Nadella was devastated.

Nadella's resultant emotional journey helped him better understand human potential and what love and ingenuity can accomplish. Around this time, Nadella stumbled on the teachings of Gautama Buddha.

Buddha was a crown prince who left the material world behind with just a begging bowl. He meditated on the nature of human suffering over many years. This journey resulted in Buddha's enlightenment.

After his enlightenment, Buddha realised that human suffering was rooted in three things:

HABIT THREE: FOSTER DEEP EMPATHY

1. Our aversion to pain.
2. Our craving for certainty.
3. Our ignorance of the illusionary nature of the world around us.

Humans remain spiritually 'asleep' to avoid pain, create certainty and reject what is. Buddha realised that the world we experience is both real and illusionary. Our personalised experience of the world is an illusion. From our 'asleep' state, we see the world as we are, not as it is. Yet, the true 'I am' that experiences the world and the world itself are both real.

Buddha used the word 'suffering' for the way we systematically define who we are by our perception of the world. Our personal story causes us to miss our true nature and the world around us.

Contrary to what one might expect, suffering is not the problem. Rather than trying to get rid of suffering, when we inquire into and meet suffering, a doorway to enlightenment opens. A willingness to suffer fully, even for an instant, without trying to escape or be saved, means that suffering is no longer an obstacle to our full surrender, beyond the door and into the mystery of our true nature.[66]

Once enlightened, Buddha had sympathy, empathy and compassion for those who were 'asleep'.

Sympathy means you can understand what another person is feeling. Sympathy and empathy are different. If a child is born with a disability, while you may not physically feel the parent's pain viscerally, from a place of sympathy, you can understand their sadness.

Empathy is visceral. Empathy means that we feel what another is feeling. Thanks to our brain's mirror neurons, empathy may arise when we witness someone in pain or joy. We cry with sadness or joy from what we are mirroring. This is why a happy, smiling person can light up a room, or a massive outpouring of grief can happen when human tragedy occurs. Interestingly, laughter and enthusiasm are two of the most contagious states on the emotional spectrum.

Enthusiasm can trigger high levels of positive energy and persistence towards shared goals.[67] Nadella's enthusiastic, eternally optimistic and imaginative ideas have helped achieve many important shared outcomes at Microsoft.

Our imagination can also be used to trigger empathy. We can trick our mirror neurons by imagining someone else's experience. Empathy is what can happen when we choose to 'imagine ourselves in someone else's shoes.'

While empathy is often considered a positive trait, empathy can also have a divisive and dark side.[68] If we frequently feel the pain of others, we can become overwhelmed and may experience burnout, which can result in mental health issues. 'Empathy fatigue' is often an issue for overworked managers, caregivers and healthcare providers. We are less likely to burn out if, when we feel empathy, we compassionately act to alleviate another's pain.

Because compassion and empathy access different areas of the brain, acting with compassion can help us combat empathy fatigue. Nadella's journey and study of the Buddha's life revealed that, instead of entering heaven, Buddha's compassion means he waits patiently at 'the gates' for all humankind to awaken and join him.

Compassion is the willingness to relieve the suffering of another. Listening actively to another with our entire presence is one of the most compassionate things we can do. Instead of listening with the intent to reply, we listen with the intent to understand without filtering anything that is being shared through our worldview.

Findings from 'The Potential Project' in Figure 3.1 reveal the dynamic between understanding and willingness to support.[69]

Active listening is becoming increasingly rare, as our devices, social media apps and busy lives keep us 'asleep' and prevent us from being present and compassionate with one another. It is little wonder that within our fragile world, unresolved trauma, mental health and their corresponding cocktail of addictions continue to rise.

In his book 'The Art of Happiness', the Dalai Lama famously said:

"If you want others to be happy, practice compassion. If you want to be happy, practice compassion."[70]

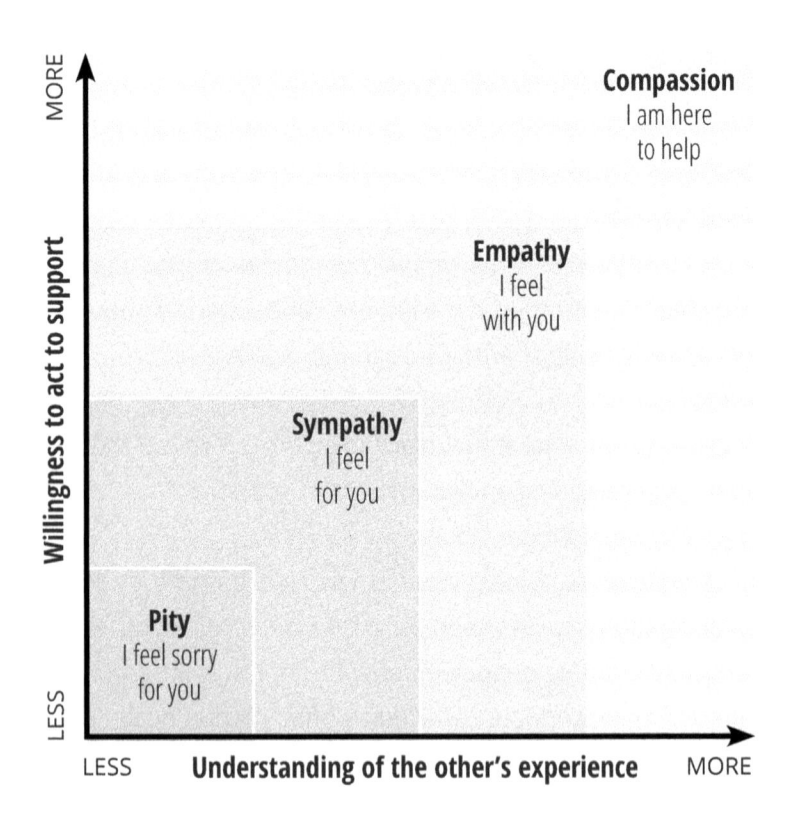

Figure 3.1 Going beyond sympathy and empathy

For CEOs, sympathy is better than pity, and compassion is a more desirable trait than empathy.

Why?

Because CEOs are responsible for leading and managing large groups of people. They need to be able to understand and respond to emotions. They also need to be able to make difficult decisions and act from both a supportive and understanding place.

To act compassionately, leading with intention and meditating are essential. CEOs can focus their best efforts on supporting others by setting an intention to be more compassionate. Through meditation, CEOs can learn to be more aware of their emotions.

CEOs can learn to respond to emotions in a more balanced, caring and purposeful way. They can practice self-care and model presence.

MODEL PRESENCE

Many CEOs spend their day listening to people.

At Microsoft, the first part of Nadella's MCC framework requires that leaders Model what they want from their people. CEOs who model the gift of presence will see the world more clearly than those less present.

Wherever possible, conscious and caring CEOs keep their doors open and encourage the design of office spaces that break down departmental silos. Without presence and empathy, CEOs will remain amiable, detached or fatigued, as demonstrated by Figure 3.2.

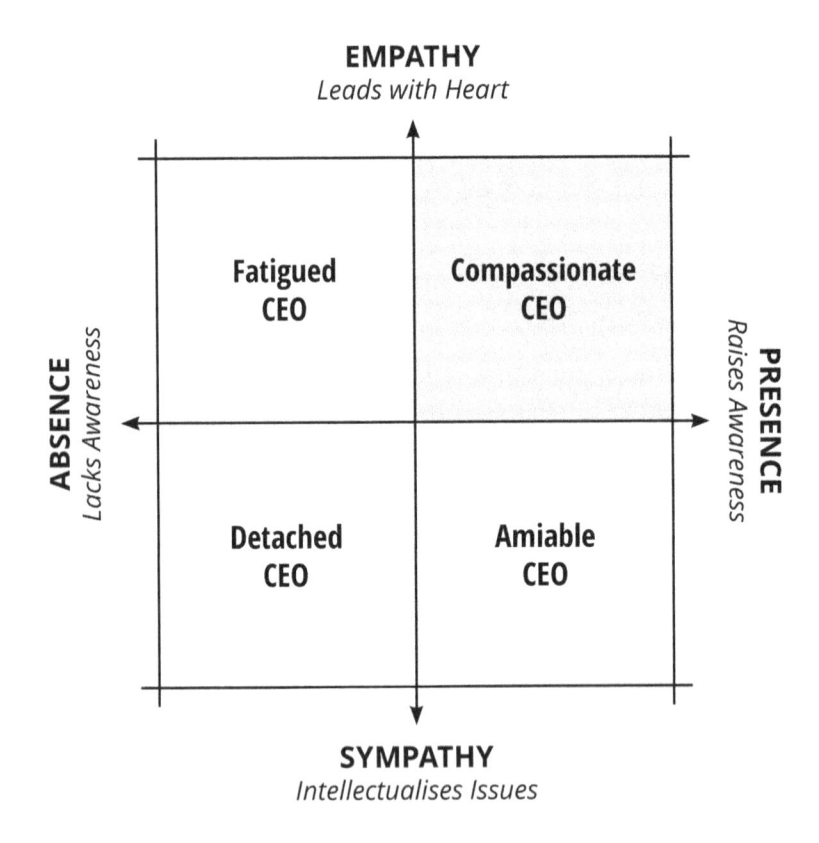

```
                    EMPATHY
                 Leads with Heart
                       ▲
        ┌──────────────┼──────────────┐
        │              │              │
        │   Fatigued   │ Compassionate│
        │     CEO      │     CEO      │
ABSENCE │              │              │ PRESENCE
◄───────┼──────────────┼──────────────┼───────►
Lacks   │              │              │ Raises
Aware-  │   Detached   │   Amiable    │ Awareness
ness    │     CEO      │     CEO      │
        │              │              │
        └──────────────┼──────────────┘
                       ▼
                    SYMPATHY
               Intellectualises Issues
```

Figure 3.2 Empathy and Presence

Being present helps us recall events and people's names. When you say someone's name, their brain's left hemisphere lights up, and they are motivated to listen. To help remember the name of someone and keep them motivated, say their name back to them when you hear it. This allows you to get their name's pronunciation correct and shows that you respect them.

To help remember the name of someone you have just met, creating a familiar, mundane or whacky visual image can improve your retention of their name by 400%.[71] For example, if the person's name is Donald or Joe, see them speaking from behind a Presidential lectern. If their name is Mary, see them as the Madonna or imagine them flying over chimney tops in London with a parrot-handled umbrella. Finally, repeat their name at the end of the meeting when saying goodbye to help cement their name in your memory.

When heading for a follow-up meeting with a stakeholder or employee, before reviewing your notes from the previous meeting, test yourself by asking:

Q1. What is this stakeholder's correct name?
Q2. What are they likely to want from me?
Q3. What is the background or history of this person?
Q4. What are their immediate and long-term objectives?
Q5. What are their pain points and what keeps them up at night?
Q6. How much time and money should I give to this issue?
Q7. What is the desired outcome of this meeting?

A multitude of psychological barriers often hinder effective listening. In his HBR article "Negotiate Like a Pro," Scott Walker shares sixteen obstacles to effective listening:[72]

1. Advising: Quick to offer solutions before fully understanding the issue.
2. Analysis paralysis: Over-collecting information, stalling solution finding.
3. Assumptions: Entering discussions with bias, lacking factual support.

4. Avoidance: Shutting down communication when there is any tension.
5. Derailing: Abruptly changing the conversation topic.
6. Dreaming: Only partially engaging in listening.
7. Experience: Over-relying on past experiences for current understanding.
8. Filtering: Selectively listening to confirm personal biases.
9. Identifying: Relating everything heard back to personal experiences.
10. Judging: Forming opinions too quickly without complete comprehension.
11. Mind reading: Assuming the thoughts and feelings of others.
12. Placating: Pretending to listen empathetically without genuine engagement.
13. Position: Feeling a lack of parity with the speaker.
14. Presentation: Imposing personal interpretation onto the information received.
15. Rehearsing: Focusing on one's own response rather than listening.
16. Stress: Allowing distractions to impede effective listening.

Preparing yourself with the seven questions ahead of time will help you stay purposefully present in meetings. Being aware of the sixteen obstacles will help you to be more empathic and ultimately become a great coach.

COACH WITH EMPATHY

The second part of Nadella's MCC framework requires that leaders become empathic coaches to help people perform at their best. When asked about the greatest secret to assisting people in innovating, Nadella says it is not diversity, talent or skill, but empathy.

Nadella relays: "Empathy is at the heart of design thinking."[73]

After all, value-driven design is about meeting the unmet needs of people. To be successful, CEOs need to coach with empathy. Coaching for success also requires a CEO to challenge their people directly, as shown in Figure 3.3.

EMPATHIC LEADERSHIP

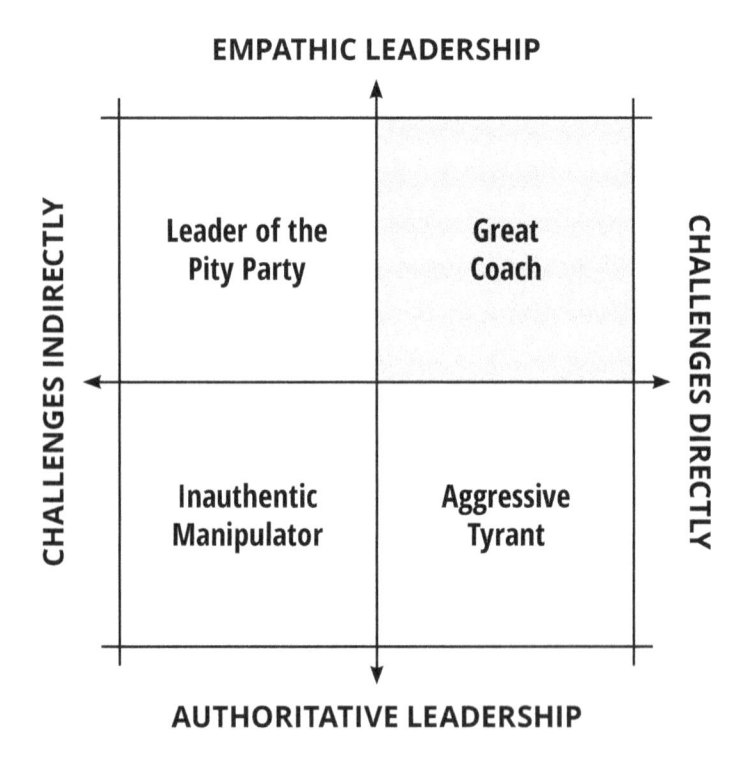

	CHALLENGES INDIRECTLY	CHALLENGES DIRECTLY
Empathic	Leader of the Pity Party	Great Coach
Authoritative	Inauthentic Manipulator	Aggressive Tyrant

AUTHORITATIVE LEADERSHIP

Figure 3.3 CEO as Coach

Empathic CEOs who challenge indirectly invite employees to behave like victims. These CEOs become the leaders of a "pity party".

Just as bad can be the indifferent CEO who challenges indirectly. Employees see such CEOs as inauthentic manipulators.

Perhaps worse still is an indifferent CEO who lacks empathy and challenges directly. Employees experience these CEOs as aggressive tyrants. A bit like the "mongrel" that my friend Rowan, perhaps mistakenly, wished he had accessed as a CEO.

HABIT THREE: FOSTER DEEP EMPATHY

Finally, there is the empathic CEO who challenges directly. To employees, they can feel like Coach Pop.

Rowan's comments reflect the dilemma of balancing challenge and empathy. Finding the sweet spot between the two is hard.

The story of the Emperor and the Prime Minister masterfully illustrates this.

Once upon a time, an Emperor made an agreement with his Prime Minister. The agreement was that each day, the Emperor would empathise with the people and their concerns, and the Prime Minister would challenge the people to behave and punish those who broke the rules. Years passed. One day, the Emperor realised that people had lost respect for him. However, they respected the Prime Minister.

After some thought, the Emperor, who wanted more respect, reversed the roles. The Prime Minister agreed. Now, the Prime Minister empathised with the people, and the Emperor punished them.

Soon thereafter, there was a rebellion, and the people dethroned the Emperor.

Without a leader, the people looked for a replacement. They realised that over many years, they had learned to respect the Prime Minister. Now reformed, the people forgot that the Prime Minister used to punish them. They felt that the Prime Minister had become more caring.

They made the Prime Minister the new Emperor.

The moral of the story of the Emperor and Prime Minister is that if we adopt an overly friendly attitude without challenges early on and become punitive taskmasters later, people will resent the change.

The ones who loved us will now resent us. The ones who do not respect us will complain.

However, if we directly challenge ourselves and others with high standards from the beginning of our reign, people will take our words seriously and respect us. Then, we can afford to be more friendly down the track. If we are initially tough and adopt a kind approach later, people will think we have grown wiser.

Nadella's journey from engineering disciplinarian to empathic leader fits the bill here and may offer some wisdom about his meteoric rise to CEO.

LEAD WITH CARE

The third part of Nadella's MCC framework is about caring enough to place yourself in the shoes of the people you lead and manage. Successful CEOs do not get stuck behind a desk. They lead by walking about, caring for others and caring for the future.

HABIT THREE: FOSTER DEEP EMPATHY

Many people have questioned their working future since the COVID-19 pandemic and the rise of Generative AI.[74] This enquiry has led them to sense which companies they would prefer to work for, for which bosses and in what roles. Research supports the notion that people do not leave firms; they leave emotionally unavailable bosses.[75] A recent Gallop survey found half of those leaving jobs in the US did so because of a lousy boss.[76]

The best CEOs practice loving kindness. With increasing awareness, they can better care for their people and the future. Both awareness and kindness are needed. A lack of awareness, kindness or both results in a cool, cold or cruel CEO, as revealed in Figure 3.4.

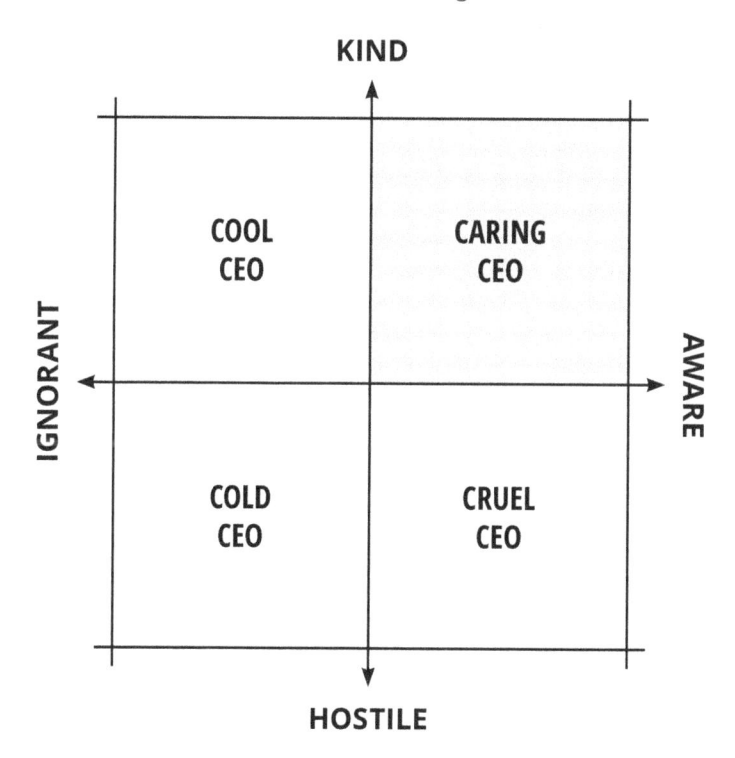

	KIND	
IGNORANT	COOL CEO	CARING CEO
	COLD CEO	CRUEL CEO
	HOSTILE	

Figure 3.4 Caring CEO Matrix

In the advancing era of AI and automation, Microsoft has implemented AI tools to develop "kindness software" that aids thousands of CEOs and leaders in modelling, coaching and caring for employees more effectively.

By 2022, Microsoft had provided the Viva app for free to all users in team environments. The name Viva, which means "Long Live" in Spanish, reflects Nadella's ethic of care.

The Viva app alerts leaders and managers if they have not recently spent time with a direct report. It alerts employees who may be at risk of burnout. It also prevents leaders from emailing their teams over the weekend, suggesting they email during work hours instead.

Viva is one of many tools CEOs can use to cultivate compassionate cultures. Over the last decade, Nadella has been recognised as one of the kindest, most caring and emotionally connected tech CEOs.

Having participated in and led men's leadership circles for over a decade, I have observed a need for more emotional intelligence in leadership, especially among older individuals and particularly in men. In sharing circles, men would constantly intellectualise their response to the question, "What emotion are you experiencing?"

To encourage men to engage with their emotions, I adopted two approaches. If they struggled to identify their resident emotions, I suggested labelling their emotional state as "numbness" until they could discern fear, sadness, anger or joy.

This method was generally effective, but some men consistently reported feeling numb. As an alternative, I invited them to close their eyes, breathe deeply and tune into their bodily sensations, which helped them reveal their underlying emotions. In time, men realised that their habitual emotional responses stemmed from their early childhood conditioning and trauma.

Recognising and understanding the sources of our primary emotions can be a transformative and life-affirming journey. While therapeutic help is beyond the scope of this book, a willingness to understand our emotional responses and those of others can be a beneficial starting point.

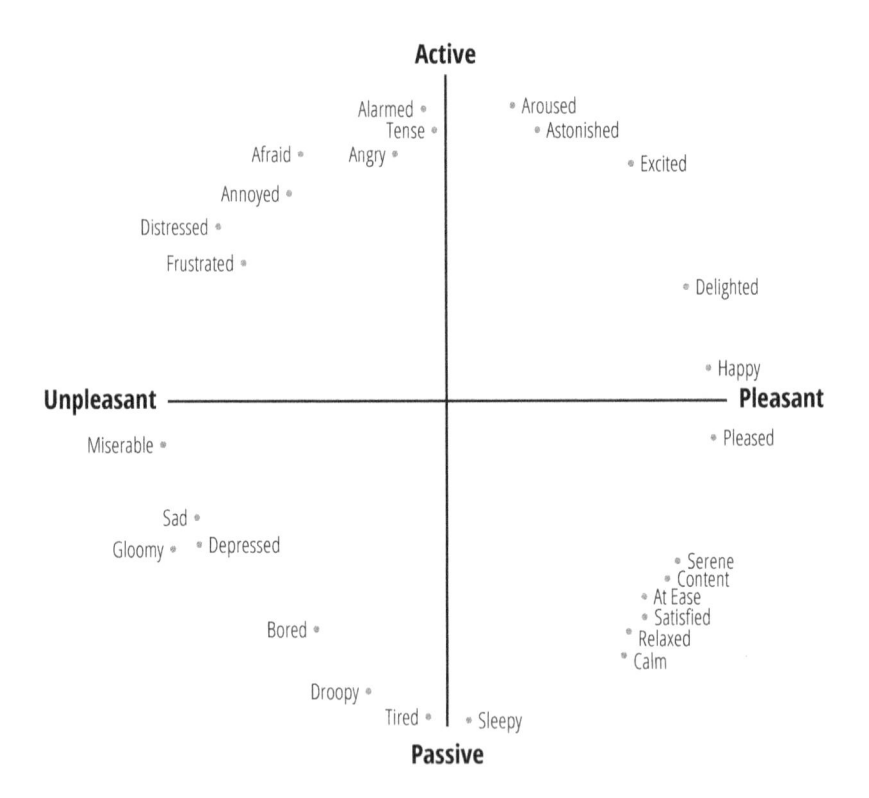

```
                        Active
              Alarmed •      • Aroused
                 Tense •     • Astonished
        Afraid •  Angry •
              Annoyed •              • Excited
      Distressed •
         Frustrated •
                                     • Delighted

                                     • Happy
Unpleasant ─────────────┼───────────── Pleasant
         Miserable •                 • Pleased

            Sad •
      Gloomy • • Depressed
                                        • Serene
                                        • Content
                                        • At Ease
                 Bored •                • Satisfied
                                        • Relaxed
                                        • Calm
                 Droopy •
                    Tired •  • Sleepy
                        Passive
```

Figure 3.5 Spectrum of Human Emotions

Imagine the spectrum of human emotions arranged in a circle. Figure 3.5 is a valuable tool for leaders navigating their emotional landscape and those of others. You can better understand how emotional states influence your communication and decision-making by familiarising yourself with the emotions listed and identifying those relevant to your role, such as delight, excitement, alarm, distress or frustration.

For instance, consider whether sadness makes you more cautious, or perhaps, whether anger leads to riskier decisions. Use the circle to become more aware of emotional states and improve emotional intelligence. Reflecting, meditating and seeking feedback will all help to build your emotional intelligence.

Consider the emotional states of stakeholders. Understanding their emotions can inform your interactions and help foster empathic relationships and better outcomes.

CEOs vary widely in their empathic abilities, from those who are keenly aware and kind to those who are less so. Deep empathy requires emotional intelligence and compassion, which arise from self-care.

A valuable first step in embracing self-care is to complete the activity in Appendix Two – ACE Quiz.

Once you have completed the ACE activity, look back and reflect on your insights from this habit and make some notes on the following blank pages.

Imagine leading a firm where active and hardworking employees are fired with little hesitation. We will meet the CEO of this firm next.

Before moving on, proceed to Activity Three.

ACTIVITY THREE

3.1 Imagine you see a beggar in the street, crying softly.

    Q1. What would you do?
    Q2. Would you be indifferent, sympathetic, empathetic or compassionate? Why?

    Suppose you recognise that person as a former employee of your firm.

    Q1. Would you do anything differently?
    Q2. What would you do? Why?

    Many leaders might empathise with the unknown beggar but act compassionately towards the former employee. Buddha has compassion for us all, especially those leaders who do not stop to help.

3.2 A significant part of a CEO's job involves being available, listening to others and taking action.

    Q1. Are you fully present when listening to others?
    Q2. When you are in your office, is your door closed or open?
    Q3. Do you smile, and are you genuinely nice to people?

3.3 Often, 'the squeaky wheel gets the oil.' Those noisy individuals who persistently make their needs or issues known are the ones

HABIT THREE: FOSTER DEEP EMPATHY

who gain the majority of a leader's time, while those who remain quiet can be overlooked.

Nadella's Viva app alerts leaders and managers to spend time regularly with all direct reports.

- Q1. Do you use the Viva app or have systems that schedule time with your key people?
- Q2. Who are some of the important stakeholders you should listen to more often?
- Q3. What questions will you ask them?
- Q4. How might you be a more compassionate coach?

3.4 'People don't leave firms; they leave bosses.'

- Q1. Is this true at your firm?
- Q2. What lessons about empathy from Nadella's Model Coach Care framework could you incorporate into your leadership development programs?

We can only heal the world when we start healing ourselves and we can only heal ourselves when we start feeling empathy for others.

Abhijit Naskar

HABIT FOUR
ELIMINATE POOR PERFORMERS

Adapted from
CC BY-SA 4.0 DEED

REED HASTINGS
NETFLIX CORPORATION

Hire All Stars
Instil Valued Behaviours
Question Your Colleagues

Nestled up in my Paris apartment overlooking the rain-drenched Panthéon, I am in awe, with one Netflix hit rolling into the next.

From where I sit, as a veteran business advisor, I know that culprits lurk in every workforce, threatening to pull everything towards chaos and stagnation.

Yet, Netflix seems to sail smoothly above it all.

Reed Hastings, the mastermind at Netflix's helm, packs his company's workforce with individuals whose fervour and skill match Netflix's reputation.

As I flick to a new series, I appreciate the craft of Netflix's employees - a stark contrast to the entropy and disorder that creep in when employees cut corners.

My thoughts drift to inertia - the human tendency to resist change. However, change is what Netflix thrives on, as it is propelled by leadership that refuses to let current behaviours stagnate.

Netflix also navigates bias, that all-too-human flaw of unfair favour or discrimination, with a conscious effort towards excellence and fairness, affecting everything from casting to promotions.

As I break for a morsel of baguette and cheese, I switch channels, only to have my musings being punctuated by the bold voice of Ricky Gervais, hosting the Golden Globes for the fifth time. Gervais' words resonate with me as he jests,

HABIT FOUR: ELIMINATE POOR PERFORMERS

"No one cares about movies anymore. No one goes to the cinema. No one watches network TV. Everyone's watching Netflix."

I laugh because it's true.

Gervais continues,

"The Golden Globes should just be me saying, 'Well done, Netflix, you win everything. Good night.' But no, we've got to drag it out for three hours!"

His honesty is refreshing, even if it stings a bit for Hollywood's traditionalists.

Then Gervais drops another truth bomb:

"The best actors have all jumped to Netflix."

I think of the stars I've been watching that weekend - De Niro, Di Caprio, Foster, Theron and Gyllenhaal - all now part of Netflix's stellar line-up. Netflix has not only captured our attention, it has also garnered acclaim.

The Hollywood Academy's attitude towards Netflix is complex. Despite the apparent resistance, films like 'All Quiet on the Western Front', 'The Power of the Dog' and 'Marriage Story' have won Oscars.

I lean back, snack in hand, a participant in the very trend Gervais skewers.

Our fourth helmsman, Reed Hastings, fills the halls of Netflix with the elite, each fervent in spirit and adept at their craft. Hastings has a round face with sharp cheekbones. His demeanour is typically calm and composed. He may be seen fidgeting when in deep thought, indicative of his intellectual and creative nature. In the digital arena, Hastings has emerged as a pioneer.

Trained in mathematics and then in the Marines, he travelled the world as an educator. After earning a master's degree in computer science, Hastings entered the software industry. In 1991, he established Pure Software, which he sold in 1997 for a significant profit.

Inspired by a hefty late fee from a video store, in 1997, Hastings invented a mail-order DVD rental service called Netflix. Initially, customers rented DVDs for a week, but by December 1999, they were offered a monthly website subscription to rent unlimited DVDs. DVDs were returned swiftly and replaced with the next available title from the customer's list.

Netflix transitioned from a mail-order DVD service to a dominant online streaming platform, premiering its original content 'House of Cards' in 2013. Under Hasting's leadership, Netflix has grown into a global giant, offering a vast library of movies and TV shows to millions of subscribers in over 190 countries.

HABIT FOUR: ELIMINATE POOR PERFORMERS

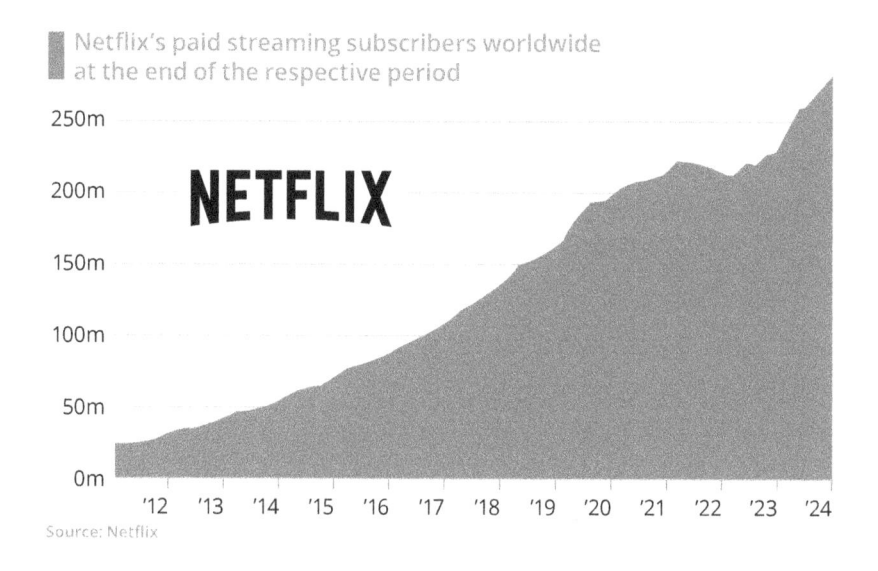

Figure 4.1 Reed Hastings' streaming prediction was right

Netflix consistently ranks among the world's wealthiest companies, with a market capitalisation exceeding two hundred billion dollars. Hastings has served on the boards of several organisations, including the California Charter Schools Association, and has contributed over a billion dollars to various charitable endeavours.

HIRE ALL STARS

Hastings was obsessed, from the beginning, with hiring stellar employees and having high-performing teams. His strategy was as decisive as it was daring – constantly 'separating the wheat from the chaff.'

Netflix's hiring policies demand that only those with the highest talent and good character be recruited. This means hiring people with proven track records in their domains of expertise, and correlating their suitability by understanding their off-the-job behaviours.[77] Referees for possible employees are never phoned but interviewed in-person or video-conferenced, making it easier to detect if a referee is overly biased or lying.

Having stellar employees is considered a precursor to employee morale. On the other hand, poor performers are deemed toxic. In an interview with Harvard Business School in 2019, Hastings elaborated:

"We're overt about the professional sports metaphor, as opposed to the "If you do a bad job, you're out" model. We're like, "If you're a good player but not the best on the planet, I will try to get the best one because that's how the team will win. That's a shift that makes some employees uncomfortable, but we are open about it and take that into account when we deliver feedback."[78]

Netflix employees who are not exceptional or exceptionally resilient often feel pressured to resign because of co-worker feedback during informal 360-degree performance reviews. The spirit of excellence combined with a bootcamp-like elimination ethic, which benefits elite military services, benefited Netflix similarly during Hastings' tenure.

> We're a *team*, not a family.
>
> We're like a **pro sports team**, not a kid's recreational team.
>
> Netflix leaders hire, develop and cut **smartly**, so we have stars in every position.
>
> **NETFLIX**

Figure 4.2 Netflix Pro Sports Team Slide

Hasting's approach contradicts Coach Pop, who avoids recruiting highly talented 'All Stars'. In Pop's mind, the team is the star, never the individual.

Exercising positive discrimination for what you deem 'right' when hiring makes sense.

To maintain a culture of excellence and innovation at Netflix, Hastings does very little to prevent his managers from firing less-than-stellar employees - a challenge Rowan grappled with. If there is any doubt that a team member is not the best fit for the role, Hastings would prefer to give that employee a generous four-to-six-month severance payout rather than have them occupy a position that a more talented new hire could better fill.[79]

> **Unlike many companies, we practice:**
>
> *adequate performance gets a generous severance package*
>
> **NETFLIX**

Figure 4.3 Netflix Severance Package Slide

Even though Hastings goes to great lengths to recruit the talent he most desires, the average employee tenure at Netflix is 2.8 years.

In the third decade of the 21st Century, average job tenure can vary significantly based on age, occupation, industry, nation, sector and education level. For instance, Gen Z individuals born between 1996 and 2010 tend to have much shorter tenures than previous generations. Gen Z individuals stay in a job for an average of only 1.7 years, perhaps due to their social media-induced multifaceted motivations and reduced attention spans. Meanwhile, the median job tenure for slightly older Gen-Y Millennials, born between 1981 and 1996, is around five years.

HABIT FOUR: ELIMINATE POOR PERFORMERS

In Australia, in 2024, job tenure sees a worker stay an average of 3.4 years. Meanwhile, European countries have some of the highest retention rates. Employees in Greece spend an average of 12.1 years with their employers, the longest average job tenure among European countries. Among surveyed European countries, Denmark had the shortest employee tenure, keeping employees an average of 6.2 years.[80]

The Netflix "Keeper Test" is a management tool Hastings devised to ensure that each position at the company is filled by the best possible candidate, not just for the present but also for the future, as company and individual roles evolve. The test is straightforward. Managers are encouraged to regularly assess their employees and consider whether they would actively fight to keep an employee should they desire to leave.

> The **Keeper Test** Managers Use:
>
> Which of my people,
> if they told me they were leaving
> for a similar job at a peer company
> would I fight hard to keep at Netflix?
>
> **NETFLIX**

Figure 4.4 Netflix Keeper Test Slide

If the Keeper Text answer is no, the manager should consider terminating the employee. This creates what Hastings refers to as 'talent density,' ensuring that only the most valued and contributing employees remain, thus making room for even better talent. From bitter experience, Hastings knows that five highly talented software programmers can easily outperform one hundred average programmers.[81]

Hastings' approach differs from traditional methods, such as stack ranking,[82] which can foster unhealthy competition and hinder collaboration. Instead, Netflix's Keeper Test promotes reassessment without pitting employees against each other since there are no firing quotas or forced rankings.

The intent is to encourage high performance and collaboration, aiming for employees to compete with other tech and entertainment companies rather than internally. Netflix adheres to the belief that if every employee excels, the company will thrive and be able to expand to accommodate more high performers.

However, this belief can create a feeling of constant risk of termination among Netflix staff.

To address this, Netflix has instituted the Keeper Test Prompt. Employees who feel insecure about their standing are encouraged to ask their manager if they would pass the Keeper Test. This transparent communication aims to reaffirm valued behaviours, clarify expectations and ensure that motivation is driven by passion and commitment rather than the fear of losing one's job.

Recent legislative changes in democratic countries like Australia require that employees be given a fair and structured chance to correct poor performance, with methods evolving to include legitimate feedback and additional support.

However, the concept of a "fair go" in unionised environments has delivered rulings from Australia's Fair Work Commission,[83] which suggest that even imperfect yet reasonable managerial actions, like the Keeper Test, towards addressing underperformance can be lawful.

INSTIL VALUED BEHAVIOURS

In Netflix's vanguard of corporate culture, employees are not merely workers but can become artisans of their destinies. There is a commitment to individual autonomy. Common sense and working for the good of Netflix replace any so-called 'rules.'

Netflix propels its workforce toward independent decision-making, valuing an individual's judgment and initiative. Information flows freely and does not trickle down through layers but spreads openly, broadly and with intent, ensuring every employee is informed and aligned.

Employees are encouraged to take their integrity seriously with the slogan:

'You only say things about fellow employees that you say to their faces.'

Netflix leaders work hard to ensure everyone continually gives each other professional, constructive feedback. At Netflix, feedback is the key to learning faster.

Netflix normalises feedback in everyday work by making it a more positive experience. Feedback is seen as a trust-building behaviour. Every employee can avoid misunderstandings by practising positive feedback.

Despite the 'no rules' ethic, to assist employees, Hastings has approved and modelled Nine Valued Behaviours he believes are characteristics and tendencies of 'fully formed adults.'[84] These valued behaviours appear on Netflix's careers webpage.[85]

Netflix's valued behaviours are highly prescriptive. They must be demonstrated during the job application process, assessed in the 'meet the referee' process, provided as a code of ethics for employees once hired, and act as a form guide for feedback between colleagues and self-reflection.

1. Judgment
    - You make wise decisions despite ambiguity.
    - You use data to inform your intuition and choices.
    - You look beyond symptoms to identify systemic issues.
    - You spend our members' money wisely.
    - You make decisions mostly based on their long-term, rather than the near-term impact.

HABIT FOUR: ELIMINATE POOR PERFORMERS

2. Selflessness
    - You seek what is best for Netflix, not yourself or your team.
    - You are humble and open-minded about others' great ideas.
    - You make time to help colleagues across Netflix succeed.
    - You debate ideas openly and help implement whatever decision is made, even when you disagree.

3. Courage
    - You make tough decisions without agonising or long delay.
    - You take informed risks and are open to possible failure.
    - You question colleagues' actions inconsistent with these behaviours.
    - You are willing to be vulnerable, in search of truth and connection.
    - You give and take feedback to and from colleagues at any level.

4. Communication
    - You listen well and seek to understand before responding.
    - You are calm in stressful situations.
    - Your writing and thinking are concise and coherent.
    - You adapt your communication style to work effectively with different people, including those who do not share your native language or cultural norms.

5. Inclusion
    - You work well with people of different backgrounds, identities, values and cultures.

- You are excited to help build diverse teams where everyone feels welcomed and respected.
- You recognise we all have biases and work to counteract them.
- You act if someone is marginalising a colleague.
- You treat everyone with respect regardless of their position at Netflix.

6. Integrity
    - You exhibit and are known for candour and transparency.
    - You only say things about colleagues that you are willing to share with them.
    - You admit mistakes openly and share learnings widely.
    - You always share relevant information internally, even when uncomfortable.
    - You act with good intent and trust your colleagues to do the same.

7. Passion
    - You care deeply about Netflix's success.
    - You inspire others with your drive for excellence.
    - You are excited about your work.
    - You are proud to entertain the world.
    - You are tenacious and optimistic.

8. Innovation
    - You develop new ideas that prove impactful.
    - You look for every opportunity to reduce complexity and keep things simple.

- You challenge prevailing assumptions and suggest better approaches.
- You are flexible and thrive in a constantly evolving organisation.

9. Curiosity
    - You learn rapidly and eagerly.
    - You seek alternate perspectives to improve your ideas.
    - You see patterns and connections that other people miss.
    - You seek to understand members' changing tastes and desires.

Here are two questions for you if you feel you could thrive in such a culture.

Q1. Why not head to the jobs section of the Netflix website and express your interest?

Q2. Better still, why not build a new work culture in your team that embodies similar valued behaviours?

QUESTION YOUR COLLEAGUES

Reed Hastings acknowledges that while it is easy to talk about valued behaviours, it takes courage to live by them.

Regarding courage, Netflix states:

'You should question colleagues' actions that are inconsistent with our valued behaviours.'

When colleagues question each other, it leads to better decision-making as assumptions are challenged and more perspectives are considered. The resultant culture fosters a sense of accountability, as employees know that their ideas and actions may be questioned, prompting them to be thorough and diligent.

Like Satya Nadella, Hastings understands that employees are more likely to emulate their leaders' behaviours than follow their words. Thus, modelling valued behaviours can quickly create a ripple effect across the organisation.

Questioning actions inconsistent with valued behaviours has prevented Netflix from making careless mistakes. This is a lesson from which other tech CEOs, like Meta's Mark Zuckerberg, could benefit from. One should always appreciate the dangers of large groups of people, especially in cultures where staff do not question one another and live in an echo chamber.

Sometimes, in a large group, it only takes two misguided individuals to create tragedy.

> **Sometimes, in a large group, it only takes two misguided individuals to create tragedy.**
>
> The negligent and flawed decision to launch the Space Shuttle Challenger, made by a NASA administrator and a prime contractor, despite repeated warnings from aerospace engineers, demonstrates the folly that can be perpetrated by two individuals who choose to live in an echo chamber.

At Netflix, failure is tolerated, but recklessness is not. Employees are encouraged to fail quickly and learn from failure just as swiftly, with the expectation that everyone should already be a talented contributor. Netflix's approach is to facilitate rapid learning from failures to prevent major setbacks and continuously improve performance.

Netflix stands out by endorsing a philosophy that values innovation and creativity over conventional rule-bound structures. Over two decades, Hastings has distilled his leadership ethos into five key lessons that reflect the company's bold business approach:[86]

Lesson 1: 'No Rules' Rules Philosophy
Employees are empowered to act in Netflix's best interest and are free from restrictive regulations. This autonomy is based on the confidence that highly talented individuals will excel and propel the company forward when given the freedom to do so.

Lesson 2: A Global Culture for a Global Company
As a leading force in global entertainment, Netflix embraces a culture that extends beyond borders, welcoming diverse ideas and perspectives. Hastings acknowledges that he initially made slow progress concerning employee diversity. Today, the company has a culture that has progressed with greater employee diversity, fostering innovation and global connection.

Lesson 3: Open Disagreement and Candid Progression
Netflix cultivates a culture where forthright discourse is not merely encouraged but expected. 'Farming for dissent' involves actively challenging ideas to improve them. This ethos of radical honesty is ultimately seen as a kindness that, in the long term, serves the best interests of Netflix employees and the company itself.

Lesson 4: Inspire, Do Not Manage
High-performing employees at Netflix are given context rather than directives, inspiring them to make bold strategic choices and seek

innovative solutions. This enhances their sense of responsibility and ownership.

Lesson 5: Financial Transparency within the Company
Hastings emphasises that only with openness can employees make sound decisions. By sharing financial information widely, Netflix ensures that its workforce is informed, enabling them to act in the company's best interest. Hastings believes this high degree of transparency is crucial within creative industries, where quality decision-making significantly influences the content and services' success.

In balancing kindness with transparency, Netflix has struck a harmony where straightforwardness is a sign of care, aligning every team member with the company's mission to entertain the world and unite people through storytelling in non-traditional ways.

In traditional firms, check-ins and performance evaluations are formal, often inflexible and structured. Ratings and performance reviews are also, despite contemporary research, "dreaded" by 90% of managers.[87] Netflix prefers informal, continuous conversations about performance rather than periodic evaluations.

Also, in traditional firms, there are formal processes with escalating warnings leading to termination. The blurred policy line between underperformance and misconduct frequently makes traditional performance reviews imprecise. Thus perpetuating fear and lack of trust in conventional hierarchies.

As we have seen, Hastings rises above this drama by hiring 'fully formed adults' who are expected to act in the company's best interests, thus avoiding the need for formal disciplinary processes. The resultant culture promotes self-discipline and personal responsibility.

Coaching is often offered as a remedial step for poor performers in traditional firms. It is also seen as a tokenistic attempt to provide a "fair opportunity to improve". Meanwhile, the delay in employment termination creates a sub-culture of poor performance tolerance. While coaching and self-improvement are encouraged, Netflix does not invest in coaching for struggling employees. Instead, it prefers to part ways with those who do not meet their high-performance standards.

Hard Work – Not Relevant

- We don't measure people by how many hours they work or how much they are in the office
- We do care about accomplishing great work
- Sustained B-level performance, despite "A for effort", generates a generous severance package, with respect
- Sustained A-level performance, despite minimal effort, is rewarded with more responsibility and great pay

NETFLIX

Figure 4.5 Netflix Hard Work Slide

HABIT FOUR: ELIMINATE POOR PERFORMERS

Netflix's operational philosophy rejects inflexible frameworks in favour of agility and versatility. This fosters a culture conducive to innovation and requires sound judgment calls, especially from managers responsible for assessing their teams' creative work.

Hastings has created a new paradigm in corporate culture, where accountability, honesty and creativity form the foundation of success. Hastings' stewardship illustrates the importance of eliminating poor performers by assembling a team comprising solely of the crème de la crème, instilling valued behaviours and fostering a culture of questioning one another.

Hastings relentlessly pursued excellence. Excellence is, after all, the pinnacle of satisfaction and the most challenging to sustain.[88]

You have now read the first four habits of this book, which have offered a range of proven methods to care for your people. In Habits Five, Six, Seven and Eight, we focus on helping you know which way to go. CEOs must facilitate the multitude of strategic conversations needed to navigate and lead their organisation's direction successfully.

Coming up is a young and visionary leader who, despite accusations by the Western World of his ruthless quelling of dissent, is profoundly transforming his country's cultural and economic landscape by anticipating future trends.

Before we move on, look back and reflect on your insights from this habit and make some notes on the following blank pages.

When you are ready, proceed to Activity Four.

HABIT FOUR: ELIMINATE POOR PERFORMERS

ACTIVITY FOUR

4.1 Could your firm foster an empowering work environment where employees are responsible for motivating each other and enhancing the customer experience without any rules?

> Q1. If so, what would be the universally understood mission for your firm that employees consistently work towards?
>
> Q2. Could you minimise the downside of radically increasing your employee's freedoms by systematically removing poor performers?
>
> Q3. Could you apply the model of continued peer accountability with the Keeper Test?
>
> Q4. Could you also use the Keeper Test Prompt?

4.2 At Netflix, some of the most talented employees take three to six months of annual leave and arrive at work full of creative energy and fresh ideas for their team's next highly successful project. Netflix's most talented employees know the value of flying business class during busy periods. Getting some decent sleep between time zones gives Netflix better outcomes than saving a few thousand dollars by squishing employees into economy seats.

> Q1. Could you give your employees the freedom to decide the number of weeks of annual leave they should take and the amount of company money they can spend?
>
> Q2. How could these ideas be adapted to your business?

4.3 Reflect on the Nine Valued Behaviours and compare them to the list of valued behaviours your firm uses to hire and develop its people. If your firm does not have a list of valued behaviours, start creating them on the following blank pages.

HABIT FOUR: ELIMINATE POOR PERFORMERS

Hire slow, fire fast.

Grant Styles

SECTION TWO
KNOW WHICH WAY TO GO

Habit Five - Anticipate Future Trends

Habit Six - Establish Shared Purpose

Habit Seven - Keep Competitors Close

Habit Eight - Enhance Personal Effectiveness

HABIT FIVE
ANTICIPATE FUTURE TRENDS

MOHAMMED BIN SALMAN
HOUSE OF SAUD

Scan The Horizon
Name The Trends
Shape The Future

Over coffee, I asked Ariana about Mohammed bin Salman (MBS),

"Just like the shifting sands, so too does the evolution of Saudi Arabia. Would you agree?"

"It's fascinating to witness," Ariana remarks, *"especially when you think about traditional Islamic society."*

"Given your aunt's role in caring for the Saudi royal family, she must see the changes up close?"

"Yes, it's like watching a flower bloom. MBS is changing things - reshaping societal norms and introducing flexibility. It's a significant transition."

"I often reflect on his academic ability. I have read that he graduated second in his law class from King Saud University."

"He's quite impressive, not one to have just jumped into the limelight. MBS worked in the private sector after university. Later, he was a government advisor to his father. By 31, he became the leader of Saudi Arabia, shaking up the line of succession."

"His presence is... commanding. He's got that look - strong jaw and piercing eyes."

"True, he exudes an aura of unbreakable confidence. He is calm and composed amidst the pace of business and politics."

"He feels like a modern leader. What do you think?"

HABIT FIVE: ANTICIPATE FUTURE TRENDS

"MBS is fluent in both Arabic and English. He is leading progressive reforms - particularly for women, by dismantling the old guard. He's navigating the twenty-first century for Saudi Arabia."

"I've noticed when he rubs his chin; it's as though I can see the wheels turning in his head, pondering the future."

"That's his intellect breaking through. He is a creative problem-solver, ready to face complex issues head-on."

"What about the West? Some view him as a paradox, an amalgamation of force and fear, like an apex predator in the political arena, with allegations of ruthlessly quashing dissent."

"To understand MBS's leadership, it's about the context. You must understand history to grasp the narrative he's creating for Saudi Arabia's future."

Ariana is right.

Pondering MBS demands context.

Around 4000 BCE, a dramatic loss of moisture and vegetation led to severe desertification in the Arab world, profoundly impacting its inhabitants. The climate's transition to drier conditions marked a shift to nomadic and water-conserving ways of living. People had to adapt to arid conditions and competition for rapidly diminishing resources.

Competition meant this period was also marked by increased territorial violence and genocide. In Figure 5.1, we see that even between 1850 and 1950, this dark competitive culture had left its imprint.

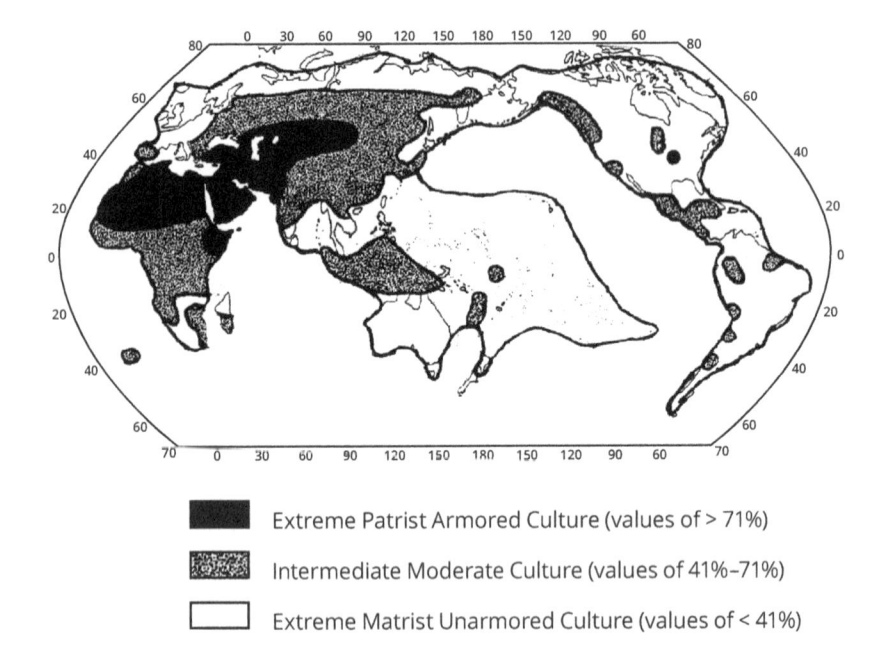

■ Extreme Patrist Armored Culture (values of > 71%)
▨ Intermediate Moderate Culture (values of 41%–71%)
☐ Extreme Matrist Unarmored Culture (values of < 41%)

Figure 5.1 World Behaviour Map (1850 to 1950)

For a Patrist Armoured societal score of 100%, the following cultural characteristics all need to be present:

1. Female premarital sex taboo.
2. Segregation of adolescent boys.
3. Male and female circumcision.
4. High bride prices.
5. Polygamous family organisation.

HABIT FIVE: ANTICIPATE FUTURE TRENDS

6. Patrilocal marital residence.
7. Patrilineal descent.
8. Patrilineal land inheritance.
9. Patrilineal movable property inheritance.
10. A high god.
11. Royal class stratification.
12. Caste stratification and slavery.

By contrast, societies with less than 41% of these characteristics are deemed Matrist and unarmoured.[89]

Amid the arid Saudi desert, lush land patches existed in areas like Riyadh. These scarce yet contrasting fertile lands allowed for flora, fauna and crop cultivation and were claimed and ruled over by the conquering royal families.

Today, Riyadh, meaning "gardens" in Arabic, is Saudi Arabia's largest city and royal capital. As Crown Prince and de facto ruler of Saudi Arabia, MBS resides in the Riyadh Royal Palace, where surveillance and protective services constantly watch his back. A stark contrast to the untamed lands of his forebears, when a moment's lapse in a leader's awareness could spell doom.

Saudi Arabia was traditionally an armoured Islamic Patrist society, where male dominance was etched into the fabric of life.[90] By contrast, unarmoured Matrist societies give women autonomy over their life choices, their bodies and their reproductive rights.

Yet, despite deep tradition, you will find in MBS a leader who has taken just one wife, not several wives. The role of women is also changing under MBS's leadership, with increased participation from the female labour force.

SCAN THE HORIZON

As MBS scans the horizon from his Riyadh palace, the cityscape unfurls like a tapestry - a striking silhouette of glass and steel spires reaching the heavens. The skyline is a silent testament to MBS's progress toward a new era for Saudi Arabia. From his residence in Jeddah, the 167-story Jeddah Tower can be seen, the tallest structure on Earth, ascending 180 meters higher than Dubai's Burj Khalifa.

To the north of Jeddah, the Red Sea coastline stretches forth like a vast pool of liquid sapphire, bathed in sunlight and brushed by the whispers of ocean and terrestrial breezes.

The Red Sea is celebrated for its stunning coral reefs and abundant marine life - a potential hub for tourism and a beacon for future holidaymakers attracted to its natural beauty. Here, where the desert edge meets the azure depths, one will see the beginnings of NEOM, MBS's ambitious project for a series of futuristic mega-cities.

HABIT FIVE: ANTICIPATE FUTURE TRENDS

When leaders scan the horizon, there are many stimuli to see and process. Much of what is coming our way remains hidden. In 2016, Bill Gates predicted a future pandemic. However, by the time people saw COVID-19 coming, it was too late. Nothing stays the same forever. We must keep sensing and seeing. Sensing and seeing are the first two steps of the six-step Strategic Mindset Process, which is explained in my book, 'The Strategy Book.'[91]

The most important strategic question every leader must continually answer is, 'What is really going on here?' It is only possible to know which direction to go once we understand what is happening around us and within us. Human perceptions matter. Each person sees the world in a unique way.

With every person perceiving the world differently, it is imperative for leaders to employ approaches like VUCA. VUCA was birthed in the late 1980s in the halls of the United States Army War College and was developed to help describe the swirling scenarios unfolding in the post-Cold War world.

Eventually, VUCA entered the mainstream world of business.

VUCA

VOLATILITY — **UNCERTAINTY** — **COMPLEXITY** — **AMBIGUITY**

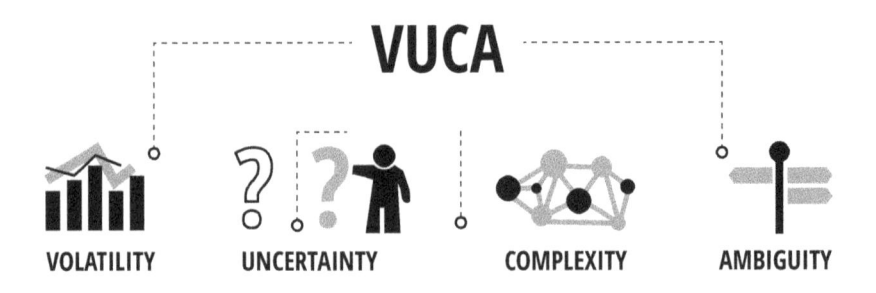

Figure 5.2 VUCA World View

Volatility is an unpredictable and whipsaw-like change that invariably hinders progress, often making it difficult for leaders to differentiate between urgency and importance.

Businesses address market volatility and fluctuating demand by moving towards more cost-efficient organisational structures, building up war-chest-like cash reserves, diversifying their product lines or services and targeting different customer segments.

Uncertainty is a consequence of volatility. Uncertainty beckons leaders to become the latest prophets of the unknown, where successful gambles can net epic results and fame. However, most prophets are found to be fools and die off from their resultant infamy.

Businesses meet uncertainty by continuously reassessing their strategy, stress-testing ideas, and keeping one eye glued on the horizon and the other to the rear-view mirror. These businesses have a proactive and fast-paced approach to transformation, constantly finding new ways to gain information and move forward.

Complexity is most often characterised by the sheer volume of relevant information present and the nature of it. Complexity is a labyrinthine intricacy where many variables can overwhelm or entwine, such that a plethora or tangle of interdependencies obscures cause and effect.

Businesses can respond to complexity by becoming ambidextrous and learning to balance short-term goals with long-term strategic planning. They also leverage advanced analytics and machine learning to sort through complex data and gain knowable, actionable insights that allow more informed decision-making.

Ambiguity is a sly trickster that clouds our vision, leaving us to question the meaning of what we see and the truth of what we think we know. Because we need something close to perfect information, we can become confused between cause and effect. Conflicts of interest, conscious or unconscious, can make understanding a situation impossible.

Businesses have learned to minimise ambiguity by fostering a culture of innovation with agile methodologies, which quickly convert uncertainty into opportunity.

In today's climate-affected world, it is not just businesses but rather the very fabric of our society that is under threat.

The first, second and third-order effects of climate change have complex implications that create what are often called 'wicked problems.' These are difficult to solve because of incomplete, contradictory and changing requirements. Wicked problems are complex and frequently involve multiple stakeholders, each with their values, preferences and priorities.

Worst of all, wicked problems are non-linear and have no clear solution. Instead, they demand creative, collaborative and innovative approaches that adapt over time and must be adjusted as the understanding of the problem deepens. Wicked problems take the task of scanning the horizon to a whole new level, with much to observe and assimilate.

Observing climate change is hard. There are a multiplicity of forces and effects at work:

First-order effects include increasing global surface temperatures, ocean warming, ice sheet melting, rising sea levels, changes to ocean currents, more frequent and intense weather events, heatwaves, wildfires, land degradation, reduced food security, increased deaths from heat stress and the spread of infectious diseases.

These first-order effects create negative feedback loops, self-reinforcing cycles that add to and accelerate the primary effects.

Dangerous negative feedback loops with global warming are numerous. For example, melting ice reduces the Earth's reflectivity, leading to greater absorption of solar radiation and further warming, which causes more ice to melt. Thawing permafrost releases methane, a potent greenhouse gas, which leads to additional warming and greater thawing of permafrost.

Warming temperatures stress forests, leading to wilting, withering and slow plant deaths. This forest dieback reduces the Earth's capacity to absorb CO_2, further increasing global warming.

Second-order effects involve the increasing and cascading impacts of first-order effects, which are nearly impossible to predict or manage. For instance, the physical destruction caused by extreme weather events can have significant consequences on social and economic systems, such as supply chain disruptions, increased likelihood of civil unrest and forced migrations.

A recent example of a second-order effect is the Panama Canal, which has had to reduce traffic due to reduced water supply. Leaders need a much deeper understanding of systemic interdependencies to understand why shipping routes are being compromised.

Third-order effects are the long-term and far less visible consequences of climate change that most leaders cannot see. They include radical changes in global geopolitical dynamics due to resource scarcity or the displacement of populations, shifts in economic power and changes in real estate valuation due to altered coastlines.

These third-order effects last for generations and permanently alter how human society functions. None of the current approaches can reverse climate change's third-order effects.

When it comes to responding to the complex, non-linear and irreversible tipping point effects of climate change, VUCA is inadequate for several reasons.

Climate change, a hyper-object, defies traditional understanding and approaches. Defining or solving it requires a paradigm shift. For instance, while one might fight an exploding Tesla battery with a fire extinguisher or large blanket, a wildfire tearing through the Amazon requires different strategies.

In our rapidly warming and fiery world, a better way of scanning the horizon and answering the question, 'What is really going on here?' is to embrace the BANI framework. BANI offers a nuanced understanding that aligns with the nature of climate change.

BANI suggests that today, many global systems are:

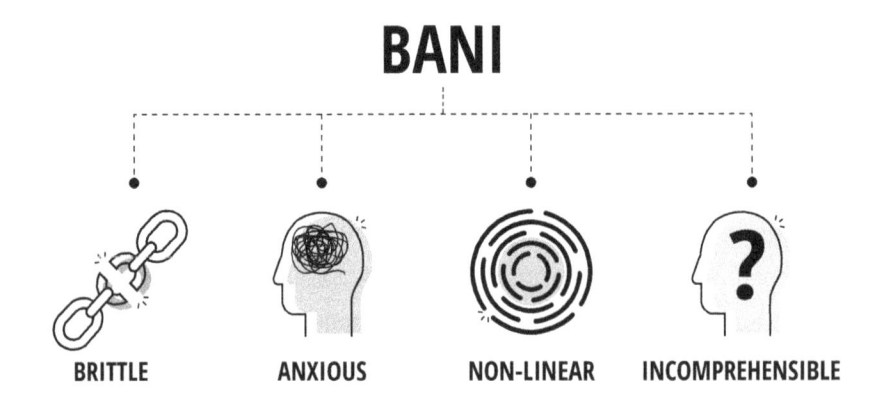

BANI

| BRITTLE | ANXIOUS | NON-LINEAR | INCOMPREHENSIBLE |

Figure 5.3 BANI World View

Brittle: They may break easily under stress rather than bending and adapting. With increasing interconnectedness, the ripple effect can be disastrous if one part fails, leading to broader system failures.

Continuously scanning the horizon for signs of brittleness can help us learn faster and remain resilient.

Anxious: The certainty that the world is becoming brittle makes us uneasy. This acknowledges the widespread anxiety about the future and adds a deep-seated emotional dimension as we contemplate such pervasive threats. We must make decisions quickly, as minutes lost may leave us behind.

Despite their anxiety, leaders must learn empathy and exhibit a degree of mindfulness, while acting decisively amid incomplete information.

Non-linear: In non-linear environments, even small decisions or inactions can have devastating consequences. The causes and effects of climate change are complex. Actions and consequences are interconnected in complex ways, making them difficult to predict or control.

This suggests and requires that leaders focus more on context and be flexible enough to engage in divergent systems thinking, embrace complexity and remain agile.

Incomprehensible: This suggests that we cannot fully understand climate change due to its vast scope and our knowledge limitations. Events can unfold so rapidly that the more we know, the less we understand.

Greater transparency helps. Here, traditional predictive models do not work. Creativity and brainstorming can help us formulate intuitive, adaptive and emergent strategies with a better chance of success. Please see Appendix Seven - Creativity.

Both VUCA and BANI are sources of disorder.

Antifragility, as coined by Nassim Nicholas Taleb, refers to systems or entities that <u>benefit from the disorder</u> caused by VUCA and BANI.

In his book, Antifragile,[92] Taleb offers a comprehensive framework for eliminating sources of fragility and champions ten strategies that reduce complexity, dependencies and vulnerabilities:

1. Embrace volatility
2. Encourage diversification
3. Utilise optionality
4. Implement decentralisation
5. Build in redundancy
6. Conduct stress testing
7. Adopt a barbell approach
8. Align incentives
9. Accept uncertainty
10. Apply *Via Negativa*

Taleb points out that *Via Negativa* is the most effective way to increase resilience by subtracting rather than adding. During the pandemic, many businesses learnt the value of using *Via Negativa* within their supply chains.

The principle of *Via Negativa* is illustrated at a personal level by Fields Millburn and Ryan Nicodemus's Minimalist Movement. This pair increased their resilience by subtracting possessions rather than adding to them. They demonstrated that owning only what we need makes people happier. With increasing bushfires, the most resilient communities remove all flammable vegetation and materials from the vicinity of homes and buildings to create defensible spaces with minimal or no flammable fuel.

Today, the fires we see on the horizon are not a mirage. We are entering a brave new world of our own making - a warming world where our past collective unconsciousness and ignorance have sown the seeds of new and profound challenges.

Leaders who understand what they are seeing are rare. They appreciate what unfolds before us. They recognise that an age of chaos is eclipsing the era of disruption.

Those with insight must articulate emerging trends clearly so they are understood by all. Collectively, this enables us to stem the tide.

NAME THE TRENDS

Like whole societies and species, trends rise and fall away.

Much like a distant tsunami, trends start as weak signals hundreds of miles out at sea and eventually head our way, patiently and with great force. Trends are like slowly moving tides, not short-lived episodic waves.

Trends also have rips called signals.

As a keen surfer for many years, I learned the impact of an incoming tide and the relative weakness of an outgoing one, except for the presence of rip currents. Rips can occur at any tide level but are more dangerous to swimmers on outgoing tides when the seaward pull is more pronounced.

Amy Webb's book 'The Signals Are Talking: Why Today's Fringe Is Tomorrow's Mainstream' explores the fascinating world of trend analysis, futurism and strategic planning using a cone concept. Webb explains the idea of "signals," which may grow into emerging trends. Many technologies and developments start on the fringes of society and have the potential to become mainstream.

CEOs with good visioning abilities listen to the signals. In Figure 5.4, Webb's Strategic Planning Cone, the "Vision" zone requires a long-term perspective (5-10 years and beyond). Here, foresight about signals is essential.

CEOs must shape the future direction in the face of ambiguous signals such as the slowly increasing sovereign debt around the globe. CEOs must also respond to highly reliable trends such as social media, climate change, AI use and a shortage of talent.[93] This strategic foresight involves preparing for multiple potential scenarios, continuously updating assumptions and being agile in response to the changing signals from the external environment.

HABIT FIVE: ANTICIPATE FUTURE TRENDS

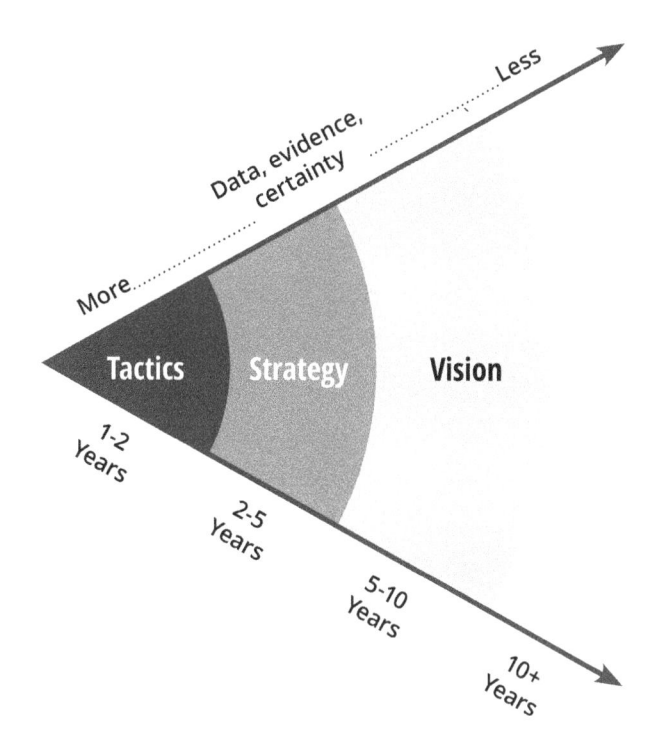

Figure 5.4 Strategic Planning Cone

Moving to the "Strategy" zone, which looks 2-5 years ahead, there is an emphasis on developing approaches to achieving medium-term goals and balancing known variables with emerging trends. For the "Tactics" zone, actions are planned for the immediate future (1-2 years) with established trends, which have more data, evidence and certainty. CEOs need a limited focus on managing the present and a significant emphasis on creating the future.[94]

In 1973, I remember my father, who had worked at Stanford, showing me an email account, where he used to message others via the ARPANET. At that time, there were only a few thousand email users globally within a tight-knit community primarily made up of university scientists and academics.

During the mid-1980s, I enjoyed using email via SMTP software on the Unix operating systems sold by the tech company I was working for. Once the World Wide Web appeared in 1991, email became mainstream. By 1997, Hotmail and Yahoo had arrived, making email usage a global trend.

Also in 1973, Martin Cooper of Motorola made the first mobile phone call on an early prototype of the Motorola DynaTAC. This first large handheld cellular phone was released in 1984. By 1987, as a sales rep who worked on the road, I was perhaps one of 250,000 fringe users globally with one of these 'brick phones.' This device cost my firm $20,000 and had an active battery life of only 2 hours.

By the 1990s, Nokia had entered the mobile phone market and by 2005, their annual sales had exceeded 250 million phones per year. Since introducing the iPhone in the last two decades, Apple has sold an estimated 3 billion iPhones.

For decades, telecommuting was a signal, not a trend, and had been practised for about twenty years by a relatively small number of global tech companies. Elsewhere, telecommuting was seen as a fringe benefit or a niche arrangement. The COVID-19 pandemic made it a trend. Hybrid and remote work have become widespread and have had a lasting impact on the future of work.

Autonomous cars and air taxis have been on the fringes of society for nearly a decade. However, as we have seen with email, mobile phones and remote working, autonomous transport will be as commonplace as receiving an email, sending a voice message or working from home.

Naming trends can be risky.

The assumptions we make are critical. If our assumptions are based on reliable knowledge grounded in evidence, it will be safer to place bigger bets. If our assumptions are based solely on hunches and wishful thinking, we might be seeing a short-lived signal, not a trend.

Back in the Saudi Royal Palace, MBS has scanned the horizon and named the trends related to his people and the world. These include global warming and transitioning the Saudi economy away from its dependence on fossil fuels. MBS's regional analysis reveals a shift towards solar, wind, green hydrogen and nuclear energy, mining, logistics, sports, music, tourism, digital services, finance and entrepreneurship.

SHAPE THE FUTURE

Shaping the future is a passion for MBS.

To even the most astute investor, MBS is an exciting leader to watch. NEOM, the brainchild of MBS, is taking shape in Saudi Arabia's Tabuk Province along the Red Sea.

NEOM's futuristic giga-project includes a network of carbon-free smart cities and resorts with research centres, innovation hubs, medical facilities, health and wellness centres, sports complexes, entertainment venues and cultural and educational institutions.

NEOM is planned to operate independently from the existing governmental framework with its own tax and labour laws designed to attract international investment.[95]

NEOM also features 'The Line', a 170-kilometre-long linear futuristic city, and 'Trojena', a year-round destination for winter sports, slated to be completed in time to host the 2029 Asian Winter Games. NEOM boasts a highly advanced transportation network that includes the new Red Sea International Airport, intelligent public transit and autonomous vehicles. Designed with sustainability at its core, NEOM aims to harness renewable energy, implement water conservation techniques and follow eco-friendly construction practices.

MBS also envisions transforming Saudi Arabia into a global investment powerhouse and a logistics hub connecting three continents: Asia, Europe and Africa.

MBS's Vision 2030 focuses on three main themes:

1. A vibrant society.
2. A thriving economy.
3. An ambitious nation.

His vision includes plans to further increase women's participation in the workforce.

These initiatives have sparked significant enthusiasm among employed and unemployed Saudi youth, resonating with a brighter future for themselves and their country.

In the next habit, we will learn about creating the future from someone who taught himself computer programming at twelve and then sold a video game he had made.

Before we move on, look back and reflect on your insights from this habit and make some notes on the following blank pages.

When you are ready, proceed to Activity Five.

ACTIVITY FIVE

5.1 As a leader, MBS proactively identifies trends and shapes the future. In response to global warming, MBS is diversifying the Saudi economy beyond oil dependency by investing in many new areas that will lead his country and its people to success.

> Q1. Which of these megatrends; global warming, water scarcity, aging populations, rapid urbanisation, the rising middle class or AI and Automation - will most impact your firm's future?
> Q2. Which framework, VUCA or BANI, offers you the best questions and creative ideas?
> Q3. Is getting to net zero one of your firm's goals? Should it be?

5.2 Apply the concept of Antifragility to enhance your firm's resilience by employing at least three of the subsequent ten strategies aimed at minimising complexity, dependencies and vulnerabilities.

- Embrace volatility
- Encourage diversification
- Utilise optionality
- Implement decentralisation
- Build in redundancy
- Conduct stress testing
- Adopt a barbell approach
- Align incentives
- Accept uncertainty
- Apply *Via Negativa*

HABIT FIVE: ANTICIPATE FUTURE TRENDS

5.3 Three of MBS's strengths are:

1. Visionary Thinking: MBS consistently identifies emerging trends.
2. Adaptability: MBS embraces the trends that will impact his region and his people.
3. Investment in Innovation: MBS invests in capabilities that help him shape the future.

   Evaluate your proficiency at these strengths, and, using the blank pages that follow, make some notes on how to improve them.

The future belongs to those who see possibilities before they become obvious.

John Sculley

HABIT SIX
ESTABLISH SHARED PURPOSE

ELON MUSK
TESLA MOTORS INC.

Communicate Your Vision
Lead By Example
Promote Confidence

Imagine growing up in the sun-baked hues of Pretoria.

Picture a past with harsh, painful days, in stark contrast to the vibrant future one might envision at night under a blanket of stars.

The violence Elon Musk endured as an early teen was barbaric and gruesome.[96] *He was routinely surrounded by bullies at Pretoria Boys' High School.*

His crime?

Taking an early stand against racism and injustice.

Musk remembers lying in a hospital bed, his broken skull and face unrecognisable - a swollen testament to the 'Lord of the Flies' like cruelty of boys,[97] *their unyielding fists and heeled shoes.*

Amidst the sterile white of the hospital, young Elon's mind raced with dreams of rocket ships and electric cars.

A resolute defiance against the gravity of his circumstances.

However, it was his battles at home that shaped him profoundly. Musk's father, Errol, an engineer by trade and aggressor by nature, imparted complex and harsh lessons. Errol's charisma was polarising; it enchanted young Elon with dreams of innovation.

Meanwhile, Errol's violent outbursts cast long shadows over his son's youth. Musk's father was both his sternest critic and an unintentional catalyst that imbued Elon with a paradoxical blend of vulnerability and an ironclad resolve.

HABIT SIX: ESTABLISH SHARED PURPOSE

This intricate dance of light and shadow propelled Musk forward, beyond the schoolyard cruelty and the earth, into the boundless expanse of space and the electric renaissance of our roads.

The road ahead is not just a playground Musk aims to own, but the future itself - a brighter tomorrow.

Architects of tomorrow are rare.

Da Vinci, Tesla, Lovelace, Berners-Lee, Curie, Turing and Musk flash forth amidst the brightest echelons of human potential.

Such architects are purposeful, luminous and as vast as the night sky.

Remaining engaged and galvanising others around a shared purpose is a defining hallmark of Elon Musk. Committed to positively impacting humanity, Musk values hard work and takes risks. Musk's journey to becoming the CEO of the world's most innovative companies is a saga of relentless pursuit and visionary ambition.

He is passionate, insatiable and curious.

Musk's gaze is intense and unpredictable. His leadership style is often unconventional and sometimes brash. Musk's success can be attributed to a myriad of factors. Some of these are his habits of leading by example, promoting confidence and the ability to communicate a compelling vision.

In 2002, he became the CEO and lead designer of SpaceX. Then later, the CEO and product architect of Tesla Inc. Musk's path has been strewn with obstacles, from the financial brinkmanship of SpaceX's early launches to Tesla's production hurdles and the woke-led backlash against his acquisition of X.

In 2018, Musk became a co-founder of Open AI. A related venture, Neuralink, founded by Musk, is improving human life through implantable AI devices to restore lost brain function.

Musk embodies a quote by famous business author Jim Collins:

"Far better to dare mighty things, to win glorious triumphs, even though checkered by failure, than to take rank with those poor spirits who neither enjoy much nor suffer much, because they live in the grey twilight that knows not victory, nor defeat."[98]

Musk knows the triumphs that come from realising a shared purpose. As an advocate for sustainable energy and technology to combat climate change, he has gained the trust of millions by:

1. Developing and bringing long-range electric vehicles to market.
2. Building an extensive network of Supercharger stations.
3. Producing solar panels and energy storage systems.
4. Constructing the Gigafactory – a large-scale battery factory.
5. Creating Tesla's vertically integrated business, from sourcing raw materials to delivery.
6. Pioneering efforts in Open AI and Neuralink.
7. Leading SpaceX and its manned missions to Mars.

8. Envisioning 700 mph Hyperloop transport systems.
9. Founding The Boring Company to create tunnels that reduce traffic.
10. Launching the Starlink Satellite Network to provide remote internet access.

Like Reed Hastings, Musk has a long list of terminated ex-employees. He constantly pushes boundaries and frontiers and 'takes no prisoners.' Some do not agree with his methods. Nevertheless, his ability to communicate a compelling vision, coupled with his competence in formulating and executing missions, is nothing short of breathtaking.

COMMUNICATE YOUR VISION

Vision and mission both guide decision-making. One is aspirational, the other embodied.

A vision statement offers a long-term view of the organisation's mission. It inspires and motivates.

A mission statement states the organisation's daily purpose. It answers the question of "what it is that we do" and "how we do it."

Tesla's vision statement is: "To accelerate the world's transition to sustainable energy."[99]

This statement guides Tesla's long-term aspiration to help transition the world to sustainable energy by developing and producing electric cars, rechargeable batteries and solar electric components.

Tesla's mission statement is: "To create the most compelling car company of the 21st century by driving the world's transition to electric vehicles."[100]

This statement describes what the company does daily and how it does it.

CEOs often communicate their firm's vision through interviews, speeches and presentations to build support for their company. The Harvard Business Review found that CEOs who give speeches are more likely to be seen as credible and inspiring leaders – building support for their organisation's vision and mission.[101]

When a vision is already compelling, simply sharing it over and over brings it to light. At other times, a vision may be less inspiring. In this instance, the way it is communicated can make it compelling. CEOs of cigarette, soft drink and fast-food companies, as well as the marketers they employ, must be excellent communicators to force stakeholders to look beyond their products' less-than-ideal long-term health impacts.

To build support for Tesla, Musk has regularly communicated Tesla's vision through interviews and presentations - sharing his vision for the future of energy, transportation and humanity. In August 2006, after the EV market's early adopters placed the first 500 orders for the Tesla Roadster, Musk announced his purposeful vision to the world:

HABIT SIX: ESTABLISH SHARED PURPOSE

"The overarching purpose of Tesla Motors is to help expedite the move from a mine-and-burn carbon economy towards a solar electric economy."

For many, Musk's purpose could have been more aspirational. To make his vision embodied, Musk then explained Tesla's mission in a four-point plan:

1. Build and sell a sleek and futuristic Roadster sports car.
2. Use that money to build and sell an affordable car.
3. Use that money to build an even more affordable car.
4. While doing the above, provide zero-emission power generation options.

By 2008, Tesla had delivered over 2000 Roadsters, which excited and delighted early customers. One early advocate was the Governor of California, Arnold Schwarzenegger, who announced,

"I test-drove this vehicle, and it is hot."

Influential advocates and brand ambassadors are helpful voices for raising awareness of your firm's aspirations. However, care is needed. Schwarzenegger was a fan of the Roadster but only sometimes of the climate change vision.

Schwarzenegger also admits:

"I have a private plane. But I fly commercial when I go to environmental conferences."

LEAD BY EXAMPLE

Conscientious CEOs like Musk prioritise sustainable futures.

Musk's active role in Tesla's electric and solar ventures underscores his dedication to a sustainable future. Leaders like Musk, who demonstrate their vision through their actions, are more likely to be trusted and respected than those who simply talk about them.[102]

By 2009, Musk demonstrated ambitious leadership by acquiring a defunct GM plant in Fremont Beach, CA, funded by a $500 million US Government loan. Its IPO in 2010, the first by an American automaker in half a century, raised another $226 million. The acclaimed Model S, launched in 2012, secured the 'Car of the Year' title in 2013.

Tesla scaled its factories and dealerships rapidly, and in 2015, released its Model X SUV for $132,000 and its Model 3 Sedan for $35,000. In late 2015, Musk solved the Tesla Model Xs' early quality control issues and improved the company's manufacturing processes.

In just a decade, Musk had shown the world that he could establish a shared purpose and deliver on it!

When his SolarCity merger in 2016 was met with scepticism and criticism, Musk continued to invest in the venture and eventually turned it into a profitable business. In 2017, Musk hoped to solve evolving production issues for the Tesla Model 3 by increasing plant capacity.

HABIT SIX: ESTABLISH SHARED PURPOSE

In late 2017, he had fixed production issues for the Model 3. In early 2018, the departure of Tesla's head of engineering and chief financial officer raised questions about the company's leadership. Musk quickly addressed the departures by highlighting the company's strong performance and the capabilities of the remaining leadership team.

Musk then announced the names of new hires and promotions to fill the vacant leadership positions and reaffirmed Tesla's mission. Employees in every organisation, at every level, need to know that at the heart of what they do lies something grand and aspirational.[103]

2018 marked a dark period for Musk. When charged by the Securities and Exchange Commission (SEC) with fraud for tweets about taking Tesla private in 2018, Musk settled with the SEC. Then his new and improved energy-saving and highly automated plant in Fremont Beach, responsible for the lion's share of Model 3 builds, was operating at too high a gear. As a result, numerous production and product market failures occurred.

By October 2018, Tesla was on the brink of financial collapse. Things had become both urgent and vital. Musk had to lead by example.

Musk stepped onto the shop floor to understand the situation.

Musk began working 120-hour weeks. Concerned family and friends asked him to slow down.

At that time, Musk said, "If you have anyone who can do a better job, please let me know. They can have the job."

An on-the-job trap that CEOs may face when trying to lead by example is that they become too focused on short-term results, neglect their health and bypass the long-term goals and values of the company.

The idea of CEOs like Musk working 120-hour weeks poses two questions:

Q1. How much stress is acceptable – how far can I safely push myself?

Q2. What can be done to lower the level of stress in my workplace?

The stress that was unacceptable to Musk's family and friends was less than Musk's threshold. They saw the situation as a 'game-changer' for his mental and physical health. Meanwhile, Musk moved from being 'on his game' to being 'okay for now,' as shown in Figure 6.1.

HABIT SIX: ESTABLISH SHARED PURPOSE

STRESS LEVEL ACCEPTABLE TO CEO

	ON THEIR GAME	OK FOR NOW	
		Musk: "I'm ok"	
	OFF THEIR GAME	GAME CHANGER	
		Musk's family and friends: "You need to rest…"	

LOW STRESS WORKPLACE ← → HIGH STRESS WORKPLACE

STRESS LEVEL UNACCEPTABLE TO CEO

Figure 6.1 CEO Game Gauge

Six months later, Musk solved his company's Model 3 production and product issues, and by late 2019, he reported Tesla's first profits.

Tesla's first profits were achieved partly by his hands-on approach and a risky investment in Bitcoin. Musk shared that Tesla was considering accepting Bitcoin as a valid way to buy Tesla cars. The Bitcoin price rose sharply. A short time later, Musk sold 75% of the Bitcoin investment, and Tesla made $1 billion in profit.

Then, with a greater understanding of Bitcoin, Musk changed gears and announced that Tesla would not accept Bitcoin for cars due to the negative environmental impact of the Bitcoin server network on the planet.

By 2021, unit production costs were under control, and sales margins had improved.

Meanwhile, in a parallel universe, Musk's SpaceX program overcame setbacks by investing in redesigns and process improvements. SpaceX's 'Starship' and 'Super Heavy' had their first flights in 2023 – ultimately aimed at various celestial destinations, including the Moon and Mars.

CEOs like Musk, who communicate their vision through actions, improve their chances of success and are more likely to be trusted and respected than those who only talk about the vision. As Musk has shown, 'walking the talk' makes for an even more compelling vision.

As Musk illustrates, the negative repercussions of stress on a CEO are not commensurate with the amount of stress. More often, the limit is determined by the CEO's acceptance or willingness to embrace stress.[104]

As we saw in the previous habit with VUCA and BANI, the future is always inconvenient and unpredictable. Healthy CEOs understand that making their work-life predictable rather than unpredictable can help them lower stress levels. The best CEOs usually only need to make a few decisions.

They solve many generic situations through rules and policies. Once a CEO determines which decisions are generic or repeated, they decide once and then communicate that to others as policy.

HABIT SIX: ESTABLISH SHARED PURPOSE

Savvy CEOs strive for a purposeful and automated set of systems around places, people, and processes. They may achieve military-like precision around many decisions – with minimal effort and mental strain. By limiting the number of urgent activities, CEOs preserve their mental capacity for unique situations.

Setbacks are unique situations where a CEO can lead on purpose and by example to demonstrate the compelling nature of the organisation's vision. CEOs, through intellect and resilience, can artfully weather many crises. Musk routinely delegates urgent and non-urgent issues that are not vital. Non-urgent vital matters are scheduled for strategy reviews.

However, issues like the combined production and product market failures at Fremont Beach were both urgent and vital to the immediate success and long-term survival of Tesla. In this case, Musk made Fremont Beach his top priority.

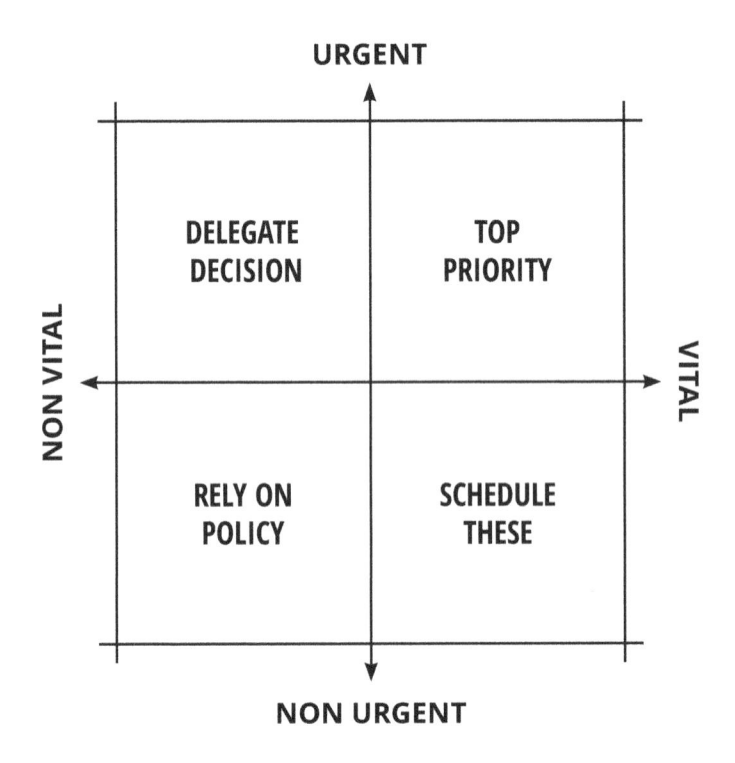

```
                    URGENT
                      ▲
        ┌─────────────┼─────────────┐
        │             │             │
        │  DELEGATE   │     TOP     │
        │  DECISION   │   PRIORITY  │
 NON    │             │             │  VITAL
VITAL ◄─┼─────────────┼─────────────┼─►
        │             │             │
        │   RELY ON   │   SCHEDULE  │
        │   POLICY    │    THESE    │
        │             │             │
        └─────────────┼─────────────┘
                      ▼
                  NON URGENT
```

Figure 6.2 Eisenhower Matrix

The more issues a CEO has in the urgent/vital quadrant of Figure 6.2, the more stress they experience. Musk's portfolio of business ventures, from SpaceX to Tesla to Neuralink and, more recently, X, routinely creates many Top Priority decisions for him. Musk is incredibly efficient and effective at managing his time and is brilliant at getting things done. He is often busy and can take on more tasks while remaining productive.

CEOs are busy people who get things done. Most of us cannot tolerate the high pressure that Musk has handled. Nevertheless, CEOs can lead by example, showing others the value of systems, policies and rules that preserve their mental capacity for top priority and unique decisions.

HABIT SIX: ESTABLISH SHARED PURPOSE

PROMOTE CONFIDENCE

When compared with employees who lack confidence, confident employees:

1. Are more engaged and productive.
2. Take greater initiative.[105]
3. Generate new ideas.
4. Accept additional responsibilities.
5. Persist in the face of obstacles.[106]
6. Make sounder decisions.[107]
7. Stay positive.
8. Are enthusiastic.
9. Remain resilient.[108]
10. Inspire others[109]
11. Promote teamwork.
12. Communicate better.[110]
13. Are more adaptable to change.
14. Are less afraid to take risks.
15. Are willing to have 'skin in the game.'
16. Raise performance in themselves and other employees.[111]

Tesla promotes a sense of ownership among its workforce by offering stock options, allowing all employees to have 'skin in the game' and share in the company's productivity gains. Musk's approach to incentivise everyone from entry-level to executives with stock that vests over time cultivates a collective commitment to the company's prosperity and engenders deep-seated loyalty and motivation within the team.

Unlike other major automakers, Tesla has avoided unionisation. In 2023, when Joe Biden made ill-informed public comments about unionising Tesla, many workers reacted negatively. Most Tesla workers have confidence in their jobs and do not want powerful 'rent-seeking' unions interfering.

Rent-seeking unions often negatively impact worker morale and performance by prioritising the interests of a few and creating a work culture of entitlement and complacency rather than focusing on collective worker welfare and productivity.

Successful CEOs also understand the role social media can play in promoting confidence. Well-managed social media can help CEOs to be more transparent, approachable and in touch with the concerns of their people, their customers and the public.[112]

Musk frequently uses X to broadcast updates about Tesla's products. He also makes known his concerns and ideas. This allows him to connect directly with customers and stakeholders and to build excitement in their shared purpose.

Sharing success stories of how a company has positively impacted customers, employees and the community is critical. Sharing successes and celebrating wins weekly, or even daily, demonstrates the ongoing importance of an organisation's purpose and promotes confidence. CEOs need to celebrate the shared purpose and routinely convey stories of their team's successes.

HABIT SIX: ESTABLISH SHARED PURPOSE

Whether a firm is public or private, transparency helps to promote confidence. A common trap many CEOs face when trying to establish confidence is that they may become too focused on controlling the narrative by always presenting a positive company image.

Being transparent about challenges and setbacks helps. When the chips are down, all is not lost. Within every fall is a chance to soar to new heights. With every lost chip and challenge comes a new frontier.

The COVID-19 pandemic caused a massive global shortage of the semiconductor chips needed to make cars. Musk divulged this news to his people. Musk and his team avoided the catastrophic shortage by creating their own chips. With this challenge came a new frontier. Tesla pursued a new material technology called silicon carbide wafers for its vehicles.

The unique properties of silicon carbide made Tesla's chips much more energy-efficient and durable than traditional silicon wafers. Due to their improved thermal conductivity, silicon carbide wafers reduce energy loss by as much as 50%.

Again, this energy-saving move aligned with the shared purpose and vision Musk initially established for Tesla. Their chip innovation inspired other companies to follow.

It is important to note that a firm's shared purpose may not have as grand a planetary impact as Tesla's. The shared purpose for any firm can be extended via corporate social responsibility (CSR) goals. CEOs should take a holistic view of their operations, looking at their firm's financial performance and its footprint on the wider world.

Musk has repeatedly demonstrated that shareholders are not his primary focus. This is why he has sometimes looked to take Tesla private, often creating sharp movements in the share price. His most important stakeholder is humanity. Musk's vision to expedite the move from a mine-and-burn carbon economy towards a solar-electric economy was embraced wholeheartedly by the share market in 2020 and has continued since, as revealed in Figure 6.3.

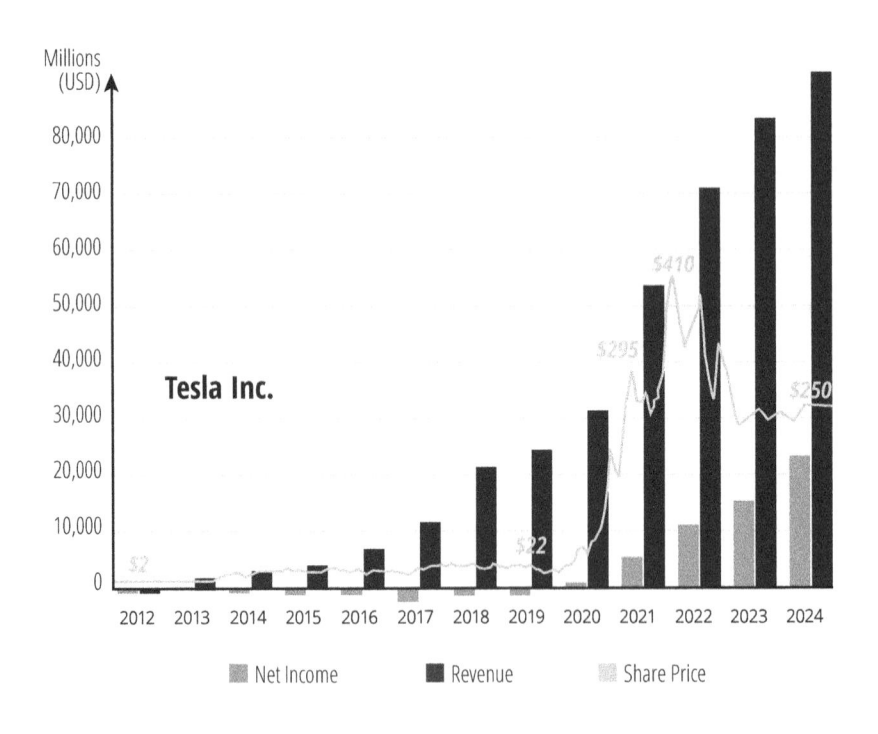

Figure 6.3 Tesla Confidence-Performance Curve

HABIT SIX: ESTABLISH SHARED PURPOSE

When taking a comprehensive stakeholder approach, astute CEOs recognise they may need extra help gaining the confidence of capital markets. Having Joe Biden set a 2035 100% clean energy target and having the US re-join the Paris Climate Agreement has helped Musk's shared purpose.

Musk shows us the importance of aligning a company's interests with planetary and interplanetary progress!

It's time to progress to the next habit, which reveals a quintessential garage-to-global-executive tale.

Before we move on, look back and reflect on your insights from this habit and make some notes on the following blank pages.

When you are ready, proceed to Activity Six.

ACTIVITY SIX

6.1 A clear and memorable purpose is essential for a successful business.

A memorable purpose can align collective efforts towards a future that benefits humanity.

As demonstrated by Reed Hastings in Habit Four, a company must have a universally understood mission so that employees are consistently working towards the same goals.

For over a decade, Netflix's mission statement has been: "To entertain the world."

Netflix's vision statement is also clear: "Becoming the best global entertainment distribution service."

In contrast, Kodak's 1990 mission was cumbersome, and its vision was overly ego-centric:

"Building a world-class, results-oriented culture that offers consumers and customers various methods to capture, store, process, output, and communicate images and pictures as memories, information, and entertainment to people and machines anywhere, anytime; and to market differentiated, cost-effective solutions quickly and flawlessly in terms of quality, through a diverse team of energetic employees with world-class talent and skills to sustain Kodak as the World Leader in Imaging."

"Our heritage has been, and our future is, to be the World Leader in Imaging."

Q1. Do your firm's vision and mission statements resonate as clearly and compellingly with your team and stakeholders as you intend?
Q2. Is your firm's shared purpose something that contributes to a sustainable future for humanity?

6.2 Musk embodies his firm's vision through decisive actions and activity, bolstering credibility and fostering trust. However, this kind of approach must be balanced using the Eisenhower Matrix.

Q1. How can you apply the Eisenhower Matrix to schedule your time better?
Q2. How will you prioritise your health and not allow stress to rule your life?

6.3 Plot your current stress position on Figure 6.1 CEO Game Gauge.

Q1. What needs to change?
Q2. What changes will you make?

When spiders unite, they can tie down a lion.

African Proverb

HABIT SEVEN
KEEP COMPETITORS CLOSE

SUSAN WOJCICKI
YOUTUBE

Analyse The Competition
Know Yourself
Master Combat

I remember the regal feeling, running hither and yonder amid the leafy environs of Stanford University.

The harmonious blend of Romanesque and Modern architecture inspiring a sense of endless possibility.

Each corridor and laboratory - a gateway to new worlds.

On sun-drenched afternoons, I would accompany my father, who taught computer science, through sprawling quadrangular courtyards and arching palm trees.

The campus air was rich with the scent of eucalyptus bushes and the hum of intellectuals clattering on typewriter-like keyboards - a symphony of progress echoing through hallowed halls.

Susan Wojcicki, also a Stanford child, was at home amidst the vibrant campus grounds. Her father, a physics professor, and her mother, an educator, instilled in Wojcicki a reverence for knowledge and an insatiable curiosity. This foundational upbringing set Wojcicki on a path of lifelong learning and achievement.

Wojcicki's academic pursuits took her from Harvard's historical and literary corridors to the analytical rigours of science, technology and economics. The early years of her career at Intel Corporation were followed by further expansion of her expertise through a master's in economics from UCSC and an MBA from UCLA's Anderson School of Management.

In 1998, Wojcicki's trajectory intersected with that of Google. She completed her MBA just as Google's founders set up their first office in her family's garage. Her entry into Google as their first marketing manager marked the beginning of a storied career, where she played a pivotal role in developing Google's initial marketing strategies, creating the famous Google logo and launching Google Image Search.

Her ascent continued. By 2003 she had become the VP of Advertising & Commerce, overseeing the growth of AdWords and the introduction of Google Analytics. Wojcicki's business acumen was evident when she perceived the untapped potential of YouTube. She advocated for its acquisition in a move reminiscent of Estée Lauder's strategy of acquiring up-and-coming threats.

Google's $1.65 billion purchase of YouTube in 2006 was a testament to her foresight. By 2014, she had ascended to the role of YouTube CEO, where she guided YouTube through expansive growth and innovation, introducing platforms like YouTube Gaming and YouTube TV. Under Wojcicki's guidance, YouTube made strides towards inclusivity and safety, implementing policies to restrict hate speech and violent extremism.

Moreover, Wojcicki's tenure saw an increase in gender diversity, with the percentage of female employees rising significantly. Her influence stretched beyond strategy with her advocacy for paid parental leave and efforts to close the gender gap in tech.

As Wojcicki stepped down from her role as CEO, her tenure at YouTube reflected her strategic acumen and her moral and ethical stances. Her legacy, punctuated by her engaging blue eyes and the strength of her convictions, enriched her company and the broader competitive landscape.

ANALYSE THE COMPETITION

A summary of the UCLA MBA Strategy Unit reads:

'The course is designed to introduce a wide variety of modern strategy frameworks and methodologies, including methods for assessing the strength of competition, for understanding relative bargaining power, for anticipating competitors' actions, for analysing cost and value structures and their relevance to competition, and for assessing potential changes in the scope of the firm.'

When it comes to strategy, bright MBA graduates like Wojcicki, have been schooled in the need to understand the competition.

Specifically, they learn to:

1. Assess the competition.
2. Anticipate competitor moves.
3. Analyse the competition's relevance to their firm's future.

CEOs need to do the same.

HABIT SEVEN: KEEP COMPETITORS CLOSE

A CEO must have an eye for their competition, unless they operate in a new or uncontested market where competition does not exist.

CEOs understand that new and uncontested markets only last for a while. CEOs pay attention to what is happening in their marketplace and assess the changing external business environment. They anticipate competitor moves and change their firm's strategy in response to the evolving competitive landscape.

In 2022, in response to the evolving popularity of TikTok, Wojcicki reported:

"It's definitely a very dynamic market. So, we're always paying attention to what's happening in the marketplace and there's constant change."

HIGH WIN RATE

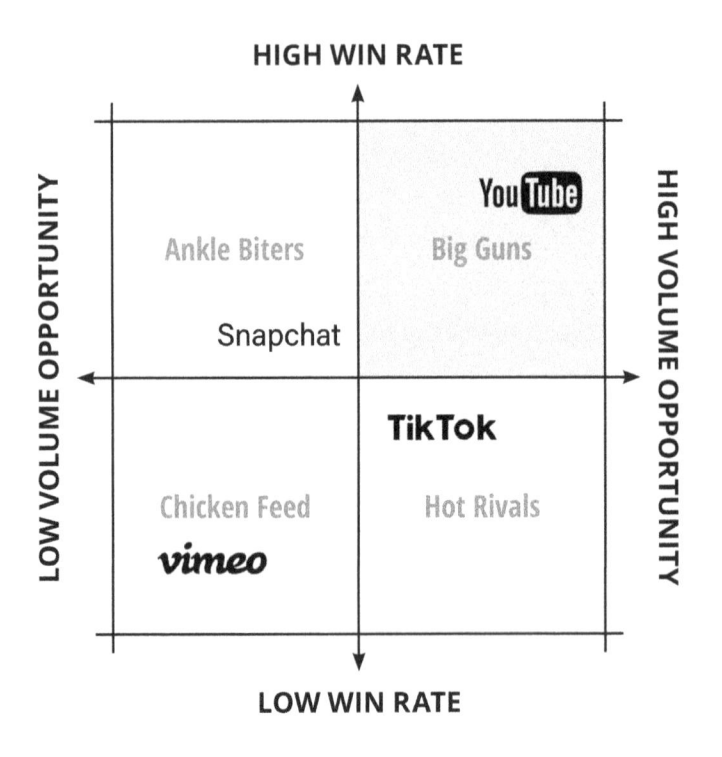

	Ankle Biters	Big Guns YouTube	
LOW VOLUME OPPORTUNITY	Snapchat		HIGH VOLUME OPPORTUNITY
	Chicken Feed vimeo	**TikTok** Hot Rivals	

LOW WIN RATE

Figure 7.1 Opportunity-Win Matrix

Wojcicki has learned when to fight and when not to fight. Buying rival YouTube was a well-timed strategic move. At the time of writing, acting on TikTok is not. As shown in Figure 7.1, TikTok has emerged as a hot rival with some benefits.

Often, the path of least resistance provides the optimal course of action. Wojcicki knows that many TikTok creators consider YouTube their home base, and they post to TikTok with links back to their YouTube accounts. She also knows that TikTok has ties to the Chinese Communist Party (CCP), and that anti-China privacy concerns may limit TikTok's progress in the West.

HABIT SEVEN: KEEP COMPETITORS CLOSE

KNOW YOURSELF

The Art of War by Chinese General Sun Tzu states:

"If you know your opponent and know yourself, you will not suffer in a hundred battles; if you do not know your enemies but know yourself, for every battle you win, you will lose one; if you do not know your enemies nor yourself, you will be imperilled in every single battle."

Business and war are similar.

When Stanford University dropout and Snapchat CEO Evan Spiegel felt threatened by the encroachment of Facebook into Snapchat's early market, he gave his team members a copy of 'The Art of War.'

I don't think his team read it or understood it.

Around that time, Spiegel declined Facebook's generous $3 billion takeover offer – a nice exit or new partnership for Spiegel.

Nevertheless, Facebook understood Snapchat well.

Snapchat colossally underestimated Facebook and Snapchat overestimated itself.

Soon after, Facebook curbed Snapchat's appeal by allowing Instagram users to personalise photos with realistic-looking digital elements.

Following the addition of 'Instagram Stories', Facebook eventually hung Snapchat out to dry.

An essential point in 'The Art of War' is that information matters and that a well-educated move can be better than most gut decisions. Sun Tzu believed that leaders should be adept at 'military calculus'. CEOs also need to account for anything and everything that could affect the outcome of a battle.

CEOs develop insight into what competitors might attempt. They know their strengths and weaknesses and those of their competitors. CEOs routinely analyse big data reports to see the field clearly. In business negotiations, knowing yourself and your opponent in detail can be vital for success.

Knowing yourself extends to knowing what employees and customers do on their devices. Today, CEOs need to understand the digital marketing channels and how channel growth and channel return on investment (ROI) vary between demographic groups.

In Figure 7.2, we see that Google AdWords, email campaigns and traditional outdoor and TV advertising are still good channel 'cash cows' for many. In most markets, search engine optimisation (SEO) tools, YouTube and Facebook are 'stars' that offer healthy channel growth.

HABIT SEVEN: KEEP COMPETITORS CLOSE

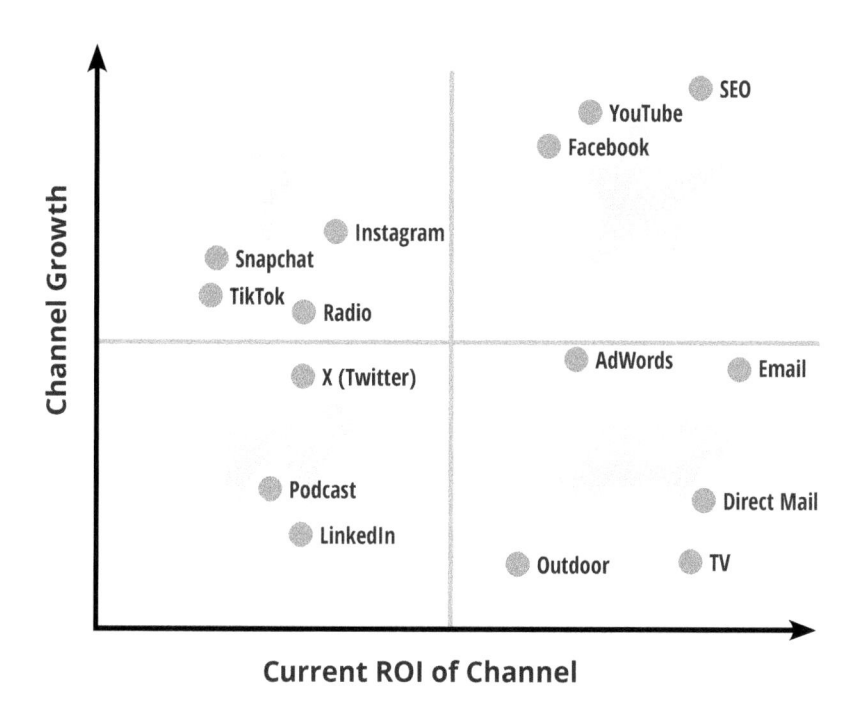

Figure 7.2 BCG Marketing Matrix

Figure 7.2 BCG Marketing Matrix does not reveal that Gen Z consumers born between 1995 and 2012 differ from the overall consumer market. Today, Gen Z is best reached via Instagram and TikTok. The Estée Lauder Companies understand this as a result of their willingness to energise their middle managers and allow them to reverse mentor their executive branches.

CEOs take time to study channel competition, and they understand The Art of War.

As a result, they have three competitive principles at their fingertips:

(i) Neither party benefits from prolonged conflict nor delayed innovation.

It is often a race to the bottom in a protracted price war. Astute CEOs like Leonard Lauder worked hard to avoid such wars. In recent history, Didi and Uber have attested to the exhaustive effects of a protracted conflict. Both firms burned through billions of dollars and fought a lengthy price war.

In the 'Art of War', Sun Tzu advises leaders to strike effectively and quickly, making victory decisive. Likewise, astute CEOs do not suffer from protracted internal conflict. They do not postpone tackling the problems they have. Like Musk, they move to strike early. If they have an innovative idea, they do not delay. They get going, lest someone with the same idea takes the field.

In 2007, when Nokia delayed the planned innovation of its mobile phone, Apple and Samsung took the field.

(ii) Amid change, there is opportunity.

Change can be one of the most critical factors in deciding the outcome of any battle. Sun Tzu emphasised that anything could happen in warfare. He proposed that leaders always prepare for the worst whilst calmly and deliberately advancing, waiting or retreating.

Astute CEOs remain calm, keep an open mind in times of uncertainty and are best positioned to leverage opportunities when they arise. Where change is inevitable in an industry, the best way to prepare for change is to be the driving force behind it.

HABIT SEVEN: KEEP COMPETITORS CLOSE

At Harvard University, Wojcicki studied history and literature as part of her humanities major. She planned on a PhD in economics and a career in academia. She changed her plans when she took her first computer science class and discovered an interest in technology.

Had she pursued a career in academia, Wojcicki would be earning a million dollars annually as a UCLA Professor. As a result of her CEO role at YouTube, her net worth is eight hundred million dollars. Wherever there are changes, fresh opportunities lie.

(iii) The best leaders subdue their opponents without fighting.

Warfare can be dangerous. Sun Tzu proposes that the best tacticians defeat their opponents with diplomacy.

Sun Tzu argues that we have more than one tool at our disposal in any situation. This applies to real life as much as it does to military conflict. A zero-sum game is a situation in economics where the losses or gains of the other participants exactly balance each participant's gain or loss.

Business is rarely a zero-sum game; there can be multiple winners because players choose to be different from each other. Apple's 'Think Different' campaign and ethos reminds us how companies can become successful, not by direct competition, but by differentiation.

Former Microsoft CEO Steve Ballmer went all out to beat Apple's sales numbers and market share. Apple never attempted to beat Microsoft. Apple always tried to improve itself and its products.[113]

Snapchat CEO Evan Spiegel denied Facebook's Mark Zuckerberg access to his valuable ideas instead of sharing them. Together, Spiegel and Zuckerberg could have created something unique and valuable.

Wojcicki knows that many TikTok creators consider YouTube their home base and they often post to TikTok with links back to their YouTube accounts. In her analysis, Wojcicki saw that TikTok provided YouTube with more new users than it could have gained by resorting to combat.

MASTER COMBAT

To master combat, CEOs keep their workforce close and their competitors closer.

Completely transparent, friendly and overtly agreeable CEOs are frequently out manoeuvred by competitors, who turn out to be far less pleasant.

Choosing respect over friendship can make a difference.

CEOs who make close friendships with their managers and employees invite jealousy, internal chaos and exploitation by others. CEOs should aim to treat their people and their competition with healthy respect.

In return, they earn the same.

CEOs are always competing for the future. CEOs master combat in many ways,[114] as shown in Figure 7.3.

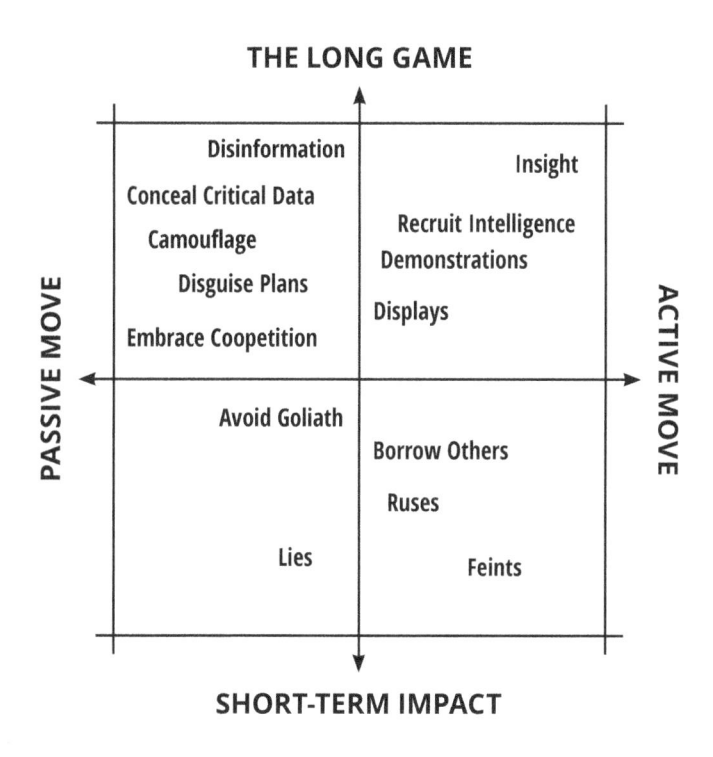

THE LONG GAME

PASSIVE MOVE		ACTIVE MOVE
Disinformation Conceal Critical Data Camouflage Disguise Plans Embrace Coopetition		Insight Recruit Intelligence Demonstrations Displays
Avoid Goliath Lies		Borrow Others Ruses Feints

SHORT-TERM IMPACT

Figure 7.3 Combat Tactics Table

Disguise Plans: Keeping your intentions and strategies hidden from your competitors is essential in a long game. One way to do this is by disguising your plans, as demonstrated by Walmart's CEO, Sam Walton.

Walton outmanoeuvred retailers like Sears, Kmart and JCPenney by initially operating in small remote towns rather than directly competing with the others' product lines. Walton also used well-protected procurement information systems to conceal information from his supply chain partners, allowing rumours about Walmart's vulnerability to spread unchecked.

By managing perceptions and waiting patiently for the right moment to strike, Walton built his company into the world's largest retailer. Like its parent company, Google, YouTube has been known to start projects under the guise of experimentation while aiming for larger goals. For instance, they might introduce new features to enhance user experience while striving to increase market share or advertising revenue.

Recruit Intelligence: This is an active move. YouTube has hired talent from all over the tech industry, including competitors' employees. These employees bring valuable insights that help YouTube navigate the market and innovate accordingly.

Following the pandemic, major software companies such as X, Meta, Microsoft, Amazon and Google made significant layoffs. This allowed Australian firms like Atlassian and Canva to hire talented software programmers and gain valuable information and market intelligence.

However, caution is advised when relying on competitors' ex-employees for information, as their perspectives may be biased, misguided or lead to patent-related breaches. In 2023, Masimo accused Apple of infringing on its patents by poaching employees to obtain pulse oximetry technology for their Apple Watches.

This intellectual property dispute resulted not only in financial consequences, with Apple being forced by the courts to halt sales of Apple Watches in the US, but also affected Apple's public image and reputation.

HABIT SEVEN: KEEP COMPETITORS CLOSE

Borrow Others to Fight: It can be strategic to borrow others to fight battles for you. Uber's founders, for example, used their knowledge of the taxi industry to create a phone app that allowed freshly minted contractors to offer ride services, effectively inciting third-party drivers and passengers to attack traditional taxi networks.

YouTube has relied heavily on content creators, who are essentially third-party contractors, to compete with traditional media companies. By providing a platform for these creators, YouTube has drawn viewers away from television and other traditional media without producing content itself.

Another example occurred when Apple hired prosecution lawyers to keep up the fight against Samsung for many years over numerous patent infringements. This was less about seeking compensation but more about forming strategic alliances with other companies, creating a united front in the tech industry to protect Apple's intellectual property and interests.

Avoid Goliath: When YouTube started, it did not go head-to-head with major entertainment companies, but instead, provided a platform for independent video creators. This strategy allowed YouTube to grow without fighting entrenched industry giants.

Harvard Business Review and other popular business publications sometimes glorify start-ups and unicorns that aim to disrupt industry giants, suggesting that David will beat Goliath. The truth, however, is that Goliath wins far more often. Thanks to quick-thinking CEOs like Wojcicki, mighty Google swallowed the disruptive start-up YouTube.

Similarly, industry giant Facebook gradually dismantled unicorn Snapchat, feature by feature.

Innovate without Disruption: YouTube has introduced various features that were not directly disruptive but built on existing behaviours. For example, the monetisation of videos through ads allowed creators to earn revenue without disrupting the existing advertising industry.

Non-disruptive innovation breaks this socio-economic trade-off by growing the economic pie with minimal social pain. Innovation can produce a positive-sum game with multiple winners rather than a zero-sum game with winners and losers.

Opportunities for non-disruptive innovation, while less glamorous, are still immense. CEOs of start-ups and established companies wisely connect the dots to the non-customers yet to be served. Some classic examples of non-disruptive innovations include Post-it Notes, Viagra and Life Coaching.

Since 3M introduced the Post-it Note fifty years ago, their usage has expanded effortlessly. By 2021, the global Post-it Note market was $2.3 billion and is expected to reach $2.5 billion by 2028.

Twenty-five years ago, Viagra and Life Coaching did not exist until someone offered brand-new ideas for helping people improve the quality of their personal and professional lives. Both have created multibillion-dollar industries that did not come at the expense of an existing player.

Befriend Distant Competitors: YouTube has partnered with hardware manufacturers like television and smartphone makers to have a pre-installed YouTube app, which indirectly competes with other streaming services. More and more, the boundaries between industries are blurring. Apple entered the music player industry with the iPod and the smartphone industry with the iPhone. Within four years of their release, Apple Watches outsold the Swiss watch industry.

How?

Apple CEO Steve Jobs was skilled at befriending distant competitors to attack ones nearby.

Jobs signed an exclusive deal with Japanese laptop manufacturer Toshiba to manufacture mini hard drives for the iPod to compete against the dominant Sony Walkman and Discman. He also surpassed the earlier models of the clunky and low-song-capacity MP3 players.

Jobs worked with distant competitors like LG and Samsung for the Apple Watch to outperform existing watchmakers. Jobs bypassed the competition and entered new industries by befriending distant competitors.

Going around your competition traditionally meant diversification into a new industry with a new product, bringing innovation to the forefront or using geographical targeting. Befriending distant competitors allows firms to leapfrog large and less agile incumbents. This indirect approach capitalises on a competitor's weaker or untapped market.

Another way to attack a dominant competitor in a desired industry or geographic location is to become 'number one' in an alternate industry or geographic location and then use that experience and momentum to challenge a competitor on their home turf. Virgin CEO Richard Branson used Virgin's top position in the record industry to fund the innovation needed to establish Virgin Airlines and successfully beat British Airways.

To beat Harley-Davidson, Suzuki and Kawasaki, Honda's CEO Tadashi Kume befriended Hero, India's largest bicycle brand and dealership network, and entered India's highly protected motorcycle market. Soon after that, the Honda Hero model reached dominance in India. This move helped Honda become the largest motorcycle company in the world.

Astute CEOs befriend distant competitors to attack ones nearby.

Embrace Co-opetition: YouTube has occasionally partnered with competitors. For example, it has allowed competitors' content to be uploaded to its platform and it has integrated its services with others, growing traffic back to YouTube.

Astute CEOs understand that reducing customer search costs is crucial to business growth. For a customer to choose a brand, they must know it, like it and trust it. Unless your brand is as well-known as Apple or Coca-Cola, most people have probably never heard of your business.

Even if a company has invested thousands in social media advertising, a Google search may fail to connect it with many potential buyers. However, leveraging your small reputation alongside a nearby competitor's reputation, via cooperation, could make a significant difference.

Conceal Critical Data: While YouTube discloses some viewership data, it maintains the confidentiality of its performance metrics and algorithms. This secrecy challenges competitors trying to decipher the factors behind the platform's success.

Astute CEOs master the art of concealment, not just with competitors but also with supply chain partners. They proactively influence how other players perceive them, which can shape the competitive landscape and benefit their business's long-term success.

Protecting information critical to an organisation's mission is typically categorised under Operations Security (OPSEC), a practice refined by adept military commanders, CEOs, managers and other leaders in decision-making roles. OPSEC strategies are also employed to assess whether actions perceived as benign might be covert attempts by competitors to gather intelligence.

The objective of OPSEC is to safeguard specific data that, if stolen by an adversary, could expose a company's strategic orientation and the extent of its resources.

Deceive Opponents: YouTube's algorithm changes are often announced or even downplayed, to surprise competitors and aid content creators as the platform evolves. Deceiving an opponent is usually more straightforward when actions align with the opponent's pre-existing perceptions of the firm, rather than trying to convince them of a new narrative.

CEOs may employ a series of ruses or strategic deceits to influence opponents to reconsider their stance. Such ruses are carefully crafted plans. They might involve laying a trail of breadcrumbs. For instance, placing misleading documents where they are likely to be found accidentally is a clever ruse. For misinformation to be effective, it must seem authentic and align with what the adversary perceives as valuable intelligence.

The amount and quality of misinformation can be crucial. The more extensive the information an adversary has, the harder it becomes to deceive them.

In mastering combat, a series of quiet actions can be potent.

Directly confronting an opponent in a market while focusing on a different business initiative is a feint in combat terms. Demonstrations, akin to feints, can have more enduring impacts. The intent behind a demonstration is to lead your adversary to an incorrect assessment of your firm's true objectives or available resources.

Susan Wojcicki's leadership at YouTube showcased the importance of having an in-depth understanding of competitive dynamics and market opportunities – highlighting the need for CEOs to know themselves and their enemies.

Next, let us move the spotlight onto a radiant leader who helped herself and her clients in a very personal way.

But first, reflect on your insights from this habit and make some notes on the blank pages that follow.

Then, when you are ready, move on and complete Activity Seven.

ACTIVITY SEVEN

A multifaceted approach is essential as YouTube navigates the increasingly competitive video content landscape alongside TikTok and X.

They may:

(i) **Disguise Plans:** Innovate their platform subtly based on user feedback.
(ii) **Recruit Intelligence:** Hire experts from TikTok, X, Open-AI and other emerging platforms.
(iii) **Borrow Others to Fight:** Attract new audiences and further bolster their partnerships with leading content creators, especially those with substantial followings on TikTok and X.
(iv) **Avoid Going Head-to-Head:** Instead of directly challenging TikTok in the short-form content arena, YouTube can play to its unique strengths, such as its diverse content range and well-established advertising platform.
(v) **Innovate Without Disruption:** Introduce new e-commerce capabilities to enhance the platform's attractiveness to creators and viewers without overhauling the core experience.
(vi) **Befriend Distant Competitors:** Form strategic alliances with distant players to gain new distribution channels and technologies.
(vii) **Embrace Co-opetition:** Consider collaborative efforts with competitors like Netflix on shared challenges such as digital rights management or advertising standards, which could

benefit the industry and create a better environment for both Netflix and YouTube.

(viii) **Conceal Critical Data:** Keep strategic metrics confidential, like algorithms and performance data, to prevent competitors from replicating their success.

(ix) **Deceive Opponents:** Leak information about new feature developments that misdirect competitors and spread their efforts too thinly. For example, suggesting investing in virtual reality content during a press conference could lead competitors to focus on VR, a less proven market than YouTube's current platform.

7.1 If you were the incoming CEO of YouTube, how would you combat threats from TikTok and X?

7.2 How good are you at assessing the competition, anticipating competitor moves and analysing the competition's relevance to your firm's future structure, strategy and scope?

7.3 How well do you know your firm?

7.4 Do other players know your firm better than you? Why? Why? Why?

The competitor to be feared is one who never bothers about you at all but goes on making their own business better all the time.

Henry Ford

HABIT EIGHT
ENHANCE PERSONAL EFFECTIVENESS

Adapted from FORBES Magazine

KATRINA LAKE
STITCH FIX

Prioritise Self-Care
Balance Work-Life
Cultivate Support Networks

Amidst a sea of desks cluttered with monitors displaying flickering graphs, the youthful Stitch Fix team stood out, a beacon of entrepreneurial spirit.

In the NASDAQ trading room, a moment of quiet fell.

Eyes were drawn to the central platform.

Before those present and flanked by her dedicated team, Katrina Lake was the youngest woman CEO to take a company public.

Lake's radiance transformed the typically staid ambience of the trading floor into a tableau of inspiration and celebration. With her young son, cradled in one arm and clutching his fluffy toy tiger, Lake rang the bell to open trading.

Above them, screens flashed with the Stitch Fix ticker symbol 'SFIX', announcing that her innovative personal styling company was now among the ranks of publicly traded firms.

Oblivious to the significance, her son smiled, mirroring his mother's happiness.

The image of Lake and her son on this defining day became emblematic of progress, work-life balance and the promise of what a woman-led, customer-focused company could achieve in the modern marketplace.

Katrina Lake is a luminary, that shattered the glass ceiling, just as Estée Lauder and Susan Wojcicki had done.

HABIT EIGHT: ENHANCE PERSONAL EFFECTIVENESS

Katrina Lake's father, John, embodied an entrepreneurial mindset and passion for building something from nothing. This passion reflected his outlook on life, a perspective he imparted to his daughter. While Lake's father encouraged her to explore expansive possibilities, her nurturing mother, Yumi, instilled the traditional Japanese family values of discipline and continuous improvement or "Kaizen."

By the time Lake was considering pre-med in college, she had developed a well-rounded and multifaceted perspective on life. This foundation would eventually propel her to business school and into the realm of entrepreneurship. In 2011, at the age of 29 and before graduating from Harvard Business School, she established Stitch Fix.

Before applying to medical school, Lake volunteered at a hospital to assess her suitability for the profession. Like the new-age healthcare expert Peter Attia,[115] who we will soon meet, Lake stepped away from hospital work and joined a business consulting firm, an environment equally as demanding. Both Attia and Lake are more driven by performance than by patient care. They came to understand and prioritise health and self-care in their lives and work.

Enhancing personal effectiveness is a multifaceted endeavour that seeks balance between work, purpose, health, authenticity and happiness. A commitment to physical and mental health is a fundamental component of personal effectiveness. Regular exercise, including high-intensity interval training (HIIT) and mindful dietary choices, fuel our systems and promote health span and life span.

Lake's company, Stitch Fix, is an online service that transformed how women approach fashion and created a new paradigm, seamlessly integrating individual style with algorithmic precision.

Lake recalls days when a monotonous uniformity characterised her retail experience. She looked beyond the conventional, imagining a service where customers felt recognised, their styles understood, and their preferences anticipated. Lake identified a market niche for highly customised clothing selections favouring quality over quantity. Each month, Stitch Fix sends customers hand-picked clothing and accessories based on their preferences, sizes, and budget, which they can try on at home before purchasing.

Stitch Fix merges advanced data analytics with the intuition of human stylists to create selections that align with the unique stories of each client. Stitch Fix's predictive AI algorithms enable exceptional customer engagement and efficient inventory management. This innovative approach allows Stitch Fix to offer a personalised shopping experience that was once thought impossible on a large scale.

Stitch Fix emerged as a David in the shadow of Amazon - a veritable Goliath with its endless styles and rapid Prime delivery. However, instead of slinging stones, Stitch Fix began by dispatching boxes of carefully selected fashion, offering a formidable value proposition.

'Personal Shopper' by Prime Wardrobe responded with personal styling preferences while maintaining its extensive, almost boundless selection. In contrast, Stitch Fix cultivated a collection of less than a thousand brands, each chosen not for its name but for the narrative it could weave when adorned by the right individual.

By concentrating on this niche, Stitch Fix was able to compete with and ultimately outperform Amazon in the online consumer fashion sector.

Stitch Fix's 'Style Shuffle' app capitalised on real-time customer feedback, continually refining its services. A continuous improvement or Kaizen-like approach to innovation kept Stitch Fix's competitive edge sharp. The company was able to expand its unique yet fashionable selection into new markets and employ even more sophisticated data analytics for trend forecasting. Stitch Fix's customer-centric model evolved, offering seamless new user experiences such as 'Shop Your Looks.'

By 2018, Lake had earned a well-deserved place on Forbes' list of the World's 100 Most Powerful Women. With her thoughtful, deep-set brown eyes, Lake personified the approachable touch and efficacy characteristic of modern leadership. As a young mother, when Stitch Fix went public, Lake balanced her personal effectiveness with her life's demands.

Shortly after Lake established Stitch Fix, I was invited to speak on strategy to the Queensland Law Society in Australia. The two women who presented on recruitment before me highlighted that, at that time, most of the CEOs of the top 100 Australian companies were male. Notably, 25% were named John or Jack, and 65% were at least 192 cm tall. They discussed women's challenges in breaking through the glass ceiling to join the C-suite.

These women shone a light on an entrenched corporate culture that favoured hyper-masculinity and the pursuit of profit over people. They pointed to a lack of emotional intelligence and empathy among traditional male CEOs like Jack Welch and Jacques Nasser. As the concluding speaker, standing at 195 cm tall and named John, I felt slightly rattled.

I recall verifying the facts at the time. These women were correct. The devil - or perhaps the 'tall white John' was in the details. Back then, a recent list of top Australian CEOs was replete with Johns.

John Ralph (CRA Limited)
John Alexander (News Corporation)
John Wylie (Toll Holdings)
John Morschel (Orica)
John Stewart (Leighton Holdings)
John Goyder (Wesfarmers)
John Hopkins (Amcor)
John Mullen (Aurizon)
John Ferrugia (Cochlear)
John Guscic (Computershare)
John Durkan (Downer EDI)
John Mulcahy (Boral)
John Fletcher (Fletcher Building)
John Grill (Worley Parsons)
John Horgan (BHP Billiton)
John Lydon (Lend Lease)
John Spark (SP Ausnet)
John Sparkes (Tabcorp)
John Stocker (Telstra)

HABIT EIGHT: ENHANCE PERSONAL EFFECTIVENESS

John Tonkin (Westpac)
John Weber (Woolworths)
John White (BlueScope Steel)
John Menzies (Wesfarmers)
John Sharp (Rio Tinto)

There have been many changes to the list in the last decade. However, with an increasing number of women in executive and leadership roles, the need for them to enhance their personal effectiveness has never been greater. Self-care, work-life balance and support networks are essential.

Research reveals that women are more productive than men in today's offices, working ten per cent harder. This finding is because men and women complete about sixty-six per cent of their assigned work, but women are assigned ten per cent more work than men. Despite the increased workload, women achieve the same completion rate as men, resulting in higher productivity.[116]

The gender pay gap is a well-documented and persistent issue that reflects the disparity in earnings between men and women. This gap has remained relatively stable in the US over the past two decades. As of 2023, women earned an average of 82% of what men earned.[117] This represents a slight improvement from 2002, when women earned 80% as much as men, indicating a slow pace of change in narrowing the pay disparity.

Women still undertake most of the domestic work globally. Over three-quarters of unpaid domestic and care work worldwide is performed by women. This proportion is sixty-five per cent in developed countries but increases to eighty per cent in developing and emerging economies.[118]

Enhancing personal effectiveness is a multifaceted endeavour that embraces the equilibrium between purpose, health and happiness. A commitment to health, both physical and mental, is an essential cornerstone of personal effectiveness. Regular exercise, including high-intensity interval training (HIIT) and mindful dietary choices, must be prioritised.

PRIORITISE SELF-CARE

Prioritising self-care is essential for enhancing personal effectiveness. Social conditioning and unconscious messages sometimes suggest that one can be Superman or Superwoman, do it all and be it all.

Lake recognises that self-care is not a luxury but necessary to sustain the energy and creativity needed to lead a pioneering company.[119] She includes running and regular exercise in her routine, practises mindfulness and maintains a diet that supports her dynamic and balanced lifestyle. Lake regularly asks herself, "What do I need in my life to survive and be my best self?"

Part of Lake's answer involves starting her mornings early with her children, which sets a tone of presence and connection for the day

HABIT EIGHT: ENHANCE PERSONAL EFFECTIVENESS

ahead. She stays away from emails and social media at home and for the first hour of her working day, which stops distraction, scattered thinking and a frazzled start to the day.[120] Her practice underscores the importance of prioritising family relationships with daily exercise amidst a busy schedule that has her out the door by 8:30am.[121]

Lake also stresses the need to disconnect from work, as evidenced by her evening routine of spending quality time with her husband and engaging in personal interests. She maintains a clear distinction between work and leisure. Lake returns home between 5:30pm and 7pm, often using the train ride to decompress.[122]

Upon arrival at home, she relieves the nanny, bathes her young children, feeds them and puts them to bed. The hours between 7pm and 10pm are reserved for her husband, meeting friends or watching TV. Evening hours are dedicated to self-care. Lake avoids the unhealthy habit of checking social media before bed, opting instead to read something on paper, not on a phone.[123]

Lake's self-care approach is woven into the fabric of her life and business. The care she affords herself is extended to her clients through Stitch Fix's highly personalised and value-added shopping experiences.

The Harvard Study of Adult Development[124] is the longest-running and most valuable study on health and happiness. The study identified two pivotal aspects of self-care that significantly impact our happiness, health and longevity.[125]

1. **Relationships are pivotal.** Deep connections with others are a critical component of happiness and robust health. Married men live an average of twelve years longer, and married women live seven years longer than their unmarried counterparts. Although the number of social interactions is beneficial, the quality of these interactions and the warmth of relationships heavily influence our mental and physical well being.

2. **Physical exercise is vital.** As little as 15 minutes of moderate to vigorous daily exercise contributes to physical, mental and emotional wellbeing.

These exercise findings are expanded upon by Peter Attia through his meta-analysis of thousands of peer-reviewed articles and included in his popular book, "Outlive."[126]

Attia outlines three potential life paths:

(i) Life by default is a sedentary lifestyle with average dietary and life habits. In this scenario, health sharply declines by age 40. By 55, individuals often experience only 50% of the mental and physical health that is possible, typically leading to death in their sixties. This was the fate of my paternal grandparents, who both passed away at 62.

(ii) Life with the best medical care means one might still lead a relatively sedentary life with average habits. Here, too, health declines sharply at age 40. However, medical interventions like stents, pacemakers and blood-thinning medications extend life.

HABIT EIGHT: ENHANCE PERSONAL EFFECTIVENESS

For instance, my father, who had a heart attack in his 70s, received such treatments, which have enabled him to live a further 20+ years. However, his physical health continues to deteriorate.

(iii) Life with the Five Pillars is the third path and prioritises self-care through:

1. A full hour of daily exercise, including interval work and some weights.
2. Soaking up Vitamin D from the sun with bare feet on the earth and meditating.
3. Device-free, quiet bedtime routines with 8 hours of sleep.
4. Adequate hydration and optimal eating regimes that may include periodic fasting.
5. Making time for great friends and, ideally, having an intimate, loving partner.

By living the Five Pillars path, one can enjoy 100% of the mental and physical health that is possible. By taking the non-Five Pillars path and relying on medical care, my father only enjoys about 25% of the physical health that might have been possible had he chosen the third life path.

My aged father's sedentary lifestyle, stiff posture and risk of a fatal fall reveal that 'our bones go where our muscles grow' and 'where muscles retreat, bones weaken and our skeletons curve.'

In Figure 8.1 below, courtesy of Peter Attia, we see that Lake's life is much closer to the rightmost dotted curve.

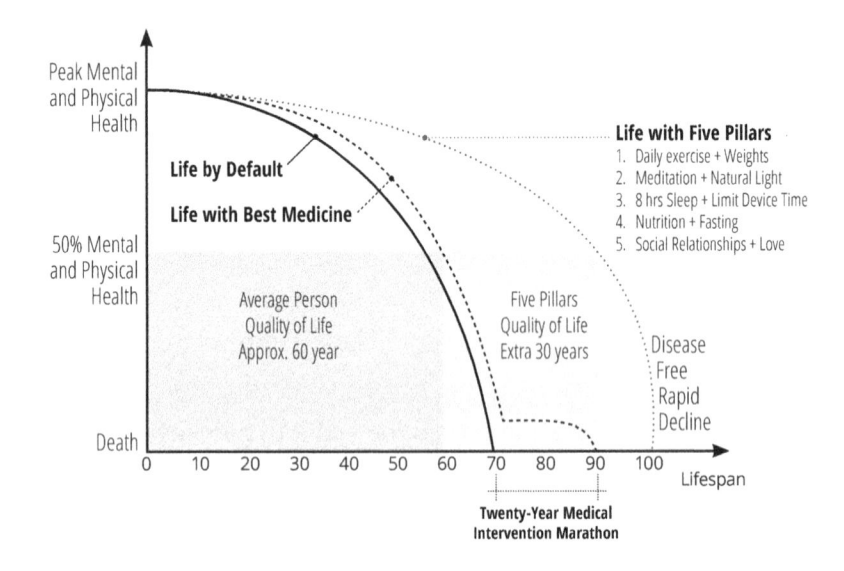

Figure 8.1 Five Pillars Life Quality

In the final chapter of *"Outlive"*, Attia reveals the significance of mental health alongside an admission of his OCD-like symptoms and vengeful outbursts, suggesting a connection to the traumatic sexual abuse he suffered as a child. As a renowned medical and wellbeing professional, Attia's mental health battle is far from uncommon.

Mental illness represents a burgeoning epidemic. The Centre for Disease Control (CDC) indicates that in 2017, US adults over the age of 18 exhibited higher rates of mental illness than in all but three of the years spanning from 2008 to 2015. Alarmingly, the youngest demographic - those aged 18 to 25 - experienced the most significant increase, with a 40% rise reported between 2008 and 2017.[127]

HABIT EIGHT: ENHANCE PERSONAL EFFECTIVENESS

The World Health Organisation (WHO) has reported that more than 10% of the global population, or one in ten people, currently suffer from mental health disorders. In the US, this figure stands at 20% or one in five people.

The lifetime prevalence rates in the US are even more startling, with data suggesting that approximately 50% of the population will fulfil the criteria for a mental health disorder at some stage in their lifetime - yes, that's half of the population.

The recent advancements in our understanding of the interconnected causes of mental health disorders bring a glimmer of hope.[128] Fundamentally, mental health correlates with metabolism, the process through which our bodies produce energy. A person with a healthy metabolism will generate a high quantity and quality of energy for their brain.

Conversely, those with insufficient available energy for their brain will exhibit a family of symptoms, which, upon evaluation by doctors and psychiatrists, may be mapped onto a constellation of problematic diagnoses,[129] such as anxiety, depression, ADHD, OCD, autism, schizophrenia and bipolar disorder, to name a few.

As illustrated in Figure 8.2, many interconnected causes disturb metabolic health and lead to mental disorders. These include stress, social media addiction, poor diet, poor sleep, obesity, lack of exercise, trauma, prescription drugs, alcohol use and substance abuse.

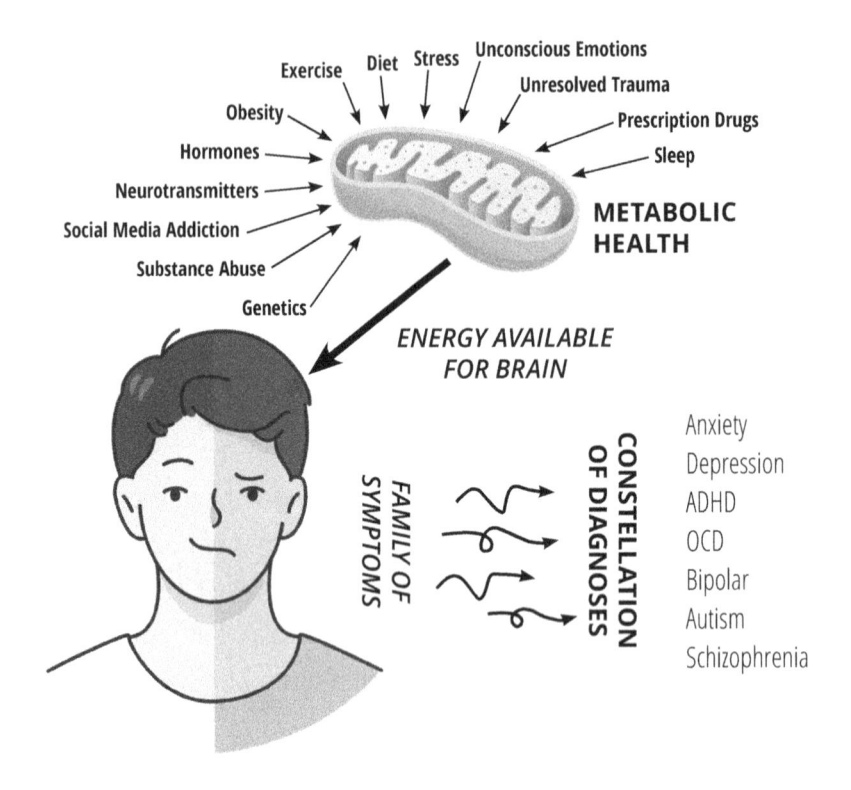

Figure 8.2 Brain Energy

CEOs who recognise that employees may have diagnosed and undiagnosed mental disorders can cultivate a workplace that champions health and wellbeing initiatives. Such programs can help staff address the various causes of metabolic disturbances that contribute to poor mental health.

Every CEO will need therapy at some point. The corporate sphere can feel bereft of love, yet life is born of love. I always appreciate my friend Dr Chris, a psychotherapist who specialises in working with overwhelmed executives.[130] Over the years, Chris has taught me how to love and allow myself to be loved. Something many people, not just CEOs, need.

Chris shares three observations from his practice:

1. Executive work often begins with passion, yet this becomes marred by a lack of awareness and an unconscious self-betrayal that mirrors deep-seated childhood coping mechanisms.
2. CEOs abandon precious shadow work, their loved ones and their health for worldly challenges and trappings like money and fame.
3. When CEOs use their false self to override their emotional and physical needs, they harm themselves and their world. Only with a balance of genuine self-love can the loving of others be possible.

BALANCE WORK-LIFE

Work and life fulfilment extend beyond the balance sheet. They are intricately tied to a sense of purpose that transcends our nine-to-five or seven-to-nine routines. Cultivating a purpose that serves others helps weave meaning into the tapestry of our work. A purpose-driven approach prioritises impactful work and meaningful relationships and affords a level of satisfaction that mere financial success cannot.

Work-life balance, especially for CEOs, represents an opportunity to harmonise professional responsibilities with life, family, and personal interests. This work-life balance sets an example for others and nurtures a culture where each member feels valued and part of a larger mission.

CEOs must navigate unique challenges in their demanding roles. To maintain equilibrium, they must establish clear boundaries, prioritise tasks effectively, delegate duties and recognise the value of personal time alongside professional commitments.

As Lake demonstrates, effective time management is crucial, emphasising productivity during work hours to safeguard personal time for relaxation and family engagements. Work schedule flexibility allows for fulfilling occasional weekday family events and needed downtime. Some CEOs will block out individual time for an hour or two per week to do something artistic, such as painting, singing or working with clay.

A work environment enriched by shared values and interests can nurture a fulfilling organisational culture. CEOs should promote a culture that supports individual growth and professional success. In our digital world, managing ubiquitous technology is imperative to prevent the encroachment of work into personal spaces. Disciplined use of tech tools, such as smartphones and laptops, is essential.

Leveraging new AI tools and digital assistants can help maintain a CEO's equilibrium and counteract job-related stress. These can be programmed to remind CEOs to exercise regularly, take time outdoors, pursue hobbies, schedule social activities and practise mindfulness.

HABIT EIGHT: ENHANCE PERSONAL EFFECTIVENESS

Lake exemplifies this integrated approach. She views work and life not as competing forces but as complementary yin-yang aspects. Striving for comprehensive fulfilment, she acknowledges family connections as integral to her leadership effectiveness. Lake ensures her presence and efficacy in both domains by integrating her personal and professional spheres, adhering to clear boundaries and practising disciplined time management.

Lake incorporates activities such as cooking and reading to detach from the virtual world and champions a company culture that prioritises well-being, advocating for mental health days and balanced lifestyles. Emulating companies like Netflix, Stitch Fix offers an unlimited vacation policy, ensuring employees return from breaks rejuvenated.

Such a vacation policy might seem ideal, but it can backfire. Fear of judgment for taking leave, especially with peer-influenced retention policies, often prevents real breaks despite official permissions.

Lake maintains a tangible and official connection with her business and clients through personal styling sessions, and like my CEO friend Graham, she is known for 'crashing' meetings to listen in and keep her finger on the pulse.[131]

CULTIVATE SUPPORT NETWORKS

Lake recognises the importance of support, both personally and within her company. In addition to self-care and work-life balance, she has built supportive networks with other women, CEO peers, past professors, alumni and her extended family.

Successful CEOs cultivate supportive networks in numerous ways:

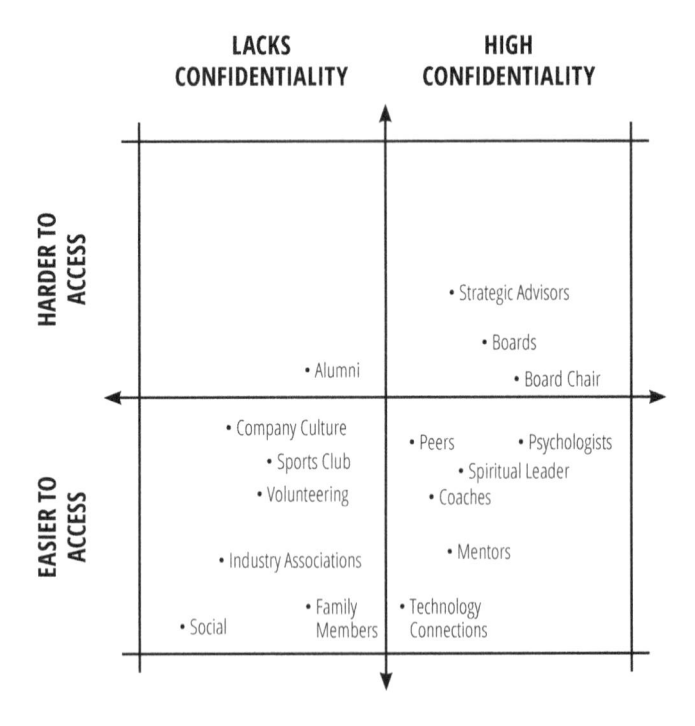

	LACKS CONFIDENTIALITY	**HIGH CONFIDENTIALITY**
HARDER TO ACCESS	• Alumni	• Strategic Advisors • Boards • Board Chair
EASIER TO ACCESS	• Company Culture • Sports Club • Volunteering • Industry Associations • Social • Family Members	• Peers • Psychologists • Spiritual Leader • Coaches • Mentors • Technology Connections

Figure 8.3 Support Matrix

Peer Networks: CEOs can join or create peer advisory groups comprising fellow CEOs and business leaders. Lake accesses these groups to air challenges and hear valuable insights from other women who have encountered similar situations.

Mentorship and Coaching: Mentors or executive coaches can be invaluable.[132] They provide guidance, serve as confidential sounding boards for ideas and give impartial advice. They can aid personal development, teach leadership skills and provide therapy.

Company Culture as a Support System: Like Lake, CEOs can foster a culture that values each employee's contribution, development and well-being. This involves programmes that promote greater trust, mental health awareness, work-life balance and continuous learning.

Strategic Advisers: A network of trusted advisers in various areas, such as finance, marketing, legal and technology, can support CEOs in making informed decisions.

Alumni Networks: Connecting with alumni groups from educational institutions can offer new perspectives. For Lake, these networks help her with decision-making and provide collaboration opportunities.

Industry Associations: Participation in industry groups or associations can provide a community and a platform to stay current with industry trends and new practices.

Social Responsibility and Volunteering: Engagement in social responsibility initiatives and volunteering can expand a CEO's network, leading to new insights and innovative ideas.

Family and Personal Relationships: Lake values her extended family network and personal relationships that provide her with emotional support.

Leveraging Technology: CEOs can use social media and professional networking platforms like LinkedIn to connect with peers, thought leaders and innovators worldwide.

Continuous Learning: Promoting a culture of continuous learning within the organisation helps CEOs stay current and fosters collective growth and resilience.

Well-structured Boards: A diverse and competent board provides strategic direction and support, ensuring CEOs are not isolated in decision-making.

As we will see in Habit Twelve, these last two elements, continuous learning and well-structured boards, are critical as firms mature.

CEOs need to have current industry knowledge. The willingness to request assistance from one's Board and to learn from its members is essential for growth. Boards can quickly become disengaged and ineffective if a CEO is overly opinionated and fails to consult with them.

Soliciting help from board members increases their investment in the cause and their CEO. A CEO who never seeks assistance from their Board risks being swiftly replaced.

Lake presents a new paradigm in personal effectiveness. She shattered the glass ceiling while demonstrating entrepreneurial, compassionate leadership that harmonises self-care and work-life balance with supportive networks. Lake emphasises the significance of maintaining high performance without sacrificing personal well-being. She has illustrated how to navigate life and business roles with an integrated approach that exemplifies her personal effectiveness.

Next, we meet a very private leader who communicates strategy clearly.

Please make any notes you need on self-care, work-life balance and supportive networks on the following blank pages.

Now, complete Activity Eight.

ACTIVITY EIGHT

8.1 Write answers to each of these questions:

Q1. How do I incorporate self-care into my daily routine, and how does this impact my effectiveness?
Q2. How might I enhance my work-life balance to benefit my well-being, family and organisational responsibilities?
Q3. What is one lesson I can apply from Katrina Lake's approach?

8.2 Complete the three most challenging and beneficial activities from the following:

(i) Daily Self-Care Audit: For one week, maintain a detailed diary of your self-care activities. Evaluate which activities contribute most to your energy levels and leadership presence.
(ii) Work-Life Balance Plan: Formulate a plan delineating specific boundaries between work and personal life. This should include time for family, exercise and hobbies. Adhere to this for at least one month to assess its efficacy.
(iii) Network Map: Develop a visual map of your current network. Identify where gender and cultural diversity is deficient and establish goals to cultivate relationships in those areas over the coming quarter.
(iv) Emotional Intelligence Exercises: Allocate 15 minutes daily to practice emotional intelligence exercises, such as mindfulness or reflective journaling, concentrating on

situations where you could have demonstrated greater empathy or adaptability.
(v) Culture Initiative Proposal: Devise a proposal for a novel company initiative aimed at enhancing employee well-being. Submit it to your leadership team for their feedback and suggestions for execution.
(vi) Digital Detox: Implement a 'no screens' rule for one hour each evening. Utilise this time for non-digital pursuits that you find enjoyable and rejuvenating.

The art of being wise is the art of knowing what to overlook.

William James

SECTION THREE
ALIGN AND ALLOCATE RESOURCES

Habit Nine - Explain Strategy Clearly

Habit Ten - Govern Resources Portfolio

Habit Eleven - Mentor Direct Reports

Habit Twelve - Maximise Board Commitment

HABIT NINE
EXPLAIN STRATEGY CLEARLY

TIM COOK
APPLE INC.

Communicate Clearly
Manage Crisis Situations
Be Media Savvy

I envision dawn's soft glow on the futuristic curves of Apple Park and the desk of Tim Cook.

As the architect of an empire, Cook may have cycled to work and is immersed in the cadence of his daily routine, which deftly balances the scales of innovation with the grounded force of operations.

With his clean-shaven face, soft blue eyes and glasses, I imagine Cook sifting through unsolicited emails. Each message is not an intrusion but a way to keep his finger on the pulse and fuel his quest for knowledge.[133] *It is telling that a CEO of Cook's stature offers his email address, tcook@apple.com, for customers to describe their experiences.*

I see Cook traversing the labyrinthine halls of Silicon Valley, not in pursuit of conflict, as Steve Jobs may have, but for the sake of clarity.

As the steward of a legacy that has elevated handheld devices to cultural icons, Tim Cook shoulders his responsibility with a humility that brings homage to his station. Cook treads a narrow path between upholding Apple tradition and charting new frontiers by telling stories that drive bold changes.[134]

My musings on Cook paint him as the keeper of a vision ever on the cusp of revelation yet perennially shrouded in a veil of anticipation. Within this dance of secrecy and illumination, Cook explains Apple's strategy clearly and in a manner that is as enduring as it is, quintessentially, his own.

Cook's biography begins in the humbleness of Alabama, where he was the youngest child of a shipyard worker. His childhood, filled with the dismantling of gadgets and toys, was a prelude to his technological acumen. Cook's parents recognised his talents and encouraged him to pursue engineering, leading him to study Industrial Engineering at Auburn University and later earn an MBA from Duke University.

Starting at IBM and moving to Compaq, Cook's expertise caught Steve Jobs' eye, prompting his recruitment to Apple in 1998.

Cook rose through the ranks to become Apple's COO. Cook was forced from his state of operational contemplation to accept the tragic unfolding of Steve Job's untimely death. Cook, without Jobs, likely found himself in a strained and introspective place. Cook understood the necessity of adaptability and assumed the CEO mantle in 2011.

Cook has guided Apple through significant growth and innovation.

Cook is known to be level-headed with a reserved demeanour. He often expresses himself in a soft-spoken and measured way and is a passionate user of Apple products.[135] Today, he is the most respected CEO in the tech industry.

Like most CEOs, Cook must explain strategy daily in dozens of settings to keep stakeholders in tune with his firm's plans and growth trajectory. Cook excels in his ability to remain strategic and understand internal and external stakeholders while staying 'on message'. He communicates clearly, leads in times of crisis and is media savvy.

COMMUNICATE CLEARLY

CEOs must have strong public speaking skills to convey their company's message to the public, industry partners and employees. They must be persuasive in front of large audiences, as well as be able to communicate clearly through written statements and social media.

One of my clients recently highlighted the importance of clear communication. Despite decades of expertise in their industry, the company's home-grown CEO needed the confidence to speak publicly. Since becoming CEO, the business and my client had lost their way. My client agreed to work on platform speaking skills, which contributed to the revival of the company.

This CEO's journey included overcoming some deep-seated trauma, which led to a liberating personal transformation. Today, the CEO speaks confidently at company conferences and events. As a result of the CEO's new speaking skills, employee morale and company results have blossomed.

Some of Tim Cook's early speaking appearances at Apple felt highly scripted. Cook looked stilted and nervous. He did not smile and lacked enthusiasm. Unlike his predecessor, Steve Jobs, who was one to smile and speak with poise and confidence.[136] Shortly after Cook's first speech, Apple's stock price dropped 5% and took two months to recover.

Like my CEO client, Cook's public speaking skills improved with time. Today, Cook's enhanced ability to communicate Apple's core values

HABIT NINE : EXPLAIN STRATEGY CLEARLY

and vision is crucial to the tech company's success.[137] Cook is confident when communicating policy and strategy to guide decision-making and achieve Apple's goals.

Apple's policies include rules and guidelines that the company uses to govern its actions and ensure compliance with laws and ethical standards. Policies are written down and provide clear direction for employees and other stakeholders.

On the other hand, Apple's strategy includes a dynamic plan for achieving the firm's overall goals. Compared to policies, strategies are less formal and more flexible. Strategies are developed to guide long-term decision-making and to align the company's resources with its key objectives.

Cook communicates strategy and policy clearly in a way that is easy to understand and ensures that everyone works towards the same objectives. Apple's product strategy is simple. Even a child can understand it. This simplicity is good because people, young and old, love Apple products. Many firms have used Apple's logic to rationalise their product strategy and reduce friction in their sales process.

As shown in Figure 9.1, Apple Store employees only need to know the answer to two questions when dealing with a prospective computer customer.

Are you a home user or a professional user?

Do you want a notebook or a desktop?

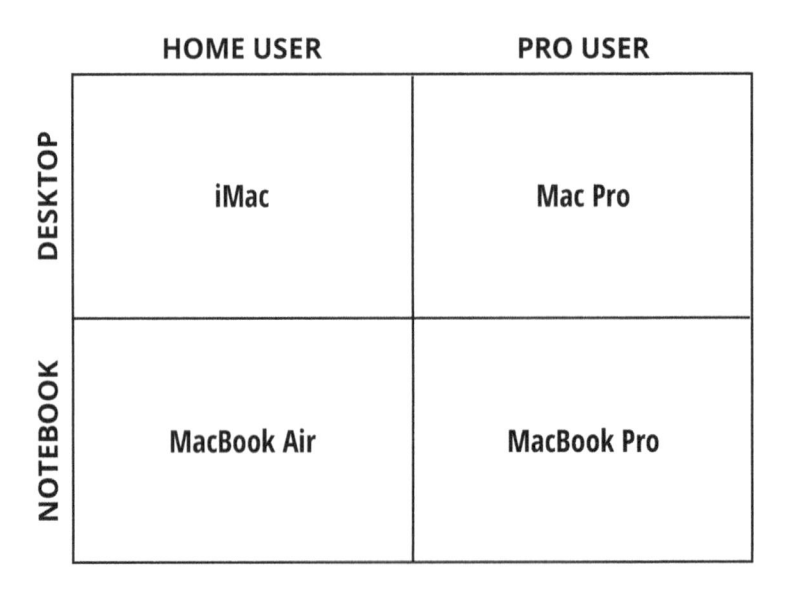

	HOME USER	PRO USER
DESKTOP	iMac	Mac Pro
NOTEBOOK	MacBook Air	MacBook Pro

Figure 9.1 Apple Product Strategy Matrix

Cook is also known for his attention to detail,[138] which enables him to effectively explain the nuances and complexities of his overall strategy in a way that is easy for employees, investors, supply chain partners and customers to understand.

His mastery of technical detail allows him to embrace new technologies, influence product innovation and design decisions, foster a culture of competitive secrecy and prioritise customer satisfaction. All of which are hallmarks of Apple's success.[139] Cook has helped to introduce numerous innovative products and technologies, including multiple generations of the Mac, iPhone, iPad, Apple Watch and Apple Vision Pro.

Thanks to Cook's ability to formulate and communicate strategy clearly, Apple remains one of the world's most resilient businesses.

MANAGE CRISIS SITUATIONS

In times of crisis, CEOs need to be resilient.

When a 'wheel falls off the bus', a CEO shows the way forward with integrity. Being honest, ethical and loyal in a crisis brings a beacon of hope in the darkest of hours. CEOs can give others the strength to keep going when things are difficult. Importantly, they respond publicly and commit their firm to action. Thus holding themselves accountable for actively managing crises.

Cook leads well in a crisis. His success is due to transparency and acceptance of the facts. He does not engage in denial, deception or spin. He is well known for being open and honest with stakeholders about Apple's performance and challenges. Cook is willing to admit when he has made mistakes or encounters dilemmas. He is open to discussing these issues and finding ways to address them. Despite Apple's many moving parts, Cook, like most CEOs, strives to do the right things the right way.

DOING THE RIGHT THINGS

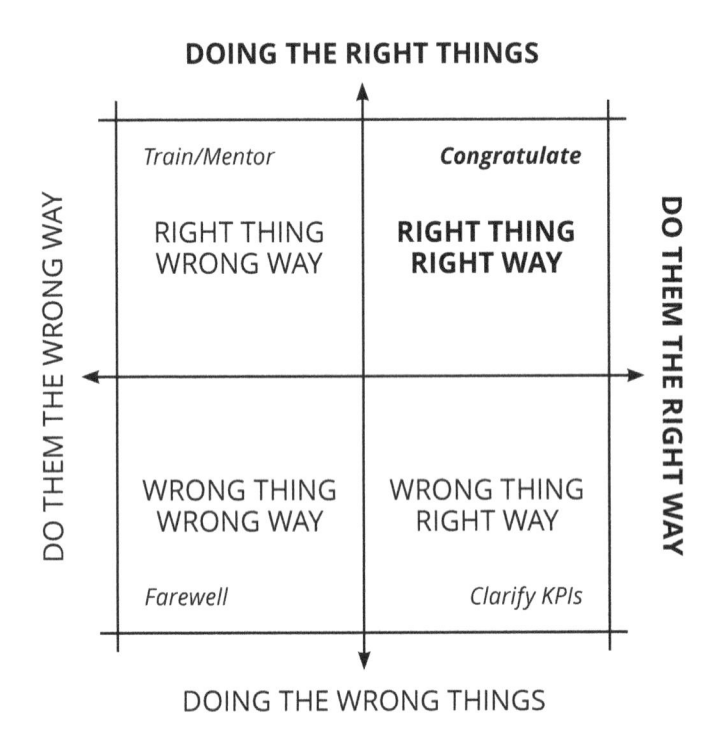

	Train/Mentor	Congratulate	
DO THEM THE WRONG WAY	**RIGHT THING WRONG WAY**	**RIGHT THING RIGHT WAY**	DO THEM THE RIGHT WAY
	WRONG THING WRONG WAY	WRONG THING RIGHT WAY	
	Farewell	Clarify KPIs	

DOING THE WRONG THINGS

Figure 9.2 The Apple Way

Applying Figure 9.2 to your people provides four ways to engage with their actions. Congratulating individuals for performing the right tasks correctly reinforces what is needed. CEOs should restate the strategy and clarify their team's KPIs if the right tasks are not being actioned. When the right tasks are executed poorly, training and mentoring are needed. When neither training nor clarification remedy underperformance, it may be necessary to adopt Leonard Lauder's reverse fault approach and farewell the individual by saying:

"Everyone has value. The fact that we have not managed to utilise your talents is not your fault. It is ours."

HABIT NINE : EXPLAIN STRATEGY CLEARLY

Like Cook, conscious CEOs acknowledge conflicts and negative public perceptions and take ultimate responsibility for any faults and issues that may have caused them. A firm's history can haunt a CEO. China-based production company Foxconn was first contracted by Apple in 2006 to assemble the iPod. Foxconn has been a source of constant concern to Apple.

In 2012, the Fair Labour Association (FLA) investigated labour practices at Foxconn and found that workers, some of whom were children, were subjected to excessive overtime and poor working conditions. This humanitarian crisis included over a dozen workers committing suicide.

Cook assumed responsibility for reforming the Foxconn supply chain. It took over a decade to implement the changes needed to bring it up to his standard. Cook responds by publicly committing to improving working conditions and labour standards throughout Apple's large and complex supply chain.

By 2018, Amnesty International accused Apple of failing to address the remaining issues of forced labour in its supply chain. Cook responded by publishing a complete list of Apple's suppliers.

During the 2019 Golden Globes, Cook steeled himself when comedian host Ricky Gervais joked, "Apple had joined the TV game with a superb drama about the importance of dignity and doing the right thing, made by a company that runs sweatshops in China."[140]

Gervais's joke did not reflect Cook's hard work of continually pushing for supply-chain audits to eliminate child labour and promoting higher-education courses at Chinese factories.[141] Today, due to Cook's insistence, Foxconn follows a code of work ethics.

This includes labour rights ranging from fair working hours, equal pay, health & safety protection, compensation and social security insurance. Foxconn now has industrial relations processes and worker integration - none of which existed a decade prior.[142]

Having workforces and suppliers across cultures is challenging. Apple works with suppliers in 43 countries and across six continents to make its products.[143] Apple's vertically integrated business model gets even more complicated when broken down into raw materials sourcing.

Japan, South Korea and China are the three main countries that have taken part in sourcing Apple's iPhone. The marked differences for 'Power-Distance' and 'Indulgence' between the USA and China in Hofstede's Cultural Dimensions speak to Cook's continuing Foxconn dilemmas.

Like Russian survivors of Stalin's depraved assault on millions of his fellow countrymen and women, restrained Chinese workers accept, without question, the hierarchy of absolute power and communist government authority.

HABIT NINE : EXPLAIN STRATEGY CLEARLY

HOFSTEDE'S CULTURAL DIMENSIONS

Dimension	USA	Japan	South Korea	China
Power Distance	40	54	60	80
Individualism	91	46	18	20
Masculinity	62	95	39	66
Uncertainty Avoidance	46	92	85	30
Long-term Orientation	26	88	100	87
Indulgence	68	42	29	24

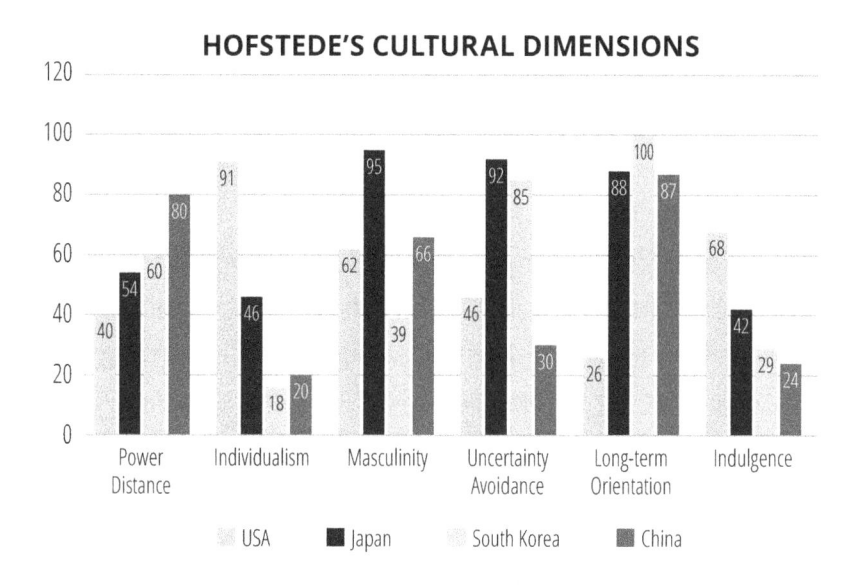

Figure 9.3 Countries for iPhone Sourcing

Non-government union movements in China are illegal. Apple Store employees in the USA are not restrained; many belong to unions. Indulgence in a society like the USA allows "relatively free gratification of basic and natural human desires related to enjoying life and having fun."[144] [145] China's low indulgence score reveals a societal practice that "controls gratification of needs and regulates using strict social norms."[146]

Erin Meyer's book The Culture Map[147] provides valuable insights for CEOs navigating cross-cultural challenges, particularly pertinent in the case of multinational corporations like Apple. Understanding cultural nuances, such as those highlighted in Hofstede's Cultural Dimensions, can significantly impact decision-making and leadership effectiveness.

In the context of Apple's sourcing operations involving countries like China, Japan and South Korea, Meyer's framework offers CEOs a roadmap for better communication and relationship-building with stakeholders from diverse cultural backgrounds.

Cook has also faced antitrust concerns related to Apple's App Store practices.[148] For example, in 2020, Spotify filed a complaint with the European Commission, alleging that Apple's App Store policies give its music streaming service an unfair advantage. Cook defended Apple's practices, stating that the company's App Store policies are designed to ensure a level playing field for all developers.

Cook stared down this mini-crisis by gaining legal advice, affirming that Apple has no case to answer for. He reiterated that the App Store is a highly attractive sales and distribution channel, allowing even the smallest start-up instant access to hundreds of millions of iOS users.

Cook and other legal commentators pointed out that developers can and do use competitors' sales platforms.[149] Apple's vertically integrated business model is competitive, and brilliant! Just because other platforms want to make their software free or cheaper for the masses does not compel Apple to join them in a race to the bottom.

In 2019, a group of Apple employees wrote a letter to Cook, calling for the company to act on the impending climate crisis. Perhaps these employees were out of the loop. Cook has been working on environmental initiatives since becoming CEO in 2011.[150]

HABIT NINE : EXPLAIN STRATEGY CLEARLY

In 2011, Greenpeace accused Apple of using dirty energy to power its data centres. Cook responded by committing to using 100% renewable energy to power Apple's operations and publicly disclosing the company's environmental impacts.

Cook then brought the climate crisis and energy use closer to his heart. Cook responded by publicly committing to addressing the issue further and published a list of Apple's environmental initiatives on the company website, compelling Apple to make products with net zero carbon impact by 2030.

Cook does not believe companies must choose between success or helping the environment. Today, Apple uses recycled materials to increase energy efficiency in retail stores, offices and manufacturing sites. Apple's corporate operations run on 100 per cent renewable energy generated from solar, wind and other renewable sources.

Soon, clean energy will be used to make every Apple product and will also account for the energy use of customers' products. Recently, Cook decided to no longer include a power adapter 'brick' with its newest Apple Watches and iPhones to reduce waste. Cook has partnered Apple with conservation funds to protect and restore 1 million acres of forests worldwide.

Another crisis occurred in 2019 when it was revealed that Apple contractors were listening to recordings of interactions between users and Siri, Apple's virtual assistant. Cook responded by suspending the contractor's program and publishing a transparency report.

Cook communicated clearly that unlike other platforms, such as Facebook and Amazon, which monetise users' personal information, Apple does not connect Apple User IDs to Siri. Siri requests are transmitted with a randomised identifier.[151]

Cook has committed to giving users even more control over their data, much to the dismay of Meta and others, who have relied on iPhones to unethically mine user information. Cook is a CEO who values his privacy and affords Apple's customers the same.

BE MEDIA SAVVY

To help explain strategy clearly, being media savvy can be a significant advantage for a CEO.

CEOs must rely on common sense, good judgement and a deep understanding of the media landscape. They must be confident and effective in public appearances. They should understand their target audience and tailor their message accordingly. Examples of various media options include:

1. Social media platforms to support messaging to both internal and external audiences.
2. Trade and industry-specific publications to help educate consumers.

3. Podcasts, blogs and interactions with common video platforms allow CEOs to present their thoughts and insights on a wide range of topics and build an audience of engaged listeners.
4. Newspapers, magazines and television also allow CEOs to reach broad audiences and shape public perceptions of their companies.

The array of media options can be overwhelming. As a result, many CEOs create an internal public relations unit or engage external communications agencies. The power of media platforms shifts over time. The best CEOs remain current with the latest trends and media platforms to stay engaged with their audience. Preferably on their terms!

Apple's use of mainstream social media platforms is different to most. Cook limits social media to annual event date announcements. This fits perfectly with Apple's brand persona and ongoing messaging - 'Think Different'.

Premium brands should not get dragged into the muck. 'The activity of large crowds inevitably sinks to the level of mob psychology.'[152] Often, social media proves itself to be the toilet of the internet with many adverse impacts.[153] Social media spawns a herd mentality, as depicted in Figure 9.4.

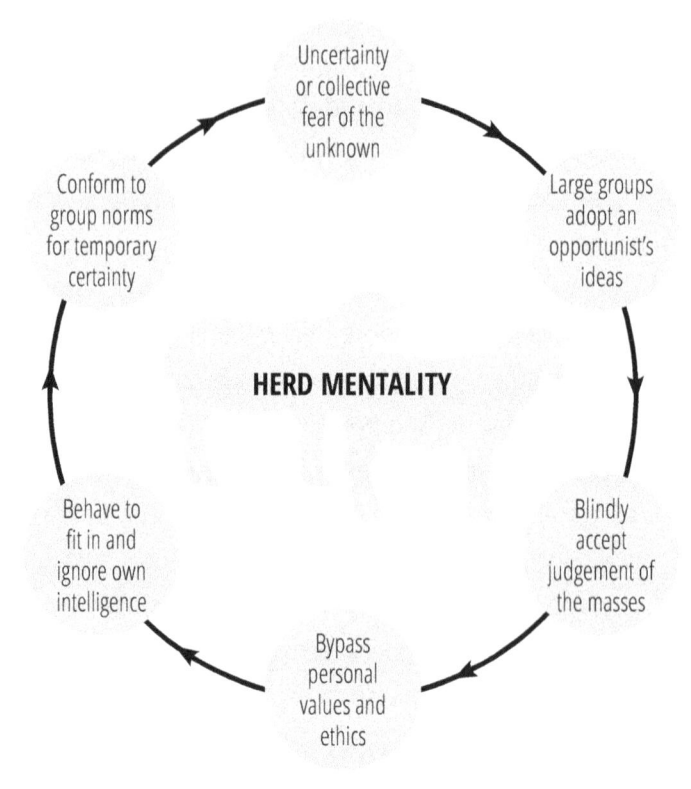

```
                    Uncertainty
                    or collective
                    fear of the
                    unknown
   Conform to                          Large groups
   group norms                         adopt an
   for temporary                       opportunist's
   certainty                           ideas

                  HERD MENTALITY

   Behave to                           Blindly
   fit in and                          accept
   ignore own                          judgement of
   intelligence                        the masses
                    Bypass
                    personal
                    values and
                    ethics
```

Figure 9.4 Herd Mentality Process

For example, social media contributed to the disruption of supply chains via panic buying during the pandemic.[154] Repeated and opportunistic Black Friday social media posts routinely cause fatal stampedes in orderly shopping malls, resulting in dozens of consumer and employee deaths and thousands of injuries.[155]

Thanks to social media, like lambs for slaughter, millions of consumers fall victim to the herd mentality. Dying to go into debt and dying to

HABIT NINE : EXPLAIN STRATEGY CLEARLY

be first in line for something that is unlikely to deliver any real joy to peoples' often-unfulfilled lives.

The main @Apple social media account on X has 7 million followers and is following zero accounts. The @Apple Instagram account is following a dozen accounts associated with Apple itself. This is fitting for a premium player that prides itself on innovation rather than following the crowd. Explaining Apple's strategy means controlling the narrative without leaving it to chance.

The premium pricing of Apple's products is often challenging for Cook in media interviews. Cook remains firm and clear in explaining Apple's pricing and strategy:

"Price is rarely the most important thing. A cheap product might sell some units. People may feel great when they pay less, but then they get it home and use it, and that joy is gone. We've always been about making the best product."

When your product and customer strategy are right, you do not have to be a great marketer; the public will do it for you.[156]

Numerous media platforms that Apple can take advantage of have emerged. These include Trend Force, MacRumors, 9 to 5 Mac and China Times. They leak new product specs and create extra demand. Individual influencers and commentators like Ross Young and Mark Gurman are also instrumental in spreading 'unofficial' news updates for Apple.

Highly trusted influencers like Marques Brownlee, with 20+ million YouTube followers, faithfully reviews the features of each new Apple product. As a result, Apple ships Brownlee all their latest products for free, ahead of in-store dates, to help raise customer awareness in the media.

In 2013, the media reported that the US Senate Permanent Subcommittee on Investigations found that Apple had avoided paying taxes on tens of billions of dollars in foreign income.[157]

Cook responded by emphasising that Apple pays all the taxes it owes and that the company is a significant contributor to the US economy. Cook also announced that the company was bringing back considerable cash from overseas and investing it in the US economy.

In 2016, Cook faced media challenges when the FBI demanded that Apple help unlock the iPhone of one of the shooters in the San Bernardino terrorist attack. Cook refused, citing concerns about customer privacy and security. Cook's stance led to a public debate about encryption and government access to personal data. In various interviews and public statements, Cook defended Apple's position, emphasising the importance of protecting user privacy.

Some leaders are born great, and others, like Cook, who work hard, have it thrust upon them. These days, Cook is very confident handling and maintaining positive relationships with the media.[158] Cook uses straightforward language in sharing Apple's strategy with the press, avoiding jargon and technical terms that might be difficult for the average person to understand.

HABIT NINE : EXPLAIN STRATEGY CLEARLY

In addition to his work at Apple, Cook is known for his philanthropy and commitment to social and environmental issues. He has donated millions of dollars to charitable causes and prioritised future sustainability and responsibility within Apple.

Rallying stakeholders towards a unified and ambitious future is the highest priority for a CEO. In the era of disruption, strategic agility and strategic clarity are paramount. The role of the CEO transcends mere management. Like Cook, CEOs must communicate clearly, lead in times of crisis and be media savvy.

In the next habit, we will meet a recently retired CEO who took on the President of the United States.

Next, make any notes about Tim Cook's approach on the following blank pages and then complete Activity Nine.

ACTIVITY NINE

Tim Cook's approach to communication at Apple is exemplary. Use the following questions to determine your communication skills. To assess your competence across all twelve habits, consider inviting others to complete the CEO Quiz in Appendix Four for you.

9.1 Consider a recent crisis in your organisation.

Q1. Did you maintain transparency and integrity as Cook does?
Q2. How could your approach be improved?

9.2 Assess the effectiveness of your public speaking.

What are your strengths, and what areas could you develop further to enhance your ability to convey strategy clearly?

9.3 Evaluate your engagement with the media.

How do you leverage different platforms to articulate your company's strategy, and what new methods could you adopt?

9.4 Analyse both your company's policy and strategy communications.

Q1. Is your company's policy and strategy clearly understood?
Q2. How might you simplify the messaging?

HABIT NINE : EXPLAIN STRATEGY CLEARLY

9.5 Complete three of the six activities. Choose activities that best support your development.

   (i)   Craft a clear and concise statement of your company's strategy, ensuring that someone outside your firm can easily repeat it.
   (ii) Role-play a crisis communication scenario and practice responding honestly and transparently.
   (iii) Organise a public speaking workshop for yourself and your leadership team, focusing on communicating complex ideas.
   (iv) Schedule a media training session to improve your effectiveness across different platforms, particularly in areas where you feel less confident.
   (v)   Create a simplified visual infographic to educate new employees and stakeholders about your company's strategy and policies.
   (vi) Host a cross-cultural communication seminar with your team, exploring the nuances of conducting business across different cultures and how to communicate effectively within these contexts.

Strategy is a commodity; execution is an art.

Peter Drucker

HABIT TEN

GOVERN RESOURCES PORTFOLIO

Adapted from
CC BY-SA 4.0 DEED
Chief Executive Magazine

KEN FRAZIER
MERCK & CO.

Protect Your Intelligence
Make Smart Decisions
Grow Digital Wings

Upon entering the modest office of Ken Frazier, you'd likely find tangible threads of wisdom, humility and resilience.

Surrounded by photos of his family and with prominent figures like Barack Obama, Warren Buffett and Pope Francis, you might expect to engage in a conversation with Frazier that reaches beyond purely fiscal achievements.

Indeed, if you lingered, a polished wood credenza might reveal a 1952 edition of TIME Magazine, with George Merck's portrait on the cover and the words beneath reading, "Medicine is for People, not Profits."

Frazier might recount his conversation with Pope Francis - a meeting that seems surprising, considering the Pontiff's religious stature and Frazier's corporate role. Yet, both men have backgrounds in chemistry.

Their ensuing conversation, a blend of morality and science.

You might anticipate Frazier reflecting on the Pope's words, which urge a deeper contemplation of our shared humanity and the role of pharmaceutical giants in addressing global suffering.

Upon closer examination, Frazier's tenure as CEO, perhaps encapsulated by the Pontiff's request, exemplifies a CEO's balancing act of managing resources in ways that account for societal needs while satisfying shareholder expectations.

Tragically, Frazier's mother passed away when he was just twelve years old. His journey is one of turning adversity into triumph. The eldest son of Otis and Clara Frazier, Frazier inherited a legacy of fortitude from

HABIT TEN: GOVERN RESOURCES PORTFOLIO

his father, who, despite growing up amidst an era of brutal lynching in the segregated South, instilled in young Ken the power of self-belief.

This lesson was echoed by Frazier's grandfather Richard, a former enslaved person whose words were, "Kenny, what other people think about you is none of your damn business. And the sooner you learn that the better off you'll be."[159] These words became an anchoring principle for young Ken.

Frazier's parents strongly encouraged education and hard work, ensuring their children knew what it took to succeed. Frazier grew up knowing, "You can be anything you want to be."[160]

Frazier's academic prowess shone brightly against the backdrop of his challenging beginnings. After graduating with the highest honours from Philadelphia's Northeast High School, he carried his pursuit of excellence to Pennsylvania State University and later to Harvard Law School, where he earned his Law Doctorate in 1978.

Frazier joined a Merck subsidiary as legal counsel in 1992, working his way up to CEO of Merck & Co in 2011, making him the first African American to serve as CEO of a major pharmaceutical company. Frazier's dedication to social justice was exemplified by his private pro bono work, including the exoneration of Willie Cochran - a man wrongfully imprisoned for two decades.

When Frazier took the CEO reins, Merck faced multiple resource challenges. Patent cliffs for many highly profitable drugs loomed large. Obama's promised Affordable Care Act was set to place downward financial pressure on prices, profitability and stock values. As Merck's CEO, governing the resources portfolio became a primary responsibility.

Indeed, a primary responsibility for all CEOs is to govern their firm's resources portfolio. Not governing resources and not reporting a firm's health can make a CEO feel safer in the short term. But this is false security. In the long term, a lack of governance spells disaster. The sins of the past are revealed all the way to the bottom line.

A firm's resources portfolio includes six assets. These are people, social resources, intellectual property, physical assets, financial investments and digital infrastructure. CEOs must ensure effective governance of all six resources. This habit touches on all six resources under the themes of protecting your intelligence, making smart decisions and growing digital wings.

PROTECT YOUR INTELLIGENCE

People

As a CEO, you must recognise that people are your most valuable resource.

HABIT TEN: GOVERN RESOURCES PORTFOLIO

With its employees' talents, creativity and knowledge, a business can function effectively. Ken Frazier understood that people and culture were critical to the success of any company.

Before Frazier's arrival, Merck's strategy was to outsource its scientific and R&D functions to reduce costs. A trend that had taken place across the industry. However, these savings paled compared to the long-run loss of employee morale, increasing bureaucracy and the reduced quality of new formulations.

Frazier and his Board realised Merck researchers and employees were pushing back against outsourcing mergers, with a 'not invented here' attitude toward new projects. Some of Merck's best people were jumping ship. Frazier has admitted:

"When I started as CEO, Big Pharma was taking resources away from R&D. We did too. We've begun to insource things we outsourced a decade ago because we realise, they are critical to Merck's long-term success. At the end of the day, the quality of Merck largely comes down to the quality of the science and the scientists."

Today, Merck is back on track. Early on, Frazier focused on three critical areas:

1. The first, and by far the most important, was to ensure that the right people were in the right jobs.
2. The second was setting the strategic direction of the firm.

3. The third was deciding how to allocate financial resources across the firm to produce the most significant long-term value for society and shareholders.

Frazier worked hard to empower his people and give them a sense of ownership by delegating important decisions to them. As a humble enabler, not a scientist, Frazier added, "And CEOs have to be willing to give up power. The most important decisions made inside Merck are not made in my office."

Social Resources

Frazier prioritised social justice at Merck and aligned it with the United Nations' Sustainable Development Goals (SDGs). Merck, in consultation with its people, allocates resources in eight SDG areas:

1. Good Health and Well Being
2. Gender Equality
3. Clean Water and Sanitation
4. Affordable and Clean Energy
5. Decent Work and Economic Growth
6. Responsible Consumption and Production
7. Partnerships for the SDGs
8. Climate Action

Frazier understood the power of the CEO's office to effect climate action and social change for the betterment of all people.

Those in other powerful offices sometimes differ. Once elected, Donald Trump exited the United States from the Paris Agreement. And in August 2017, after a white power march in Virginia that killed a protestor, Frazier believed, from media reports, that Trump had made comments sympathetic to white supremacists. Reports that political analysts have since disputed.

At that time, Frazier and Merck took a stand at what they perceived as intolerance by Trump.

Frazier resigned from the President's Manufacturing Council, inspiring other members to quit. That day, the Merck share price climbed, and the Merck Board backed Frazier's decision and statement:

"America's leaders must honour our fundamental views by clearly rejecting expressions of hatred, bigotry and group supremacy, which run counter to the American ideal that all people are created equal. As CEO of Merck and as a matter of personal conscience, I feel a responsibility to take a stand against intolerance and extremism."

Frazier echoed the sentiment that everyone should be respected and treated equally.

As a humanistic leader, Frazier treated people and the planet as assets.

He sought to empower people and increase their sense of ownership by delegating essential decisions to them. He recognised there were generous pockets of intelligence in many areas at Merck.

INTELLECTUAL PROPERTY

CEOs need to consider their firm's intellectual property (IP) assets, which include patents, copyrights, trademarks, brands, proprietary knowledge, partnerships, joint ventures and customer information.

Only a few firms should be overly concerned with IP. Speed-to-market often transcends waiting for patent approvals before deciding to scale up. Nevertheless, copyrights, trademarks and brands should be registered to protect against future capture by competitors.

Patents in the pharmaceutical industry are fundamental intellectual property resources that must be managed at all costs. A drug can take a decade or more to make its first sale, while drug patents only last twenty years. Frazier re-affirmed:

"As CEO, I need to ensure our decisions don't make sense for only the short-term. In Pharma, it takes 12 to 15 years to bring a drug to market. Our patents have a 20-year life, after which we lose exclusivity. We must keep inventing. If we don't create products that drive short-term value with new ones, we'll be out of business. Otherwise, Merck would be borrowing value from the future and bringing it to the present, which would be a mistake."

MAKE SMART DECISIONS

As a CEO, it is essential to make smart decisions regarding physical assets and financial investments to avoid borrowing from the future.

Physical Assets

Physical assets are integral to any business, and include manufacturing plants, buildings, equipment, systems and logistical infrastructure. The investment concepts of 'smart money,' 'just money', and 'dumb money' can be applied to the governance of physical assets and other financial investments.

Physical assets have an expected lifespan, and costs are incurred at each stage of an asset's life, with the highest costs occurring during the planning, acquisition and installation phases. The next phase, asset use, involves preventive, predictive and routine maintenance to extend the asset's life.

However, at some point, the additional maintenance costs and frequency of unscheduled downtimes will make the continued use of an asset non-viable. It will be time to make the 'smart money' decision to dispose of the asset or replace it.

In considering the lifecycle of physical assets, it is often more financially beneficial for a CEO or CFO to recommend leasing or a sale-and-leaseback arrangement rather than making a 'dumb money' decision to purchase assets outright.

There may be instances where the 'smart money' decision is to own an asset, especially if it is closely tied to a core competence, unique process or mission-critical function.

However, it is often advantageous to get assets off the company's balance sheet, as they can quickly become liabilities.

Financial Investments

CEOs should aim to make 'smart money' decisions whenever possible. This means intelligently allocating financial resources to produce the most significant long-term value for society and shareholders. Frazier believes that value is created for all stakeholders through careful financial management.

A firm's financial resources include:

Acquired funds.
Cash from the business.
Lines of credit from banks and capital markets.
Stock options for employees.
Vendor finance.
Foreign currency holdings to hedge currency risk from foreign transactions.

When managing the resources portfolio, CEOs must be careful to make the 'smart money' decisions shown in Figure 10.1. Eighty-three percent of CEOs name 'smart money' decisions as a key driver for growth.[161]

HABIT TEN: GOVERN RESOURCES PORTFOLIO

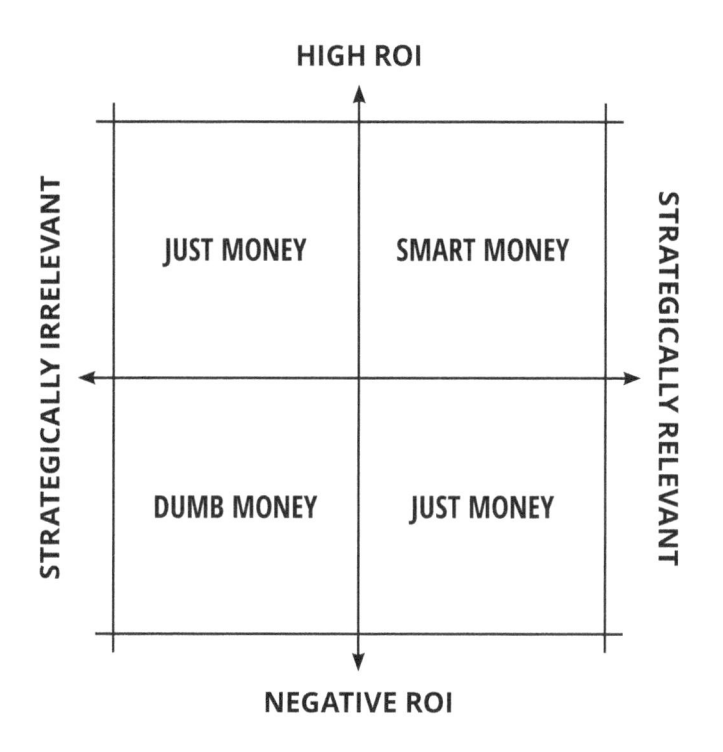

	HIGH ROI	
STRATEGICALLY IRRELEVANT	JUST MONEY	SMART MONEY
	DUMB MONEY	JUST MONEY
	NEGATIVE ROI	STRATEGICALLY RELEVANT

Figure 10.1 Investment Decision Matrix

This is where sensitivity analysis using a range of funding alternatives and earnings scenarios will help.[162] For example, suppose your new enterprise is considering three alternative financing structures:

Your Enterprise:

Projected earnings before interest and tax (EBIT) = $4M pa.
Pessimistic earnings before interest and tax (EBIT) = $1M pa.
Total funds required = $12M.
Debt may be obtained at 10% interest (fixed) repayable over 5 years.
Shareholders expect a dividend of 10 cents per share.

Shares will be sold to the public at $1 each.
Tax rate is 30%.

Three financing alternatives:

All shareholder equity.
20% debt, 80% shareholder equity.
40% debt, 60% shareholder equity.

	Alternative One	**Alternative Two**	**Alternative Three**
	All shareholder equity	20% debt	40% debt
Share Capital	$12M	$9.6M	$7.2M
Debt Capital	0	$2.4M	$4.8M
EBIT (Projected)	$4M	$4M	$4M
Interest Payable	0	$240,000	$480,000
Profit before Tax	$4M	$3.76M	$3.52M
Tax Payable (30%)	$1.2M	$1.13M	$1.06M
Profit after Tax	$2.8M	$2.63M	$2.46M
Principal Repayment (PR)	0	$480,000	$960,000

HABIT TEN: GOVERN RESOURCES PORTFOLIO

	Alternative One	Alternative Two	Alternative Three
Available to Shareholders	$2.8M	$2.15M	$1.5M
Number of Shares	12M shares	960,000 shares	720,000 shares
Earnings Per Share (EPS)	23 cents	22 cents	21 cents

This sensitivity analysis shows that with projected earnings of $4M annually, even a 40:60 debt-to-equity ratio delivers good shareholder earnings. Shareholders expecting 10 cents per share are delighted. Now, let us alter the scenario from projected earnings of $4M annually to pessimistic earnings of $1M annually.

	Alternative One	Alternative Two	Alternative Three
	All shareholder equity	20% debt	40% debt
Share Capital	$12M	$9.6M	$7.2M
Debt Capital	0	$2.4M	$4.8M
EBIT (Pessimistic)	$1M	$1M	$1M
Interest Payable	0	$240,000	$480,000
Profit before Tax	$1M	$760,000	$520,000
Tax Payable (30%)	$300,000	$228,000	$156,000

	Alternative One	**Alternative Two**	**Alternative Three**
Profit after Tax	$700,000	$532,000	$364,000
Principal Repayment (PR)	0	$480,000	$960,000
Available to Shareholders	$700,000	$52,000	($596,000)
Number of Shares	12M shares	960,000 shares	720,000 shares
Earnings Per Share (EPS)	6 cents	0.54 cent	(8 cents)

This second sensitivity analysis using the pessimistic earnings projection of $1M annually shows that taking on any structural debt erodes shareholder value. Regarding financial risk, the best CEOs do not gamble with shareholders' funds by taking on debt when sensitivity analysis does not stack up under all probable scenarios.

This is a hard rule to follow when you are a CEO looking desperately for capital to grow your firm. Yet too many CEOs have allowed debt to erode shareholder returns. Other times, CEOs incur financial risks by miscalculating their firm's Cost of Capital.

To learn how to calculate your firm's Cost of Capital, please refer to Appendix Three - Cost of Capital.

GROW DIGITAL WINGS

Digital Infrastructure

Information technology (IT) systems must be strategic assets, not liabilities. IT assets allow businesses to grow the digital wings they need to fly.

Adopting the right technologies can be crucial, when it comes to growing a business. These technologies can be classified into five digital wings.[163]

In the early business growth stages of Existence and Survival, a business should focus on the digital wing of Reach, allowing it to reach more customers and suppliers.

As the business grows and moves into the Success stage, focusing on the digital wing of information Richness, such as data mining and information management, helps with decisions and strategic planning.

During the Take-off stage, it is essential to grow the digital wing that helps with quicker Response times. This wing provides real-time updates on production, supply chain logistics and customer experiences.

In the Maturity stage, growing the digital wing of Range delivers a variety of beneficial business metrics within an integrated system that can be easily transmitted to suppliers, employees and customers. Range becomes critically important as the number of employees approaches 150 and the workplace evolves from informal and undocumented to structured and codified.[164]

THE CEO BOOK

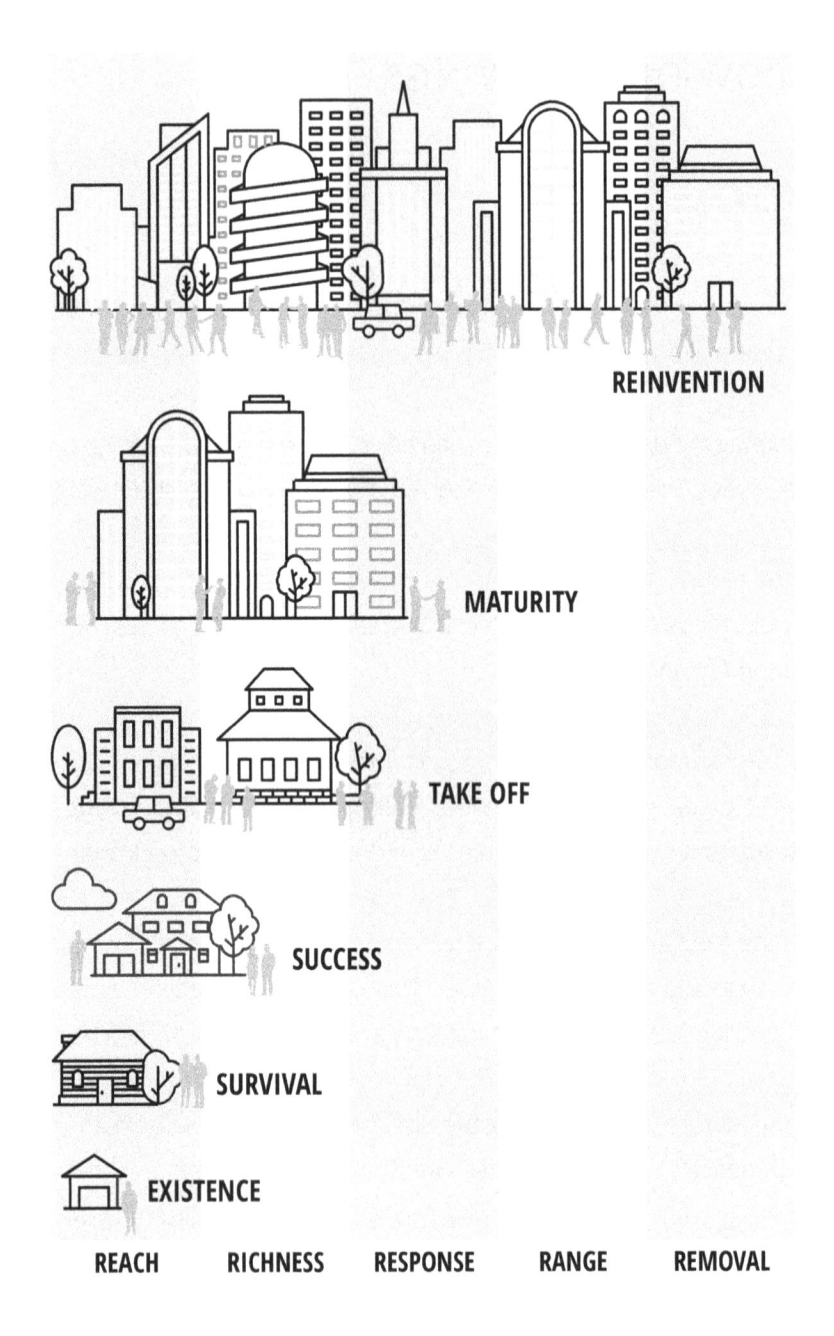

Figure 10.2 Growing Digital Wings

HABIT TEN: GOVERN RESOURCES PORTFOLIO

Finally, at the Reinvention stage, the digital wing of Removal will include technology like automation and AI to remove people, pain and processes from the business, enabling it to remain lean, competitive and profitable.

By adopting the right digital wings at the appropriate stages of business growth, a company can set itself up for continued success.

Investment in technology needs to increase intelligently as a firm grows.

Intelligence can mean repatriating back in-house, a former reliance on cloud services which, month by month and year by year, are spiralling in costs. To recap, we can think about the business value of technology in terms of five digital wings:

Reach – information pathways across geographic and virtual domains.
Richness – the usefulness of data and information.
Response – the speed at which information is delivered to the user.
Range – the breadth of functionality within an integrated system.
Removal – automation that eliminates people, pain and processes.

As their business matures, CEOs should analyse their firm's digital maturity and a level of customer focus.[165] From this exercise, four scenarios emerge, thanks to the efforts of MIT Sloan research scientists Stephanie Woerner, Peter Weill and Ina Sebastian.

This MIT Sloan team created a playbook to help CEOs ensure their firms are top performers in the digital economy and remain future-ready. Their Future Ready framework includes four scenarios.[166]

TRANSFORMATIVE CUSTOMER EXPERIENCES

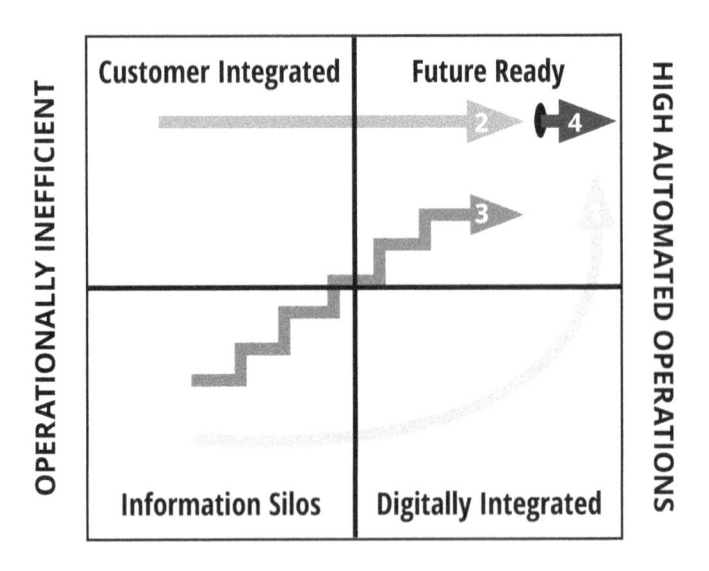

	Customer Integrated	Future Ready	
OPERATIONALLY INEFFICIENT			**HIGH AUTOMATED OPERATIONS**
	Information Silos	Digitally Integrated	

LACK OF CUSTOMER FOCUS

Figure 10.3 Corporate Digital Strategy

Scenario One: The first scenario has three options - moving up the curved line in Figure 10.3 from the bottom left to the top right.

For example, in Australia, the dominant telco, Telstra, has always been owned wholly or partly by the Government. With regulatory protection, Telstra allowed itself to be less customer-centric and less automated than its more customer-focused competitors, Optus and Vodaphone.

AT&T, the dominant telco in the United States, found itself in a similar place some thirty years ago. AT&T and Telstra were digitally challenged, operationally inefficient and needed more customer focus.

HABIT TEN: GOVERN RESOURCES PORTFOLIO

When firms are digitally challenged and customer indifferent, business and customer data are stored in poorly planned and disparate IT systems. Here, information is usually kept in departmental silos and employees find it difficult or impossible to exchange information with one another in real time. Sadly, at Telstra, a series of organisational restructures by successive CEOs did little to help their silo problem.

The first option in becoming future-ready in scenario one involves improving operational efficiency through automation and standardisation, followed by a focus on transforming the customer experience.

The second option involves prioritising the transformation of the customer experience before improving operational efficiency. Telstra eventually took this option despite considerable resistance and cultural inertia, as middle managers hesitated to accept that the customer was a genuine and valued stakeholder.

The third option in becoming future-ready involves improving operational efficiency and transforming the customer experience simultaneously. AT&T took this path while also evolving its organisational culture.

Scenario Two: Moving horizontally from left to right makes sense for a company that is digitally challenged and operationally inefficient but already delivering transformative customer experiences. Here, the path to future readiness is to prioritise improving operational efficiency through digital solutions.

Trader Joe's, Costco and Southwest Airlines in the United States, along with Aldi Stores and JB Hi-Fi in Australia, all have strong reputations for transformative customer experiences. Yet, all had to play digital catch-up.

Trader Joe's and Costco eventually caught up and reaped benefits from digital solutions that streamlined customer interactions and inventory management. Southwest Airlines moved to the right with new mobile services and improved online customer support.

During the pandemic, JB Hi-Fi deployed off-the-shelf enterprise supply chain management software to adapt to online and virtual sales when physical stores were closed.

Aldi was caught unprepared with its store-based information silos. As the pandemic set in, Aldi could not offer click-and-collect or home delivery services, unlike other major supermarkets.

Scenario Three: Here, we see a digitally and operationally adequate company with adequate customer focus. A stepwise path can be taken, where both aspects are worked on consistently and sustainably in stages. An action-learning approach to assess customer needs and automation requirements is applied, and then an Agile development methodology can be used.

To become ready for the future, in his early years, Frazier supported Merck & Co by investing in improved customer experiences and increasing operational automation. Like Merck & Co, this stepwise approach can be a good path for many large firms playing catch-up in customer experience and automated operations.

HABIT TEN: GOVERN RESOURCES PORTFOLIO

Scenario Four: This future-ready company is digitally mature, operationally efficient and already offers transformative customer experiences. They stay ahead of the competition through innovation and expanding the frontiers of customer experience and automation. Two examples of such companies are Apple and Whole Foods, which is now part of Amazon.

Since its acquisition, Whole Foods has also made significant strides in the digital space, particularly with the surge in online grocery sales. They have worked on projects to optimise the fulfilment of online orders, including improving the substitution process for items not available at the time of fulfilment, thereby enhancing the end-customer experience.

Under Frazier's leadership, Merck & Co enhanced its digital infrastructure and improved its customer experience to become future-ready.

Frazier understood that if any IT investment did not offer a strategic advantage operationally or in the marketplace, it was a strategic liability, and its continued deployment was bad governance.

By the end of Frazier's tenure, Merck & Co's annual R&D investments had reached $13.5 billion.[167] These investments were directed at technologies and programs that addressed significant global health challenges, with an emphasis on expanding Merck's social outreach goal to impact more than 50 million customers in less affluent regions and underserved communities by 2025.

Frazier steered Merck to harness data science, spurring innovation and the creation of critical medications. This strategy included partnering with Corning to improve predictive models for drug development and implementing AI for image recognition and processing large datasets, like journal articles and patents.[168]

Furthermore, Merck engaged in strategic partnerships to enhance AI-driven drug discovery efforts, focusing on biomarkers and the development of new treatments.[169] In addition, Merck launched the Digital Sciences Studio to expedite the advancement of healthcare start-ups, thus fostering digital innovation in healthcare.[170]

Merck's approach to growing digital wings emphasised Response, Range and Removal with AI, automation, cloud computing, big data analytics and 3D printing. Investment in information and communications technology (ICT) is substantial, amounting to $3 billion annually.[171]

Frazier's dedication to growing digital wings has been acknowledged with Merck's ranking in the ARC Industrial Digital Transformation Top 25 report,[172] highlighting the company's ability to remain future-ready.

Ken Frazier's ascent through adversity to the helm of Merck and his stewardship over Merck's assets, while facing industry pressures, reveal the complexity and importance of governing the resource portfolio.

In the next habit, we will meet a leader who makes it known that the best decisions transcend hierarchy.

Make any notes on governing your resources on the following blank pages.

Then, complete Activity Ten.

ACTIVITY TEN

How do you govern resources in your firm?

10.1 Reflect on a time when your company faced adversity.

   Q1. What rules and methods did you employ to govern limited resources?
   Q2. Was a turnaround possible?
   Q3. How could you apply lessons from Frazier's leadership to future challenges?

10.2 Reflect on your major financial decisions as a CEO.

   Q1. Have you ever made 'dumb money' decisions?
   Q2. How do you balance short-term gains with long-term sustainability?
   Q3. How do you approach asset ownership?

10.3 How can your firm integrate social justice into its core values and business practices, as Frazier did, without compromising long-term profitability?

10.4 Decide which stage of growth your firm is at. Then, review the five digital wings - reach, richness, response, range and removal.

   With investments in digital infrastructure, what are your 'smart money' and 'just money' options?

10.5 Select one of the following three activities to increase dialogue, raise intelligence and build capability within your firm to better govern the resource portfolio.

   (i) Cultural Resilience Workshop: Host a workshop where leaders and employees can impart personal and team resilience stories and discuss how these lessons can be incorporated into the firm's governance models.
   (ii) Financial Governance Seminar: Host a seminar with your executive team and financial experts on how to make 'smart money' decisions, emphasising long-term thinking over short-term gains while explaining how your firm calculates and governs investment decisions with its Cost of Capital.
   (iii) AI Governance Think Tank: Form a think tank to explore the implications of AI in your business, focusing on ethical considerations and the agreed rules of engagement with large language models (LLMs), AI and Cloud Storage Providers, along with future employee roles and responsibilities.

Beware of little expenses. A small leak will sink a great ship.

Benjamin Franklin

HABIT ELEVEN
MENTOR DIRECT REPORTS

DAVE COOPER
NAVY SEALS

Lead With Vulnerability
Encourage Critical Thinking
Review After Action

Harsh winds scolded the icy desert road.

Visibility worsened.

Plagued with ruts and bomb craters, the 110-mile route between Bagram and Jalalabad still haunts Dave Cooper.

On a cold New Year's Eve, Cooper found himself amidst a perilous mission, traversing that desolate road.

Why?

Because of orders.

Orders that placed him and his men on a reconnaissance mission reaching into the night. The road was infested with landmines and shadowed by bandits and insurgents.[173]

Notwithstanding the apparent dangers, Cooper's superior commander, hundreds of miles away and with no skin in the game, was brimming with a confidence that bordered on recklessness.

Despite Cooper's grave reservations, his superior insisted on proceeding with the mission. The final plan involved navigating this hazardous road in an armoured suburban equipped with specially reinforced tyres, promising speed and stealth.

Despite harbouring doubts, Cooper, ever loyal to the chain of command, reluctantly agreed to proceed. As his unit ventured from Bagram that morning, their mission quickly unravelled. Far from the navigable path they had anticipated, the road resembled a treacherous trail, severely limiting their pace.

By nightfall, they reached Jalalabad.

Common sense suggested they pause and wait for daylight. Yet, defying all logic, the superior commander ordered them to return to Bagram under the cover of darkness. Cooper's protests, born from a mix of genuine concern and frustration, clashed with the commander's directives until the orders from the higher-ranking commander overruled any further debate and silenced Cooper.

With a heavy heart, Cooper re-entered the vehicle, facing a night of dangerous certainty.

Cooper's worst fears materialised soon after, when an enemy ambush swiftly encircled them. In the ensuing chaos, as their vehicle faltered and gunfire enveloped them, the situation descended into a desperate fight for survival.

One of Cooper's men was severely wounded in the leg.

The grim reality of their predicament settled in.

Surrender became their only option, a decision that miraculously spared their lives.

Some hours after this near-death experience, an allied nation's rescue team arrived, providing safe passage to Bagram.

Cooper had an opportunity to reflect and change.

Dave Cooper was born in Los Angeles. He is a confident, sun-tanned man with sharp cheekbones and blue eyes. Cooper is known for his cheerful demeanour. He enjoys swimming, running and playing chess. He grew up in a military family. His father was a Vietnam veteran. Cooper wanted to follow in his father's footsteps and serve his country. After high school, he earned a degree in Molecular Biology from Juniata College in 1987. That same year, he entered the military, specifically to become a US Navy SEAL.[174]

The SEALs are elite soldiers trained to operate in the most complex and challenging environments. They are known for adapting to any situation and overcoming any obstacle.

Cooper, while not the most skilled combatant or strongest swimmer, enjoyed the challenges of SEAL training. After 22 years of service, from September 2009 to September 2011, Cooper served as the Command Master Chief of the Naval Special Warfare Development Group. Cooper is one of only a handful of SEALs to ever hold this position.[175]

Cooper was a loyal SEAL who carried out expeditious assassinations. Cooper embodies integrity and a dedication to a cause greater than himself. At times, having to make difficult decisions at significant personal risk.

Fellow Navy SEAL Bill McRaven, in his book 'Make Your Bed,' recounts that when the SEALS captured and cared for Saddam Hussein in an accommodation setting superior to their lodgings, Saddam never made his bed. Saddam's covers were always crumpled at the foot of his bed, never bothering to straighten them.[176]

Once the SEALs handed Saddam to the Iraqi government, Saddam was executed for his role in the massacre of his people. McRaven says that life is hard. Whether you are a Navy SEAL, a dictator or a CEO, having faith can come from making your bed and starting your day with a determined and orderly mindset. Something Katrina Lake, in Habit Eight, would advocate.

McRaven reveals that self-leadership habits are the first step in changing the world. Below are ten commandments by McRaven, inspired by his decades of service.[177] [178]

1. Make your bed in the morning.
This should be your first accomplished task in the morning, giving you pride and motivation to keep going for the rest of the day. It is the little things in life that matter. If we fail to accomplish the little things in life, we will fail to get the big things right. If someone is going through a bad day, at the end of the day, they will return to the comfortable bed they made, giving them the encouragement needed for the next day.

2. Everyone must paddle.
We all need the help of friends, colleagues and strangers daily. We must find people to paddle with to change the world.

3. Everyone must be measured by the size of their hearts, not the size of their flippers.
Your education, social status or background do not matter. What matters is a person's courage and will to succeed. Even if you were not born great or with flipper-sized feet, greatness can still be yours.

4. Get over being a "Sugar Cookie."
When a superior officer decided a Navy SEAL's conduct was anything less than perfect, that SEAL had to immediately hit the cold surf and then roll around wet in the sand until they succeeded at looking like a cookie covered in sugar! Nothing will ever be good enough. There's no such thing as a perfectly starched uniform. We have to keep moving forward, no matter the obstacles. It is just the way life is.

5. Do not be afraid of circuses.
Life is full of circuses. These are designed to challenge you and test your resilience. We often fail in life. It will be painful and discouraging. Circuses offer fresh chances to build your inner strength.

6. Slide down the obstacles with your head first.
We must take chances and risks, even if it seems foolish and dangerous. Come up with new strategies and techniques that have yet to be considered or implemented.

7. Never back down from the sharks.
There are a lot of sharks out there in the world. But to not be eaten by sharks and complete the swim, you must be grounded and not give in to the sharks.

8. Be your very best in the darkest moments.
When your tactical skills, physical power and inner strength have failed you, you must be calm and composed.

9. We must all believe in the power of hope and the power of one person.
One centred person can muster the power to give people hope and help those around them 'keep their heads above the mud.' And with the power of all united, the mud will seem a little warmer and the wind a little tamer. But it all starts with hope and one voice.

10. Lastly, never give up or ring the Bell if you want to change the world.
Most Navy SEAL candidates who start basic training do not complete it. Most recruits quit. They walk up to the Bell and ring it three times.

Why?

Because the average SEAL performance standards are much higher than those of any other armed forces section.

Those SEALs who make it often talk about the 40% rule. The 40% rule says that when you know you are mentally and physically done, you are at 40% exhaustion, with 60% of hidden reserves yet to be unlocked.

Anyone who has completed a marathon will appreciate this idea. The best CEOs never give up. These CEOs always find a way. Like a successful SEAL, the best CEOs remain determined so that one day, future generations will live in a better world than the present one.

Dave Cooper's perspective on leadership was grounded in Bill McRaven's ten commandments and then matured in the high-stakes and high-pressure environment of the Navy SEAL global deployment operations. Contrary to the traditional view of leadership, where showing weakness is avoided, Cooper underscores the notion that leaders who are open about admitting and sharing their mistakes create a culture of trust and openness within their teams.

Indeed, with mission-critical operational units like Seal Team Six, selection often focused on two dimensions, performance and trust.

Trust is about personal character and the true strength that comes from vulnerability. A trusted SEAL is honest and can be trusted with the lives of others. Trust is something Cooper was held in high regard for.

Performance is measured in skills and achievements, both in training and combat. By his admission, Cooper was not an elite performer. Cooper was above average. Yet, Cooper was appointed leader of Seal Team Six and many other mission-critical operational units in his time.

Figure 11.1 shows how Navy SEALs are sorted into five categories based on performance and trust:

HABIT ELEVEN: MENTOR DIRECT REPORTS

Highly Skilled Performer

4. High Performing but Untrustworthy SEAL	1. High Performing and Trusted SEAL
	'Coop'
5. Average Performing and Untrustworthy SEAL	2. Above Average Performing and Trusted SEAL
	3. Average Performing and Trusted SEAL

Not Vulnerable, Humble or Trustworthy — *Vulnerable, Humble and Trustworthy*

Average Skilled Performer

Figure 11.1 Picking SEAL TEAM SIX

#5. Average Performance with Low Trust: Not suitable for mission-critical operations.

#4. High Performance but Low Trust: These individuals were often considered toxic team members. SEAL leaders preferred to exclude them from mission-critical operations despite their high performance.

#3. Average Performance but High Trust: Trustworthiness is so highly valued that SEAL leaders often select these individuals over those with high performance but low trust.

#2. Above Average Performance with High Trust: Individuals like Dave Cooper, who frequently fell into this category, were often highly successful and decorated SEAL leaders. They enjoyed a healthy mix of ability and trustworthiness.

#1. High Performance with High Trust: Such SEALs were considered ideal. They were team members who were both highly skilled and trustworthy.

In business, numerous performance metrics often do not relate to trust or teamwork. There is a considerable risk that firms will be tempted to reward such metrics, promote toxic leaders and ultimately harm their firm. Measuring both performance and trust in leaders and team members can minimise harm and foster high levels of cooperation. Cooper was a highly cooperative SEAL who was trusted implicitly by those around him.

Cooper was deployed to Iraq and Afghanistan multiple times during his career and participated in many high-profile missions. He was involved in the rescue of Captain Richard Phillips from Somali pirates and a member of the team that killed Osama bin Laden. Cooper, or 'Coop', was known for his dedication to his team. He was an exemplary mentor to younger SEALs, and he always put the needs of his team before his own. He was respected and admired by his colleagues. Today, Coop is remembered as a true hero.

Coop freely admitted that the term *Military Intelligence* was an oxymoron[179] - especially where orders were formulated using hierarchy and chains of command rather than with the eyes and ears of those on the ground. Coop's approach to leadership transcended the conventional military framework, fostering an environment where mentorship was predicated on three things:

1. Vulnerability
2. Critical Thinking
3. Continuous Improvement

Coop's methods have left a permanent mark on the SEALs and leadership thinking in high-stakes environments.

Coop stayed in the trenches for a long time early in his career and was not one of those guys who climbed the leadership chain to move up. He always understood the bigger picture, and his men could talk to him. As we read at the start of this chapter, Coop's life as a SEAL changed when he could not "convince" his superior officer to delay the next mission. He followed orders and placed precious lives on the line.

Eventually, Coop decided to find other ways to implement orders coming down from the hierarchy and chains of command. He learnt to rely on the eyes and ears of those on the ground and less on those stateside. After all, the ones from afar often have little or no skin in the game.

Coop learnt that humans in organisations often have a trap or bug of *authority bias*. When our superior orders us to do something, we find it very hard not to do it, even if we see problems for us down the line. Coop wanted to ensure his team were not automatic 'yes men'. They needed to be reprogrammed.

He mentored them to all contribute to the learning process. Coop wanted his team to have the ability to ask the right questions, challenge erroneous assumptions and learn how to deal with poorly thought-out orders coming from above.

LEAD WITH VULNERABILITY

Coop started small. He stopped letting people address him by his rank. If a new team member called him by his title, they were quickly corrected: *"You can call me Coop, Dave or Fuckface; it is your choice."* Coop steered away from giving orders and instead asked team members lots of questions. A common question Coop asked of his team was, *"Does anybody have any ideas?"*[180]

Coop sought opportunities to spotlight the need for recruits to learn to speak up. He was not subtle. If a SEAL stands in front of a window in an urban environment, they are an easy target. Coop would ask new team members, *"If you see me standing in front of a window in Fallujah, what will you say?"* When a recruit answered, *"I'll tell you to move."* Coop said, *"Damm, right. That's exactly how you should always conduct yourself around here, with every single decision."*[181]

Coop championed the 'vulnerability loop' - a powerful conduit for building trust and fostering genuine team connections. Admitting mistakes was not a display of weakness but a rallying cry for collective strength and growth. By owning up to his errors with a simple "I screwed that up," Coop was not just taking responsibility. Coop inspired a culture of humility and learning with his direct reports.

Coop's direct reports could freely admit mistakes without fearing retribution or loss of face. This loop initiated a domino effect of vulnerability and trust, where every admission of a misstep by the leader was silent permission for others to own their errors and, most importantly, learn from them.

ENCOURAGE CRITICAL THINKING

If vulnerability and humility are the bedrock of Coop's leadership philosophy, then critical thinking is its superstructure. As his time in the field increased, Coop began to develop tools to mentor and teach his men.

If Coop gave an opinion, he attached phrases that encouraged others to ask questions. When Coop presented his ideas, he would accompany them with phrases like, *"Tell me what's wrong with this idea."*

Coop's knack for questioning rather than ordering nurtured a problem-solving ethos within his team. He created a safe space for intellectual sparring, where the best ideas were honed through collective interrogation and the veracity of a strategy was tested through the crucible of group scrutiny.

Coop fostered a culture where questioning and critical analysis were valued. There was the "no rank in the room" concept to encourage open dialogue. Coop often prefaced his briefings with phrases to stimulate discussion and critique, such as, "*Now let's see if someone can poke holes in this.*"[182]

This habit of critical thinking in SEAL operations is transferable to leadership in business settings.

Renowned author on business and organisational leadership Pat Lencioni has identified five temptations leaders must overcome:

- Prioritising status over results.
- Seeking harmony over productive conflict.
- Desiring certainty over clarity.
- Avoiding accountability to preserve popularity.
- Being invulnerable instead of trusting their team.

OVERCOMING THE FIVE TEMPTATIONS

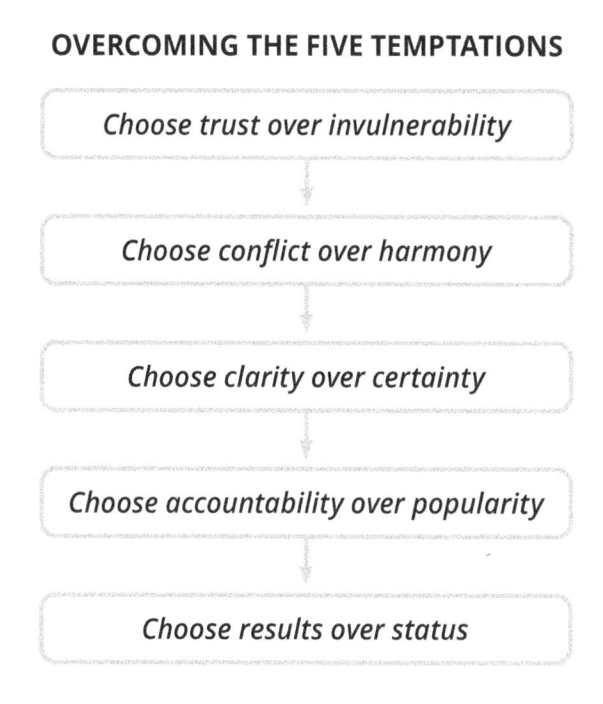

> Choose trust over invulnerability
>
> Choose conflict over harmony
>
> Choose clarity over certainty
>
> Choose accountability over popularity
>
> Choose results over status

Figure 11.2 The Five Temptations

Coop avoided the five temptations by prioritising results over rank, seeking productive conflict with open communication, and encouraging his team to challenge ideas and admit mistakes. He also embraced the notion that every mission can become a circus.

Towards the end of his military career, in early 2011, Coop and his team disagreed with the ill-informed orders from above regarding a daring circus-infested plan to kill Osama bin Laden. Coop was ordered to fly next generation helicopters at dangerously low altitudes towards bin Laden's compound in Pakistan and land men in tight spaces.

In preparing for the covert 'Capture and Kill bin Laden' mission, Coop spent months with SEAL Team Six developing dozens of 'off the books' mid-mission disaster and circus scenarios. The SEALs repeatedly practised recovering and advancing until all pivots became part of their DNA.

On the night of the raid, a worst-case scenario occurred. A Blackhawk helicopter clipped the top of fence wires and plummeted to the ground. Back in DC, President Obama and the Executive Military Command watched on in horror. Surprised at the turn of events but not alarmed, Coop's men kept their heads and changed tack in a heartbeat because of all the unofficial scenarios they had rehearsed repeatedly, just in case. Coop's team stormed the compound's main building, killing bin Laden and his security detail.

Coop dismantled traditional hierarchical barriers that stifled free thought and encouraged a culture where challenging the status quo was accepted and expected. He understood that in the volatile world of military operations, adaptability and ingenuity are paramount and critical thinking is the catalyst for such traits.

REVIEW AFTER ACTION

To ensure clarity always trumped certainty, Coop committed to after-action reviews (AARs) after each operation.

AARs were one of Coop's most enduring legacies for mentoring direct reports. He developed an unwavering commitment to reviewing after action in the field and assessing the outcomes. For SEALs, the AAR was not merely a debrief; it became a sacred rite that encapsulated the essence of learning and growth. Coop championed AARs to dissect every facet of a mission, celebrating successes and, more crucially, understanding failures without assigning blame.[183]

AARs were candid forums where vulnerability was not a weakness but a cornerstone of collective wisdom. AARs became the backbone of humility. Every team member, from the greenest recruit to the most seasoned operator, was expected to contribute their perspective on the six 'what' questions from Figure 11.3.

Figure 11.3 After Action Review

These reviews were never about individual performance but the team's journey towards operational excellence.

Coop's approach to AARs was methodical. He emphasised the need for honesty and clarity, ensuring every voice was heard and every lesson was assimilated. This meant that even in the aftermath of the most harrowing missions, Coop's team emerged stronger and more prepared for the challenges ahead.

HABIT ELEVEN: MENTOR DIRECT REPORTS

To drive innovation and strengthen resilience in today's rapidly changing business environment, CEOs can take a great deal from Dave Cooper. CEOs can foster a culture where vulnerability is valued as a strength, not a weakness. By openly admitting and sharing mistakes, CEOs set a precedent of trust and transparency, encouraging team members to do the same.

CEOs should prioritise mentoring direct reports to critically assess situations and contribute ideas. CEOs can implement AARs to cultivate a cooperative and learning culture where every investment and project is dissected to understand successes and failures without blame. By emulating the SEALs' balance between performance and trust and avoiding authority bias, leaders can ensure they promote the right individuals and prioritise team success over individual glory.

Dave Cooper demonstrates transformative leadership born from high-pressure SEAL experiences, emphasising vulnerability and critical thinking over hierarchical command. CEOs should foster workplaces of mutual accountability where owning mistakes is paramount. This will foster a culture of trust, self-leadership and adaptability in the face of adversity.

Post-military, Dave Cooper's pursuit of advanced education and the establishment of Verge, his consulting company, reflect his commitment to applying his team performance expertise and complex systems science knowledge to organisational health and leadership assignments.[184] Through Verge, Cooper blends military precision with scientific inquiry to enhance organisational resilience and sustainability, demonstrating a unique approach to leadership and change.

In our last habit, we will meet an institutional champion who, as a teenager, played cricket and was a guitarist in an all-girl rock band.

Make notes about Coop and mentoring direct reports on the following blank pages.

Then, complete Activity Eleven.

ACTIVITY ELEVEN

Reflect on the leadership lessons of Dave Cooper to address the following:

11.1 Did you make your bed this morning? If not, why not?

11.2 Describe a 'circus' your company faced. How did you lead your team through it, and what was the outcome?

11.3 Recall the 'darkest moment' your company has faced. How did you find the strength to be your best in that moment?

11.4 How do you demonstrate vulnerability to your team and improve trust and communication?

11.5 What practices can you implement to ensure team members are judged by their trustworthiness and team contributions rather than their titles or individual achievements?

11.6 How can you use the 'no rank in the room' concept to encourage open dialogue and collaboration in your firm?

11.7 Select one of the following three activities to enhance trust, creativity and cooperation.

- (i) Leadership Swap Days: Temporarily swap roles within the company to understand different perspectives, foster empathy, and improve problem-solving.
- (ii) Heart Over Flippers: Host a 'reverse job fair' where employees present their passion projects that contribute to the company's mission, regardless of their usual roles.
- (iii) The SEAL Escape Challenge: Simulate a crisis scenario in total darkness that requires perseverance, teamwork, determination and calmness under pressure, with no option to quit the exercise until the entire team is out.

My best successes came on the heels of failures.

Barbara Corcoran

HABIT TWELVE
MAXIMISE BOARD COMMITMENT

INDRA NOOYI
PEPSICO INC.

Build Outstanding Boards
Know Your Stakeholders
Tackle Difficult Assignments

As guests took their place in the White House, the air carried the soft murmur of conversation, a blend of languages and accents.

Light slipped in through the tall windows. The fog outside added mystique to the occasion.

Gracefully, Indra Nooyi travelled the intricately patterned carpet. Above, portraits of past presidents watched on, witnessing a woman with sparkling brown eyes, olive skin and long black hair.

Nooyi, a consummate stakeholder champion, appeared confident, professional and wise.

Like Ken Frazier before, Nooyi was about to meet President Obama.

Also present was Manmohan Singh, Prime Minister of India, the supreme leader of the country where Nooyi had grown up.

Her excitement was palpable.

As formal introductions were being made, Singh remarked with pride,

"She's one of us!"[185]

Not to be outdone, a swift and embracing response from Obama asserted,

"Ah, but she is one of us, too!"[186]

HABIT TWELVE: MAXIMISE BOARD COMMITMENT

This exchange showcased the mutual respect between the two leaders. It also underscored Nooyi's diplomacy skills and her dual identity, which is deeply rooted in her Indian heritage and her success as a global CEO in corporate America.

Born in Chennai, India, Nooyi's upbringing in a Brahmin family respected and supported diversity, education and scholarly rigour. This heritage set the stage for her future achievements. She honed her leadership skills early, influenced by her mother's unique dialectical methods and her grandfather's insistence on accountability.

Nooyi is a Hindu by faith and abstains from alcohol, which bodes well for maintaining control and remaining accountable.[187]

As a teenager in India, she played cricket and was also in an all-girl rock band, where she played guitar.[188] Nooyi's educational journey took her from Madras Christian College to the Indian Institute of Management Calcutta for her MBA and finally to Yale University, where she completed her master's degree in public and private management.[189]

Nooyi's career began in India but quickly moved to international arenas. She held positions at Johnson & Johnson and textile firm Mettur Beardsell.[190] Her move to the United States and subsequent roles at the Boston Consulting Group, Motorola and Asea Brown Boveri provided her with a comprehensive view of corporate strategy and operations.[191]

Joining PepsiCo in 1994, Nooyi rapidly climbed the corporate ladder, taking on roles that showcased her institution-building acumen and stakeholder management abilities, culminating in her appointment as

CEO in 2006. Under her guidance and with full Board support, PepsiCo underwent a stepwise growth transformation.

Nooyi oversaw a significant restructuring of the company's portfolio.[192] She galvanised Board commitment for the divestiture of Tricon (now Yum! Brands) and the acquisition of Tropicana and the Quaker Oats Company.[193] Nooyi then integrated both brands into PepsiCo's operations with meticulous attention to Board consultation.

Nooyi won ongoing respect and support by prioritising Board composition and fostering strong relationships with Board members. She also earned respect by having an intimate knowledge of her industry and fearlessly tackling the 'elephants in the room.'

BUILD OUTSTANDING BOARDS

Recognising that an outstanding Board was a catalyst for corporate success, Nooyi took deliberate steps to ensure each Board member was not just informed but invested in PepsiCo's mission of Performance with Purpose (PwP).[194]

Here are eight ways to maximise your Board's impact.

HABIT TWELVE: MAXIMISE BOARD COMMITMENT

1. Engage with the Board of Directors

As a board-appointed CEO, Nooyi knew her ultimate stakeholder was her Board.

She met individually with Board members to ensure they were fully committed to the PwP mission. This personal touch was essential in fostering a Board culture that understood PepsiCo's long-term strategic initiatives.[195]

2. Set Up Advisory Boards for Strategic Diversity

Creating specialised advisory boards, like the African American Advisory Board and the Latino/Hispanic Advisory Board, was a forward-thinking move by Nooyi. These Boards were integral to PepsiCo's growth and helped build a diverse talent pipeline at the leadership level.[196]

Despite their obvious value, shadow and advisory boards are less common in Australian publicly listed companies.

3. Engage Stakeholders

Nooyi navigated the complex range of stakeholder interests, balancing them with the Board's vision and external investors' expectations. Her approach involved consistent communication and alignment of the company's strategic conversations with various stakeholder interests.

4. Commit to a Sustainability Focus

Nooyi steered the Board to prioritise environmental sustainability and corporate social responsibility. During her tenure, strategic decisions were aimed at profits and at ensuring that long-term sustainable growth aligned with societal goals.

One way to champion a sustainability focus is to include women on boards. Research suggests that women on boards are less concerned with conforming to board norms and more focused on ensuring their Boards make the best possible decisions for the environment.

Each additional female director correlates with a 17.5% increase in a firm's environmental rating. The EU, with a strong sustainability track record, has mandated that by 2026, women should hold 40% of non-executive director roles in listed companies.[197]

It is also worth noting that each additional director of colour raises a firm's environmental score by 18.4%.[198]

5. Embrace Board Education

Recognising the dynamic nature of the consumer goods industry, Nooyi promoted a culture of continuous learning within the Board. This approach increased Board agility and creativity, allowing PepsiCo to adapt rapidly to market changes and maintain its competitive edge.

Board education must include cyber resilience training and scorecards, alongside broader business risks and strategies to ensure effective Board oversight.[199]

For more, please read Appendix Six - Cyber Resilience.

6. Align Board Incentives with Results

Nooyi aligned executive compensation with PwP-related metrics. She ensured that her Board was not just overseeing but was actively incentivised to drive PepsiCo towards its purpose-driven goals.

7. Build a Values-Based Institution

As an institution-builder, Nooyi infused the Board and PepsiCo's culture with enduring values. This approach helped navigate volatility and maintain coherence, ensuring that Board decisions and company actions were consistently aligned with agreed-upon values.

8. Influence Board Personalities

Ultimately, CEOs like Nooyi can influence their Board's composition. Understanding some of the typical personalities attracted to boards can help. Below are six types of common personalities.[200] Understanding each board member's personality can help a CEO influence them.

The Narcissist: Characterised by a high opinion of themselves and a need for praise, they are sensitive to any criticism that may suggest a lack of competence. Influence is achieved by highlighting how decisions impact their reputation, albeit with caution to avoid direct challenges to their competence.

The Data Chaser: Prefers decisions based on hard data and is sceptical of conclusions drawn from anecdotal evidence. They can be reminded that not all decisions require exhaustive data analysis and that timely action is sometimes more critical.

The Deferential: Often influenced by senior executives like the CEO, they typically avoid taking a stand that contradicts the CEO's position. Building a coalition of less deferential board members can provide them with the confidence to express their views.

The Status Hound: Overly concerned with their status, they may have a close relationship with influential shareholders. Persuasion requires respecting their status and framing discussions as a presentation of new ideas rather than changing positions.

The Unprepared: They may not prepare adequately for meetings, relying instead on improvisation. Engaging them in side-conversations prior to meetings can help influence their stance by ensuring they are informed about key issues.

The Stakeholder Champion: Focused on the interests of a specific stakeholder group, they may view board decisions through the lens of that group's interests. Persuasion involves demonstrating how the company's success benefits their stakeholder group while seeking win-win outcomes.

KNOW YOUR STAKEHOLDERS

Much of a modern CEO's time involves broader social responsibilities and public relations (PR). Aside from Board members and direct reports, CEOs must maintain regular communication with diverse stakeholders, each with their expectations and interests.

Success in the relationship-building space often comes down to authenticity and industry knowledge.

HABIT TWELVE: MAXIMISE BOARD COMMITMENT

1. **Authenticity** - When a leader is authentic, the moment-to-moment traits and success habits they need tend to shine through.

2. **Industry Knowledge** - If authenticity is the heartbeat of relationships, then industry knowledge is the blood that gives life to a CEO when communicating with stakeholders.

CEOs must carefully balance the often-competing interests of stakeholders, aligning them with the firm's strategic goals.

Listening to stakeholders and obtaining industry knowledge operate in a paradoxical yet virtuous cycle. The more time a CEO spends listening to stakeholders, the greater their industry knowledge can become, and the less time they will need to listen to stakeholders.

By engaging with the following stakeholders, CEOs can demonstrate authenticity and increase their industry knowledge.

Board of Directors

Nooyi's goal was to maximise her Board's commitment and performance.

CEOs report to their Boards on many things, including company performance, strategic directions and challenges. Boards assist CEOs with corporate governance and provide oversight.

CEO authenticity must be extremely high to build trust with their Boards, thus raising Board commitment and performance.

Investors and Shareholders

CEOs must update shareholders on financial performance and strategic initiatives while garnering support for critical decisions and directions.

A CEO's industry knowledge must be moderate to high with investors, as CEOs may need to reveal company specifics within the context of current market conditions.

Authenticity is crucial, as transparency is required for fiduciary reasons and genuine communication is crucial for maintaining shareholder confidence.

Nooyi routinely communicated financial results and strategic initiatives to shareholders. She addressed concerns and justified strategic decisions. For example, she resisted the splitting up of PepsiCo's business units as she diversified the product range.

Direct Reports and Employees

With employees, CEO authenticity needs to be very high. CEOs must convey the company's vision, values and overall health to all employees.

Also, CEOs must communicate changes and business achievements to engage and motivate their employees. For this, moderate levels of industry knowledge are needed.

For Nooyi's work with direct reports, more in-depth industry knowledge was needed to ensure strategic alignment and allocation of resources.

Customers

Nooyi allowed consumer trends to guide PepsiCo towards low-sugar beverages and align it with societal health reforms.

In general, moderate industry knowledge is required with customers, yet detailed industry knowledge is beneficial if understanding customer needs becomes mission-critical.

With all customer groups, authenticity must be high, as customers value trustworthy communication.

Suppliers and Partners

Nooyi negotiated contracts to ensure stable supply chains, support strategic shifts and acquire healthier product lines.

With suppliers and industry partners, moderate industry knowledge is needed; however, detailed knowledge of supply chains can be crucial.

With supplier groups, authenticity must range from moderate to high, as reliable and honest communication is the cornerstone of solid supply chains.

Regulators

CEOs must understand their regulators' needs to ensure compliance with laws, ascertain when reporting is obligatory and respond to any legal issues that may arise.

Nooyi navigated challenges such as sugar taxes and increasing regulatory compliance.

With regulators, high levels of industry knowledge are imperative to understand and comply with regulations. Authenticity must be high, as integrity is indispensable in compliance matters.

Industry Analysts and Advisors
Nooyi valued insights from analysts and advisors to inform her and her Board's strategic decisions.

With analysts and advisors, industry knowledge should be moderate to high, as familiarity with industry trends is essential to engage effectively.

Authenticity needs only be moderate, as analytical exchanges often necessitate less emphasis on authenticity.

Media
The media is a pivotal stakeholder.

Nooyi excelled at public relations, communicated company news and valiantly defended strategic choices, such as integrating the snack and beverage divisions.

Industry knowledge must be moderate with the media, as media communication typically involves more general messages.

Nevertheless, authenticity must be high, as media narratives significantly influence the brand image.

Community Leaders and Local Communities

Feedback from community members aids CEOs in formulating corporate social responsibility (CSR) goals for local operations, including environmental impacts and social contributions.

With community representatives, industry knowledge and authenticity need to be high.

High-context cultures, like ethnically diverse communities, demand dialogue and complex arrangements, with many things unspoken due to big-picture understandings and verbal agreements.

In low context or print-based cultures, such as corporations, people are obedient and focus on the task at hand without much thought of the bigger picture.[201]

Trade Associations and Industry Groups

CEOs must engage with industry-specific issues, standards and practices.

Industry knowledge must be high here, as specific industry issues are central to these dialogues.

Where collaboration is mission-critical, authenticity needs to progress from moderate to high.

Custodians of Country

In genuine democracies, which are uncommon, there is a tendency to uphold the UN Declaration on the Rights of Indigenous Peoples. Such democracies will implement inclusive policies and legal measures to redress historical wrongs. For instance, in Australia, the Native Title Act of 1993 acknowledges the unique cultural heritage and land rights of Aboriginal and Torres Strait Islanders.

The Treaty of Waitangi, ratified by New Zealand in 1840, is a foundational document that recognises Māori rights and its principles are vital to governance. In Canada, the rights of First Nations, Inuit and Métis peoples are recognised through the Constitution Act of 1982.

CEOs operating in democratic nations may need to engage in treaty negotiations and truth and reconciliation processes. At their worst, such processes can become an ordeal of profound and broad complexity, characterised by condescending attitudes, deep-rooted resentments, and intergenerational attitudes of 'payback' and 'rent-seeking' behaviour.

In these contexts, the concept of the land or 'Country', illustrated in Figure 12.1, as the supreme stakeholder may become paramount. Mutual respect, re-established trust and reciprocity are requisite to reconciling and collaborating with indigenous peoples. Only then can the enlightened process of co-designing the future of forests, farms, facilities, factories and freeways commence.

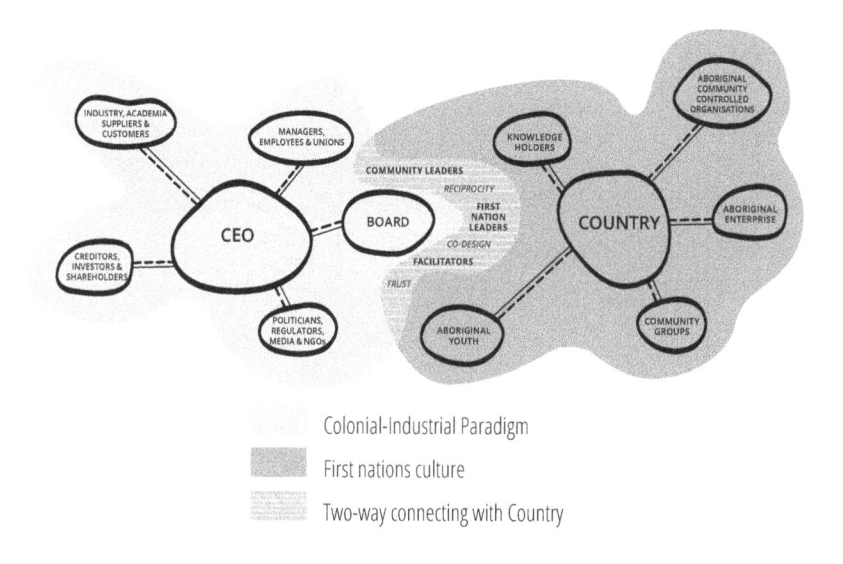

Figure 12.1 Co-Designing with Country

In compromised democracies, such as the United States, CEOs may opt to exceed the usual free market standards of practice. With the assistance of adept facilitators, CEOs can engage in the commendable practice of collaboratively shaping our world alongside Indigenous peoples. In the United States, these groups include the Sioux, Diné, Anishinaabe, Hopi, Ho-Chunk, Haudenosaunee, Tsalagi, Estelusti, Tsitsistas and Kanien'kehá:ka.[202]

Government Officials and Political Leaders

CEOs lobby for legislation and regulations that positively impact their businesses and on occasion cultivate public-private partnerships.

In these contexts, a profound understanding of the industry and the law is imperative, as is grasping the political landscape for effective advocacy.

A high level of authenticity is also essential, since sincere involvement can sway policy and legislation.

Competitors

On certain occasions, CEOs convene with their competitive counterparts at industry gatherings, as part of collaborative ventures or while deliberating on industry norms. Here, comprehensive industry knowledge can be critical.

Authenticity may only need to be moderate, as it may be all that is required to maintain professional candour. Nooyi adopted a defensive competitive posture when competitors were present during extensive industry deliberations.

Unions and Employee Representatives

CEOs engage with trade unions to deliberate on labour relations, hammer out collective bargaining agreements and address employee issues.

In negotiations with unions and when addressing employee matters, the importance of industry-specific knowledge diminishes. However, a high degree of authenticity is indispensable as trust is the cornerstone of labour relationships.

HABIT TWELVE: MAXIMISE BOARD COMMITMENT

Creditors and Financial Institutions
CEOs liaise with financial entities concerning corporate finance, borrowing and credit lines. Here, a moderate grasp of the industry is required; nonetheless, a thorough comprehension of the various financial instruments is essential.

Authenticity is crucial, as it underpins the foundation of financial rapport.

Academia and Research Institutions
CEOs nurture relationships with academic bodies to collaborate on research and development projects and to recruit emerging talent.

Engaging with academic circles requires moderate levels of industry acumen and authenticity.

In her interactions with academic institutions, Nooyi frequently concentrated on design thinking, innovation ideas and talent acquisition.

Consultants and External Experts
A moderate level of industry awareness is sufficient in dealings with consultants, as consultants are expected to contribute the necessary expertise and provide fresh perspectives.

CEOs need only exhibit moderate authenticity with consultants, provided there are clear expectations from the outset.

Nooyi regularly collaborated with consultancies such as BCG to gain specialised knowledge and tackle difficult assignments.

TACKLE DIFFICULT ASSIGNMENTS

In Indian folklore, there is a tale called 'The Brahmin and the Mongoose', which cautions against making hasty consequential decisions.[203] This story involves a Brahmin man who leaves his child at home with a loyal mongoose. Upon returning, he finds his child safe but upset and the mongoose with a bloody mouth. Assuming the worst, the Brahmin decides to kill the mongoose. Only later does the Brahmin discover it had saved his child from a snake.

	CONSEQUENTIAL	
REVERSIBLE	GATHER EVIDENCE	SPEND TIME DECIDING
	DELEGATE	DELEGATE
	INCONSEQUENTIAL	IRREVERSIBLE

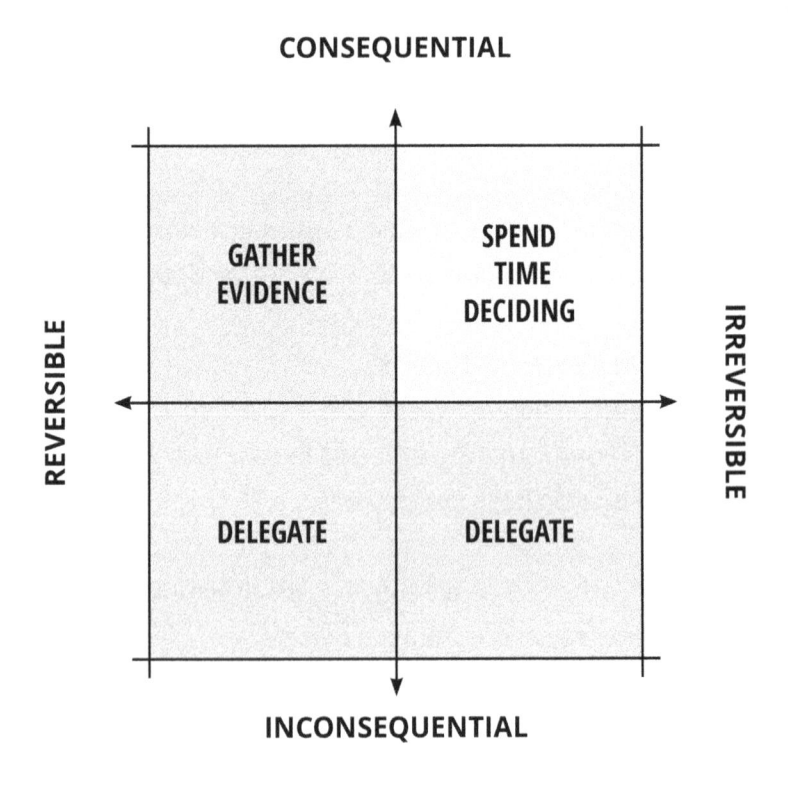

Figure 12.2 Consequential Decision Matrix

Irreversible and Consequential Decisions

As depicted in Figure 12.2, irreversible and consequential decisions cannot be undone and have significant impacts. The Brahmin's act of killing the mongoose was irreversible and consequential. CEOs and boards often face decisions that can define or significantly alter the course of their companies. The use of probability trees and the calculation of expected monetary values (EMVs) can reduce the risks of suboptimal decisions.

Reversible and Consequential Decisions

Reversible and consequential decisions can be changed but still have significant implications. Had the Brahmin potentially restrained the mongoose to investigate further, this would represent a reversible yet consequential decision.

CEOs and boards may find value in reversible decisions as they allow flexibility and adaptability. CEOs can backtrack or change course as new information emerges or situations evolve. For example, Elon Musk is famous for his about-face decision-making style.

Inconsequential (Irreversible or Reversible) Decisions

For CEOs and their Boards, inconsequential decisions should not occupy their time. Inconsequential decisions are either routine or have a negligible impact on the company's mission and should be delegated. Boards and CEOs should ensure they invest their time and resources in areas with the most significant impact.

Like most long-standing corporate CEOs, Nooyi's public record does not reveal all the difficult moral decision-making victories and defeats experienced in office. However, Nooyi did not shy away from difficult decisions that enabled ongoing growth at PepsiCo.

She tackled challenging assignments that tested the limits of her capabilities and pushed the boundaries of her company's traditional practices. Change at PepsiCo was often met with fierce resistance, commonly a harsh reality in any large, established corporation. Nooyi frequently stepped out of her comfort zone and challenged the status quo.

In reviewing Nooyi's 25-year tenure at PepsiCo, it may be informative to use Figure 12.3, the Seven S Model, developed by McKinsey & Company.[204]

HABIT TWELVE: MAXIMISE BOARD COMMITMENT

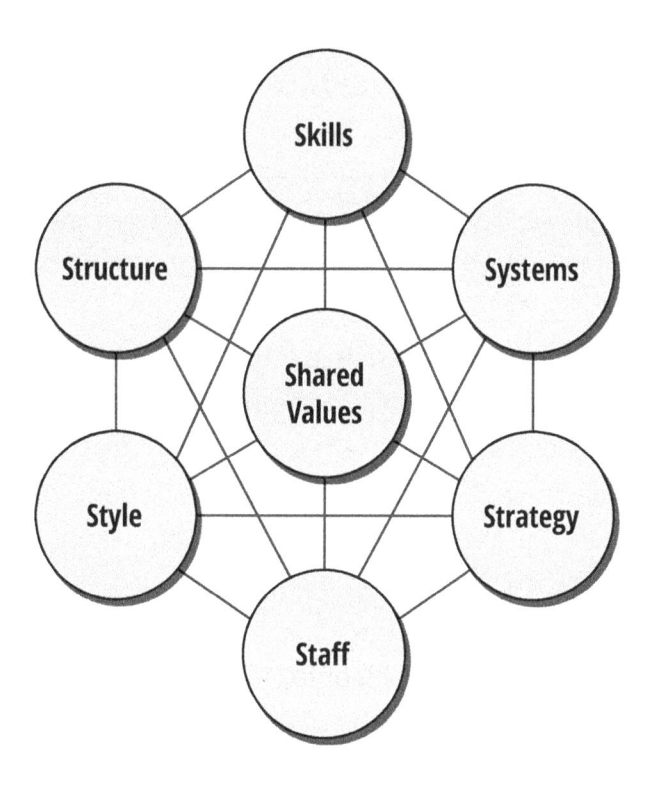

Figure 12.3 McKinsey 7S Model

Corporate transformation using the Seven Ss usually requires board commitment and a patient and persistent CEO. In these settings, conventional wisdom suggests that CEOs and boards tackle no more than two Ss over any eighteen-month timeframe to ensure effective transformation.

Nooyi's impact on PepsiCo can be linked to her early years. Nooyi began to influence the company's culture as soon as she started working for them. Here are some examples of Nooyi's most challenging assignments during her 25-year tenure, along with their Seven S theme and approximate time frame.

Cultural Shift for Innovation and Accountability [STAFF] Circa 2000.
Nooyi fostered a corporate culture that balanced innovation with accountability. Through employee development programs and performance incentives, she cultivated a workforce willing to take risks and focus on achieving strategic goals that supported PepsiCo's growth.

Optimising Internal Processes [SYSTEMS] Circa 2001.
As CFO in 2000 and 2001, Nooyi spearheaded the optimisation of supply chain operations, improved marketing strategies, and invested in technology to enhance data analytics. Growing these digital wings was essential for aligning PepsiCo's operations with the evolving industry space.

Future-Focused Strategic Planning [STRATEGY] Circa 2004.
Between 2002 and 2006, Nooyi served as President at PepsiCo. She was responsible for the company's global strategy, including its major restructuring and the divestiture of its restaurants into Yum! Brands. Nooyi played a pivotal role in various portfolio changes, including the acquisitions of Tropicana, Quaker Oats and Gatorade.

Stakeholder Engagement [SHARED VALUES] Circa 2006.
Beginning in 2006, PepsiCo pledged to engage stakeholders through its Performance with Purpose (PwP) initiative. Nooyi navigated the challenge of adapting PepsiCo to a growing consumer preference for healthier food choices. This initiative represented a significant shift in shared values around consumer health, future relevance and social responsibility.

HABIT TWELVE: MAXIMISE BOARD COMMITMENT

Redefining Product Portfolio [STRATEGY] Circa 2007.
Nooyi transformed PepsiCo's portfolio by focusing on nutritious options and acquiring relevant brands. In her decision-making, Nooyi assessed the strategic value of maintaining integrated business units against the strategic disadvantages, carefully considering the impact on operations, future growth and market demands.[205]

Environmental Impact Initiatives [SKILLS] Circa 2008.
In addressing the environmental footprint of PepsiCo's operations, Nooyi allocated resources towards sustainability. She led efforts to enhance her firm's skills in water usage efficiency, reducing carbon emissions and transitioning to sustainable packaging.

This improved operational efficiency and positioned PepsiCo as a leader in corporate environmental responsibility.

Diversity and Inclusion Initiatives [STAFF] Circa 2010.
By recognising the value of employee diversity, Nooyi implemented inclusive hiring and leadership selection processes. She advocated for a global expansion of inclusion strategies. She understood the importance of a multi-talented, multicultural and multigenerational workforce.

Strategic Integration of Business Units [STRUCTURE] Circa 2011.
Nooyi led the 'Power of One - Americas Council'. This council was formed to synergise the company's snack and beverage businesses across North, South and Central America.

She engaged in careful analysis to determine the optimal configuration of products, channels and distributors. To maximise synergies, Nooyi evaluated various organisational structures, including matrix structures and self-managed teams.

Performance Accountability [SYSTEMS] Circa 2012.
In focusing on measurable outcomes, Nooyi accelerated the practice of tracking diversity metrics and tying executive bonuses to these objectives. This approach held executives accountable for meeting PepsiCo's diversity goals.

Global Expansion Strategies [STRUCTURE] Circa 2013.
As PepsiCo expanded into new global markets, Nooyi developed a nuanced understanding of various cultural and regulatory environments. She directed resources to adapt products to local tastes and managed complex international operations effectively.

Willingness to Tackle Resistance [STYLE] Circa 1994 - 2018.
Nooyi's leadership style, particularly her willingness to confront resistance, was evident throughout her time at PepsiCo, especially when she shifted the company's focus toward healthier products.

She faced resistance and criticism. Despite scepticism from employees, investors and stakeholders, Nooyi persevered, demonstrating her willingness to undertake difficult assignments that grew the company sustainably.

HABIT TWELVE: MAXIMISE BOARD COMMITMENT

Board Chair [STYLE] Circa 2019.

Appointed as Board Chair in 2019, Nooyi became the penultimate stakeholder[206] and continued her authentic and knowledge-driven conversations with Board Members. She worked with incoming CEO Ramon Laguarta to foster a shared commitment to the company's future growth and to impart her success habits to her successor.

When Nooyi joined PepsiCo, the slogan was 'Change the Script.' During her CEO years, the slogan evolved to 'Change the Game', which is precisely what she did.

Her tenure saw the US stock market grow fivefold.

With the backing of her Boards, she achieved a twentyfold increase in PepsiCo's market value, from ten billion dollars to two hundred billion dollars, while raising productivity and reducing her global workforce by two-fifths, from five hundred thousand to three hundred thousand employees.

Nooyi ran a great race and passed the baton successfully.

ACTIVITY TWELVE

On the blank pages that follow, write down your answers to these questions:

12.1 How can you maximise Board engagement and commitment?

12.2 How can you develop a more profound, intimate knowledge of your industry and leverage this to tackle challenging assignments more successfully?

12.3 What steps can you take to build a corporate approach to strategy that aligns growth and profitability with a deeper purpose?

12.4 Select two of the five activities below and implement them.

- (i) Conduct a thorough review of your Board's composition, ensuring diversity and expertise are balanced and initiating a strategic plan that aligns with the company's mission and vision.
- (ii) Create a 'Board Engagement Scorecard' that measures the level of each Board member's active participation and commitment to strategic initiatives.
- (iii) Organise a challenging 'Cybersecurity and AI Bootcamp' for your Board and senior management team to deepen their understanding of the current digital and security landscape and enhance governance in these critical areas.

HABIT TWELVE: MAXIMISE BOARD COMMITMENT

(iv) Design and participate in a 'Capital Allocation Simulation' that forces your senior team to make tough decisions regarding investment in innovation versus immediate financial returns, while reflecting on the sustainability and long-term growth of the company.

(v) Establish a 'Stakeholder Engagement Initiative' where you must engage with various stakeholders, from employees to investors, to discuss and align on the ethical use of AI, capital and intellectual property in your firm.

If you want something said, ask a man. If you want something done, ask a woman.

Margaret Thatcher

CONCLUSION

ROWAN   DOLORES   GRAHAM   NICOLE   ROBERT

Dancing with Wolves
Twelve Consequential Habits
Wisdom from Friends

There is no finish line in this baton-passing game.

CEOs run their leg of the race. Their habits and those of their people rippling across the world stage.

As captains of industry, CEOs must navigate the future and be caring leaders of their tribes.

DANCING WITH WOLVES

Sometimes, I imagine CEOs sitting at the centre of a vast circle, surrounded by wolves. Some wolves are hunting wolves, representing astute competitors, demanding customers and powerful suppliers. They stalk the edges of the circle, ready to pounce on any opportunity or weakness. Others are beta wolves, ambitious leadership contenders, union bosses and unproductive workers who make ambitious claims.

COVID-19 and generative AI have been rogue alphas visiting from distant territories and alternate universes, here to test a CEO's wit. There is an omega wolf called time - a silent thief that steals moments, days and years. They are a constant reminder of fleeting success and the urgency of action. The delta wolf represents the unending 'devil in the details', with audit-like eyes and the teeth of compliance.

CONCLUSION

Beyond the vast circle sit the sentinel wolves, a cue to the ever-present dangers and threats facing an organisation in the form of volatility, uncertainty, complexity and ambiguity. The noisy pup wolves represent a CEO's family, whining for safety and attention. For now, they are being looked after by senior wolves to ensure their proper care and development.

Dancing with wolves can also be an internal struggle.

Our inner critic acts as a helpful and, at times, not-so-helpful internal compass. When negative self-judgments growl like wolves, a CEO who has mastered dancing with their inner wolves will tune out the noise.

If we fall prey to a barrage of shame or guilt, we feed the dark wolf within.

This tumultuous inner struggle can require help from a coach like Dolores[207] or a therapist like Dr Chris.[208]

CEOs will do well to nurture the empathic wolf, which thrives on emotional intelligence and compassionate action.

The Native American parable of the two wolves within reveals that the victor of our inner struggles is the wolf we feed.

Finally, there are the elder wolves. These are board members and shareholder groups with experience.

They sit in judgment, ready to anoint a new alpha when the mood takes them. Some CEOs, especially transformational ones, miss the writing on the wall and do not initiate a graceful exit with their legacy intact.[209]

Instead, their life becomes a circus until they are unceremoniously replaced.

Dancing with wolves is hard.

Great habits are needed.

Amidst wolves and possible choices, CEOs make consequential decisions. Never quite ready for what awaits them, their plans must remain speculative.

If a CEO is in the habit of making inconsequential decisions and avoiding consequential ones, their authority will be quickly usurped.

TWELVE CONSEQUENTIAL HABITS

CEOs are made, not born. Repetition and practice give rise to habits, and habits have consequences.

Habits can be both positive and negative. Great habits deliver great success; like building genuine safety, establishing a shared purpose and maximising board commitment.

CONCLUSION

The role of a CEO is multifaceted, requiring the navigation of complex issues and the ability to adapt to the changing needs of an organisation. Thanks to the journeys of our twelve-chapter leaders, you now have the twelve habits of highly successful CEOs:

Build Genuine Safety: Like Coach Pop, CEOs must establish a foundation of trust and safety in the workplace. This enables employees to operate at their full potential and fosters a culture of respect for diversity and open communication.

Energise Middle Managers: Taking a leaf from Estée Lauder's book, it is crucial to empower middle managers. They link the company's vision, the operational workforce and the customer. By energising this cohort, CEOs will realise the potential that middle managers afford a company.

Foster Deep Empathy: CEOs should emulate Satya Nadella's approach and intertwine empathy with technology to create an adaptable and progressive work environment. Leaders must demonstrate empathy, understand their teams' needs and challenges, and act with compassion.

Eliminate Poor Performers: Reed Hastings' methodology underscores the importance of cultivating high-performance teams. CEOs must set recruitment standards, uphold rigorous accountability and encourage the relentless pursuit of excellence.

Anticipate Future Trends: Like MBS, CEOs must possess the foresight to anticipate and prepare for future trends. Proactively driving forward-looking initiatives allows their firm to capitalise on approaching societal and economic opportunities.

Establish Shared Purpose: Elon Musk's visionary leadership and alignment of people's collective efforts towards common goals demonstrate the power of a shared purpose. All CEOs can take inspiration from Musk.

Keep Competitors Close: Susan Wojcicki shows us the benefits of understanding and maintaining a degree of proximity with competitors. CEOs must stay abreast of their market and find the right mix of competition and cooperation.

Enhance Personal Effectiveness: Katrina Lake's integration of self-care into her professional life reminds us that personal well-being is essential for sustained performance. CEOs must prioritise their health and well-being to maintain their effectiveness.

Explain Strategy Clearly: CEOs should take a cue from Tim Cook and explain their strategies clearly and confidently. Clear communication ensures that the organisation's vision is understood and embraced internally and externally, reinforcing the company's direction.

Govern Resources Portfolio: Ken Frazier shows us how to govern with ethical considerations. CEOs must astutely manage their company's resources portfolio, balancing intellectual, human, physical, financial and digital assets, while optimising profits and societal benefits.

Mentor Direct Reports: Following Dave Cooper's example, CEOs should invest time mentoring their direct reports. By fostering a culture of continuous learning and robust analytical thinking, leaders can build resilient teams equipped to tackle complex missions.

CONCLUSION

Maximise Board Commitment: Indra Nooyi's tenure highlights the importance of active board engagement. CEOs must work closely with their Boards, ensuring diversity of thought and a shared commitment to their organisation's strategic goals.

Context and timing matter. Embrace the habits that work for your context and leave aside, for now, those that do not.

So, there you have them - twelve habits for you to navigate on your unique journey towards the twin goals of humility and greatness.

WISDOM FROM FRIENDS

Great firms, like great civilisations, eventually crumble from within.

Great CEOs are needed.

As this book neared completion, I met up again with my friends. I offered my idea of dancing with wolves, which resonated with them.

I asked for their ideas on how to lead a healthy, happy and purposeful life.

Rowan believes in regular exercise. He engages in high-intensity interval training (HIIT) three times a week and takes long walks on holidays.

Graham, the marathon-running CEO, exercises five days a week, often at an easy non-fatiguing (Zone 2 Heart Rate) pace.

The combination of regular hour-long endurance sessions complemented on other days with high-intensity interval training is something Peter Attia from Habit Eight advocates for health span and lifespan.

My friends did not mention therapy, sleep, diet or sex.

At times, everyone needs therapy.

Sleeping eight hours per night is desirable, as is eating a whole food plant-based diet with B12 supplementation where needed.

Finally, consensual, safe and mutually satisfying sex aids health span and lifespan. Although, due to deeply ingrained Puritan values in American society, Attia and other health commentators often do not mention it.

Opening yourself and your love in sensual and orgasmic ways is good for you!

What are your physical health habits?

For mental health, Rowan emphasises the value of shedding negative emotions, such as bitterness and envy and cultivating a life guided by strong values. Rowan feeds his empathic wolf by being simultaneously accountable for his actions and practising forgiveness.

CONCLUSION

To the same end, Graham advocates having friends both inside and outside of work with whom to socialise every fortnight or month, including long Friday afternoon lunches.

Dolores has the daily appreciation of beauty at the forefront of her mental health routine. She makes time to smell the flowers and emphasises the importance of allowing herself to relax and unwind.

How do you stay mentally well?

Happiness for Nicole is about living authentically and embracing a practice of unconditional love. For her, giving back by courageously expressing her truth gives her the greatest joy.

Robert finds happiness by treasuring the innate beauty of the world as an essential aspect of being.

Graham finds happiness in spending quality time with family, allocating one to three hours a week to doing something he loves, and regularly reading and listening to books - both business and fiction.

Dolores finds happiness in prioritising moments with family and loved ones and cherishes the exchange of laughter, joy and thought-provoking dialogue.

Rowan finds happiness in cultivating gratitude for life's blessings and focusing on meaningful relationships while showing love to all. He suggests that our societal principles are deeply rooted and recommends exploring their origins through books like 'Dominion' by Tom Holland or 'The Air We Breathe' by Glen Scrivener.

What stands between you and happiness?

Having a purpose that transcended his interests was vital for Rowan, as were his habits of self-improvement, spiritual faith and compassion. Rowan also embraces graciousness and generosity in his interactions with others.

For Graham and Dolores, engaging in meaningful work that contributes positively to the world was vital, as was their courage in embracing the mysteries of the future.

Nicole's purpose is to champion acts of love and make decisions that resonate deeply with her core values of authenticity, courage and unconditional love.

Robert's purpose comes from profoundly appreciating relationships as part of his journey toward contentment.

Are you on a purposeful journey of service that you love?

Our journey with this book has ended. Yet, re-reading it after some reflection may be worthwhile.

Tomorrow will be the first day of the rest of your life and your career.

CONCLUSION

Navigating with the twelve habits will help you succeed in your role as a CEO and in your life. Your CEO journey will be an inner and outer transformation, often amidst harsh realities. Indeed, direct personal experience and continuous learning remain the de facto finishing school for executives.[210]

May your journey and habits allow you to create a deeply purposeful legacy.

And, oh, I nearly forgot!

Like Rowan, along the way, cultivate a smile as warm as the sun's embrace.

Throw me to the wolves and I will return leading the pack.

Seneca

APPENDIX ONE
ZHĀGĒN DE XIÀ DĀNTIÁN

The lower dantian (下丹田, Xià Dāntián) is the body's centre of balance, gravity and primal intelligence.

It is approximately two inches below the navel and is the bodily intersection between space and time. This is the centre of one's actual intelligence. From here, one can sense an attack faster than the intellect. If you can learn to listen to your centre, you will be better protected than hiring a full-time bodyguard.

Place your hand on the point approximately two inches below your navel to find your centre. Relax and gradually allow your concentration to be on the spot where your hand rests. Imagine that your focus, life force and energy are coming down from your forehead (where most of us live), down from your chest (where we imprison most of our energy) and into your lower belly.[211]

Keep your breathing slow and relaxed.

Once you feel that your focus has arrived in your Dantien, keep your attention there. If it helps, visualise that point and imagine your eyes have been relocated there. You should feel all your muscles relax, especially your chest and shoulders.

Assuming you have not relaxed too far and dozed off, you will experience an expanded awareness of yourself in space and time. Essentially, you have returned to yourself and are one with each moment.

Practice locating your centre for ten to fifteen minutes each day. Eventually, you can connect with your centre without using your hand. Practice sitting in your centre at first. Later, stand with one foot slightly forward, your weight distributed evenly across both feet with slightly bent knees. Notice how centred, grounded and balanced you feel.

Gradually begin to move, walking while living from your centre. Repeated practice will teach you to become centred in your life and work. Regular meditation, yoga, or tai chi practice can help immensely.

APPENDIX TWO
THE ACE QUIZ

The ACE (Adverse Childhood Experiences) Quiz is a tool developed to measure the prevalence of various types of childhood trauma. The foundational ACE study involved over 17,000 participants. It examined the long-term effects of childhood abuse and neglect, along with other forms of household stress, on health and well-being later in life.

The quiz accounts for specific experiences such as emotional abuse, physical abuse, sexual abuse, substance abuse, mental illness, parental separation or divorce, and the incarceration of a household member. Early results from the US population indicated that emotional abuse was reported by 11%, physical abuse by 28%, and sexual abuse by 21%. Household challenges such as substance abuse were reported by 27%, mental illness by 20%, and an incarcerated household member by 5%. In the realm of neglect, emotional neglect was reported by 15%, and physical neglect by 10%.

The ACE score is calculated based on the cumulative number of these experiences a person has had. It's critical to understand that a higher ACE score suggests an increased risk for adverse health, mental health, and substance use outcomes in adulthood. However, the ACE score is not a definitive predictor of individual outcomes since factors like resilience and supportive relationships can mitigate the impacts of ACEs.

The quiz comprises ten questions that pertain to ACEs. Each "Yes" response increases the ACE score by one. While this quiz is a valuable tool for assessing potential risks linked to childhood trauma, it does not capture all potential traumatic experiences, nor does it consider protective factors and individual variations in responses to trauma.

TAKE THE ACE QUIZ

Please answer 'yes' or 'no' to the ten questions below.

Prior to your 18th birthday:

Q1. Did a parent or other adult in the household often or very often…
   Swear at you, insult you, put you down,
   or
   Humiliate you, or act in a way that made you afraid that you might be physically hurt?

Q2. Did a parent or other adult in the household often or very often…
   Push, punch, grab, slap, or throw something at you,
   or
   Ever hit you so hard that you had marks or were injured?

APPENDIX TWO: THE ACE QUIZ

Q3. Did an adult or person at least five years older than you ever...
Touch or fondle you, or have you touch their body in a sexual way,
or
Attempt or have oral, anal, or vaginal intercourse with you?

Q4. Did you often or very often feel that...
No one in your family loved you or thought you were important or special,
or
Your family did not look out for each other, feel close to each other, or support each other?

Q5. Did you often or very often feel that...
You did not have enough to eat, had to wear dirty clothes,
or
You had no one to protect you, or your parents were too drunk or too high to take care of you or take you to the doctor if you needed it?

Q6. Were your parents ever separated or divorced?

Q7. Was your mother or stepmother:
Often or very often pushed, grabbed, slapped,
or
Had something thrown at her or ever repeatedly hit over at least a few minutes or threatened with a gun or knife?

Q8. Did you live with anyone who was a problem drinker or alcoholic, or who used street drugs?

Q9. Was a household member depressed or mentally ill, or did a household member attempt suicide?

Q10. Did a household member go to prison?
Add up your "Yes" answers. This is your ACE Score.

Your ACE Score: _____

When compared to individuals with an ACE Score of zero, those with an ACE score of four or more were twice as likely to smoke, five times more likely to suffer from depression, seven times more likely to be alcoholics, ten times more likely to have injected street drugs and twelve times more likely to have attempted suicide. Most sobering is the finding that 64% of the US prison population had an ACE Score of six or more.

These findings highlight the stark link between childhood trauma and its subsequent effects on our adult lives. Each affirmative ("Yes") response correlates with a unique pain or grief experienced by the child or young person. In most cases, this grief remains in the unconscious for the rest of their lives unless it is addressed therapeutically and brought into conscious awareness.

It's also worth discussing two effects.

APPENDIX TWO: THE ACE QUIZ

First, individuals with a high ACE Score can partially recover through resilience and supportive relationships, eventually leading to a healthier life. However, without therapy and self-work, many of an individual's adverse childhood experiences may remain hidden.

Secondly, individuals with a zero ACE score might still suffer from depression, addiction, and suicidal thoughts due to unconscious and unaddressed pain or grief that may have been experienced by one or both of their parents. Therapies such as Family Constellation work or Jungian Healing Through Art can assist in identifying the sources of grief that have been passed down or inherited from our parents' adverse childhood experiences.

As leaders, and especially as parents, one of the kindest actions we can take is to 'do the work' - to take responsibility for our healing to mitigate our unconscious impact on our children and colleagues.

APPENDIX THREE
COST OF CAPITAL

CEOs like Merck & Co's Ken Frazier understand that when it comes to company-wide expenditures, there are three types of money: dumb money, smart money, and just money. Dumb money refers to expenditures that do not add value. Once the firm's opportunity cost, or Cost of Capital, is considered, investments classified as dumb money negatively impact shareholder returns.

'Just money' describes expenditures that neither destroy nor add value. After factoring in the firm's Cost of Capital, 'just money' investments have a neutral impact on shareholder returns. Conversely, 'smart money' refers to expenditure decisions that add value and positively affect shareholder returns, after the Cost of Capital is considered.

The Cost of Capital is the minimum rate of return or profit a firm must earn to generate value. A CFO calculates the Cost of Capital to assess the financial risk level and determine the viability of a business investment. Experienced managers understand that surpassing the firm's Cost of Capital is crucial to gaining support for their projects or proposals. The Cost of Capital is also significant to investors and analysts when determining stock prices and the potential returns on acquired shares.

The initial step in determining a firm's Cost of Capital is to calculate the cost of debt. If the firm has no debt, then the Cost of Debt is zero, and consequently, the Cost of Capital is equal to the firm's Cost of Equity. A CEO should only sanction investments in projects and initiatives that meet or exceed the firm's Cost of Capital.

If the firm has debt, the Cost of Debt will be the current debt interest rate (after-tax) multiplied by the proportion of debt to total assets. Consider the enterprise example in Habit Ten – Alternative Three, which has a 40% debt and 60% equity financing structure; the before-tax debt interest rate is 10%. With a tax rate of 30%, the after-tax debt interest rate is 7%.

Thus, the Cost of Debt is calculated as 2.8%, which is derived as follows:

$$\text{Cost of Debt} = \frac{7\% \times 40\%}{\text{Total Assets}} = \frac{280}{100\%} = 2.8\%$$

The second step is to calculate the Cost of Equity for the firm.

The Cost of Equity is the rate of return that must be earned on the market value of the shareholders' funds to maintain the current dividend and to provide for the annualised growth in both the dividend and the market price of the firm's shares. This calculation considers the volatility of the company's stock relative to the market. The Cost of Equity is more theoretical than the Cost of Debt and incorporates factors such as Beta (company-specific risk), stock market rates, and prevailing interest rates.

APPENDIX THREE: COST OF CAPITAL

The Cost of Equity formula is expressed as:

Cost of Equity = risk-free interest rate + beta (market rate – risk-free rate)

Beta measures the volatility of a company's stock relative to the market. According to investors, a higher Beta indicates a riskier stock. If a stock rises and falls at the same rate as the market, its Beta will be close to 1. If the firm's stock price is more volatile, rising and falling more than the market, its Beta might be closer to 1.5. Conversely, if it is less volatile, like the stock of a utility provider or consumer staple, the Beta might be closer to 0.75.

The market rate is the expected annual return on the overall stock market. While there is typically much debate about the exact Beta values, they generally result in a value between 10-12%. The risk-free interest rate is the return on a risk-free investment, such as a treasury bill, which is often between 1-4%. This figure is also subject to some speculation.

If our enterprise example above has a Beta of 1, uses 2% for the risk-free rate and 11% for the market rate, then the Cost of Equity equals:

2% + 1 (11% – 2%) = 11%

It is important to note the vital role Beta plays in determining the result. For example, if a firm's Beta were 2 instead of 1, the Cost of Equity would be 20% instead of 11%.

Finally, the firm's Cost of Capital is the sum of its Cost of Debt and its Cost of Equity:

Cost of Capital = Cost of Debt + Cost of Equity = 2.8% + 11% = 13.8%

While a CEO will only approve investments for projects and initiatives that exceed the firm's Cost of Capital, they also constantly challenge their CFO regarding the firm's Cost of Capital. They keep asking questions like:

What did you use for our Cost of Debt?

How did you come up with our Cost of Equity?

Why do we use a Beta of 1?

Why do we use 11% as the market rate?

CEOs understand that a firm can miss opportunities when it sets excessively high standards. This is particularly evident when the Cost of Capital leaves no room for risk. For example, Ken Frazier presided over renegotiations of the Cost of Capital for riskier R&D projects at Merck. Some R&D projects are so risky that adjusting the Cost of Capital to a rate that matches the project's newness can foster smarter financial decisions in the long run.

Setting a higher Cost of Capital rate builds a cushion. The extent of this cushion depends on a firm's risk tolerance. Risk-averse CEOs might increase the Cost of Capital even further, to as much as 15-20%. Conversely, if a firm seeks to stimulate investment, it might temporarily lower the Cost of Capital.

APPENDIX THREE: COST OF CAPITAL

When physical assets like large centrifuges and cooling towers are worn out, and replacements are needed at Merck, a much lower rate is applied to such investments. These types of purchases may be considered 'just money' decisions. However, when the replaced equipment is essential for the entire business's operations, such purchases quickly become 'smart money' decisions.

APPENDIX FOUR
CEO QUIZ

This 360-degree CEO Quiz invites colleagues and direct reports to provide comprehensive feedback on a CEO's leadership across the twelve habits.

The scoring for each question is as follows: a=10, b=7, c=4, and d=1.

Quiz scores provide insights into the CEO's effectiveness and help identify areas for improvement.

HABIT ONE: BUILD GENUINE SAFETY

Q1. How does your CEO show care for team members?
- (a) Regularly checks in and provides support.
- (b) Occasionally asks about my well-being.
- (c) Focuses more on work-related discussions.
- (d) Rarely engages in personal chats.

Q2. How does your CEO maintain trust within the team?
- (a) They are transparent and consistent.
- (b) Tries to be open but sometimes withholds information.
- (c) Prioritises company needs over transparency.
- (d) They are reserved and often keep information to themselves.

Q3. How does your CEO handle conflict in the team?
- (a) Encourages open dialogue and resolution.
- (b) Addresses conflict when unavoidable.
- (c) Avoids conflict, hoping it resolves itself.
- (d) Ignores conflict unless directly impacted.

HABIT TWO: ENERGISE MIDDLE MANAGERS

Q4. Does your CEO ensure women have an equal voice?
- (a) Actively promotes diversity and inclusive decision-making.
- (b) Supports diversity without specific initiatives.
- (c) Believes in meritocracy without particular focus on gender.
- (d) They still need to take steps to empower women.

Q5. Does your CEO hire people smarter than themselves?
- (a) Looks for talented people who can challenge and teach.
- (b) Tries to hire skilled people but sometimes feels threatened.
- (c) Prefers to be the most knowledgeable in the room.
- (d) Avoids hiring those who might outshine them.

Q6. How does your CEO choose their company at work?
- (a) Surround themselves with diverse, challenging thinkers.
- (b) Has a mix of perspectives.
- (c) Prefers people who agree with them.
- (d) Keeps a close circle that aligns with their views.

HABIT THREE: FOSTER DEEP EMPATHY

Q7. How does your CEO model presence in interactions?
- (a) Is fully present and engaged.
- (b) Usually present but sometimes distracted.
- (c) Often multitasks during interactions.
- (d) Finds it hard to focus during discussions.

Q8. How does your CEO coach the team?
- (a) Prioritises understanding perspectives and feelings.
- (b) Tries to be empathetic but focuses more on performance.
- (c) Shows sympathy when it is obvious.
- (d) Concentrates solely on business outcomes.

Q9. How does your CEO demonstrate care?
- (a) Demonstrates concern for personal and professional growth.
- (b) Cares about the team but sometimes prioritises tasks over people.
- (c) Occasionally considers personal needs.
- (d) Primarily focused on results and tasks.

HABIT FOUR: ELIMINATE POOR PERFORMERS

Q10. How does your CEO manage poor performance in the team?
    (a) Addresses it immediately and provides support for improvement.
    (b) They overlook it and hope things improve.
    (c) Rarely addresses it unless critical.
    (d) Avoids confrontation around performance issues.

Q11. How does your CEO promote valued behaviours in the team?
    (a) Leads by example and recognises those who embody these behaviours.
    (b) Occasionally mentions valued behaviours in meetings.
    (c) Falsely assumes the team knows the expected behaviours.
    (d) Has not clearly defined or promoted specific behaviours.

Q12. How often does your CEO question and challenge colleagues?
    (a) Regularly, to promote critical thinking and growth.
    (b) Occasionally, when necessary.
    (c) Rarely, to avoid conflict.
    (d) Rarely - stick to their views.

HABIT FIVE: ANTICIPATE FUTURE TRENDS

Q13. How well does your CEO scan the horizon for market signals and changes?
- (a) Proactively seeks out and analyses market signals.
- (b) Occasionally, they look into signals that are brought to their attention.
- (c) Focuses more on current operations than future needs.
- (d) Rarely considers the future beyond immediate business needs.

Q14. How does your CEO address established trends in your industry?
- (a) Identifies and communicates trends to the team.
- (b) Recognises trends but rarely articulates them.
- (c) Struggles to identify relevant trends in the industry.
- (d) Rarely pays attention to industry trends.

Q15. How does your CEO shape the organisation's future in response to trends?
- (a) Actively adapts strategies to align with trends.
- (b) Makes some changes but generally sticks to traditional methods.
- (c) Is hesitant to change current strategies.
- (d) Prefers to maintain the status quo.

HABIT SIX: ESTABLISH SHARED PURPOSE

Q16. How does your CEO communicate their vision to the team?
    (a) Clearly articulates a compelling vision and inspires others.
    (b) Communicates the vision, but it may need to be more inspiring.
    (c) Mentions the vision but needs to be more focused on it.
    (d) Rarely talks about or focuses on the vision.

Q17. How does your CEO lead by example to establish a shared purpose?
    (a) Consistently demonstrates behaviours that reflect your shared purpose.
    (b) Tries to embody our purpose, but only sometimes.
    (c) Occasionally references the purpose in their actions.
    (d) Rarely aligns their actions with a shared purpose.

Q18. How does your CEO promote confidence and commitment to a shared purpose among the team?
    (a) Actively engages and motivates everyone towards common goals.
    (b) Supports the team but could do more to motivate.
    (c) Focuses more on tasks than on fostering a shared purpose.
    (d) Does not prioritise building team commitment to the purpose.

APPENDIX FOUR: CEO QUIZ

HABIT SEVEN: KEEP COMPETITORS CLOSE

Q19. How does your CEO analyse and learn from competitors?
- (a) Thoroughly understands competitors and learns from them.
- (b) Keeps an eye on competitors but focuses more on the business.
- (c) Occasionally notices what competitors are doing.
- (d) Rarely considers competitors in strategy processes.

Q20. How well does your CEO know themselves and the company's strengths and weaknesses?
- (a) Has a deep understanding of our relative strengths and weaknesses.
- (b) Has some understanding but could know more.
- (c) Is not very aware of how we stack up against competitors.
- (d) Does not think about our position relative to competitors.

Q21. How does your CEO manage the competition in your industry?
- (a) Proactively strategises and innovates to stay ahead of competitors.
- (b) Takes some actions to stay competitive.
- (c) Reacts to competition rather than proactively managing it.
- (d) Does not actively engage in competitive strategies or tactics.

HABIT EIGHT: ENHANCE PERSONAL EFFECTIVENESS

Q22. How does your CEO prioritise self-care and manage stress?
- (a) Consistently practices self-care, self-love and stress management.
- (b) Manages stress but only sometimes successfully.
- (c) Occasionally thinks about self-care.
- (d) Rarely prioritises their well-being.

Q23. How does your CEO balance work and personal life?
- (a) Maintains a healthy work-life balance consistently.
- (b) Tries to balance, but work often takes precedence.
- (c) Struggles to keep work and personal life separate.
- (d) Work is the primary focus; personal life is last.

Q24. How does your CEO cultivate supportive networks?
- (a) Actively builds and maintains robust and diverse support networks.
- (b) Has a support network but could cultivate others.
- (c) They have a few people they rely on.
- (d) Rarely seeks help from a support network.

HABIT NINE: EXPLAIN THE STRATEGY CLEARLY

Q25. How does your CEO communicate the strategy to the team?
   (a) Articulates the strategy clearly and ensures everyone understands.
   (b) Communicates the strategy, but it may need to be clarified.
   (c) Discusses strategy occasionally, but it is not a priority.
   (d) Rarely talks about the strategy in any detail.

Q26. How does your CEO lead in times of crisis?
   (a) Takes charge effectively, providing clear direction and support.
   (b) Manages crises but could be more effective.
   (c) Is hesitant and sometimes unclear during crises.
   (d) Struggles to lead effectively in crises.

Q27. How media-savvy is your CEO when representing the company?
   (a) Very comfortable and strategic in media engagements.
   (b) Handles media interactions well but could improve.
   (c) Not very comfortable with media interactions.
   (d) Avoids media engagements whenever possible.

HABIT TEN: GOVERN RESOURCES PORTFOLIO

Q28. How does your CEO manage the company's resources?
- (a) Actively and effectively manages all company resources for optimal performance.
- (b) Manages resources well, but there's room for improvement.
- (c) Could be more involved in resource management.
- (d) Rarely engages in managing company resources directly.

Q29. How does your CEO integrate digital technologies like AI into the business?
- (a) Actively pursues digital innovation to enhance the business.
- (b) Adopts digital solutions, but not aggressively.
- (c) Cautious about new digital technologies.
- (d) Prefers traditional methods over digital solutions.

Q30. How does your CEO make investment decisions?
- (a) Consistently makes well-informed, strategic financial decisions.
- (b) Makes good financial decisions but could be more strategic.
- (c) Financial decisions are often reactive rather than proactive.
- (d) Not involved in financial decision-making.

APPENDIX FOUR: CEO QUIZ

HABIT ELEVEN: MENTOR DIRECT REPORTS

Q31. How does your CEO demonstrate humility and vulnerability?
- (a) Shows humility and openness to learning from others.
- (b) Tries to be humble but sometimes finds it challenging.
- (c) Occasionally shows vulnerability but generally maintains a strong front.
- (d) Rarely shows vulnerability or admits mistakes.

Q32. How does your CEO encourage critical thinking in the team?
- (e) Fosters an environment where critical thinking is valued.
- (a) Allows critical thinking but only sometimes encourages it.
- (b) Occasionally engages in discussions that involve critical thinking.
- (c) Prefers not to challenge things.

Q33. How often does your CEO conduct post-project or after-action reviews with the team?
- (a) Regularly conducts reviews to learn and improve processes.
- (b) Conducts reviews occasionally, but they are not a priority.
- (c) Rarely conducts reviews.
- (d) No value is seen in reviews.

HABIT TWELVE: MAXIMISE BOARD COMMITMENT

Q34. How does your CEO approach the composition of the Board?
　(a)　Encourages a wide range of backgrounds and expertise.
　(b)　Recognises the need for diversity but does not actively seek it.
　(c)　Sees diversity as a compliance issue, not an advantage.
　(d)　The Board is a homogenous group with similar views.

Q35. How does your CEO engage with the Board to ensure they are aligned?
　(a)　Has in-depth discussions with Board members and advisory groups.
　(b)　Updates Board and seeks input on significant decisions.
　(c)　Has limited ongoing interaction with the Board beyond formal meetings.
　(d)　Rarely consults the Board beyond governance requirements.

Q36. How does your CEO maximise the Board's commitment to the company's shared vision?
　(a)　Aligns the Board with the vision and involves them in strategic planning and performance metrics.
　(b)　Communicates the vision but could do more.
　(c)　Updates the Board on the vision and strategy in formal presentations.
　(d)　Does not actively engage the Board in the visioning process or strategy.

though they did not admit it.

APPENDIX FOUR: CEO QUIZ

APPENDIX FIVE
SCORE CEO QUIZ

Ensure each question is scored as follows: a=10, b=7, c=4, and d=1.

Quiz scores provide insights into a CEO's effectiveness and help identify areas for improvement.

Calculate your CEO Score = (Scores from Q1 + Q2 ... + Q36) = ?

Interpret your score.
Under 170: This book could be your wake-up call.

170 to 220: There is still lots of room for improvement.

221 to 270: This book will help you become a more caring, visionary or competent CEO.

271 to 320: Your leadership ability is an inspiration to others.

Above 320: You can safely give this book to someone else.

Review the questions you scored lowest on. Investing time and resources in these areas will increase your success as a CEO.

APPENDIX SIX
CYBER RESILIENCE

Cyber resilience is not merely a technical issue but a strategic one.

High levels of system availability are a strategic issue for CEOs and boards, as they directly impact a firm's operational continuity and resilience.

The notion of achieving 99.999% uptime, or 'Five Nines', encompasses a complex and multifaceted challenge that incorporates hardware, software, planned and unplanned events. This level of uptime, which translates to less than 5 minutes and 26 seconds of downtime annually, requires meticulous operational planning and investment.

Cyber attacks exacerbate the risk of failing to maintain high-availability standards, pushing firms into failure mode.

Involving boards in cyber resilience is paramount. By grasping the threat landscape, establishing a robust cyber resilience framework, and promoting a culture of cyber awareness through ongoing training and continuous enhancement, boards and CEOs can significantly fortify their organisation's defence against cyber threats.

Boards can opt for an integrated cybersecurity training platform.[212] These integrated platforms are built with offensive technology (OT) defence systems that offer value-added services such as penetration testing, red teaming, and incident response activities. Such platforms proactively identify and mitigate security risks, monitor for threats, and detect and respond to attacks while implementing security measures to minimise cyber threats.

Here are ten proactive ways boards and CEOs can bolster cyber resilience and effectively guard against, respond to, and recover from cyber threats.

1. Understand the Landscape

The initial step in boosting cyber resilience is comprehending the current cyber threats' landscape. Threats can vary from data breaches and ransomware attacks to more complex nation-state assaults. It's crucial for boards and CEOs to familiarise themselves with the most prevalent threats within their industries and evaluate their organisation's risk profile.

Such understanding is vital to prioritising cybersecurity initiatives and investments.

2. Develop a Cyber Resilience Framework

Developing a cyber resilience framework means establishing policies, procedures, and capabilities that tackle the entire lifecycle of a cyber threat, from identification and protection against it, to detection, response, and recovery from cyber incidents.

This framework should be woven into the broader business continuity and disaster recovery strategies.

3. Allocate Resources Wisely

Cybersecurity should be seen as a 'smart money' decision. It is an essential investment in your organisation's future and reputation. Appropriately allocating resources, budget, staff, and technology are vital for constructing and upholding cyber solid defences.

Boards and CEOs must ensure cybersecurity budgets align with their risk profiles and strategic aims.

4. Practise Active Risk Management

Active risk management entails identifying, assessing, and mitigating cyber risks. This includes regular risk assessments, penetration tests, and vulnerability scans to gauge the organisation's vulnerability to cyber threats.

Boards and CEOs should also integrate cyber risk into their overall risk management strategies, treating it as a board-level matter.

5. Foster a Culture of Cyber Awareness

Cultivating a robust cyber awareness culture throughout the organisation is among the most effective shields against cyber threats. This involves ongoing training and awareness sessions for all employees, highlighting the critical role of cybersecurity and the part every individual plays in safeguarding the organisation.

Boards and CEOs can lead by example, committing to cybersecurity in their deeds and communications.

6. Test Incident Response Preparedness
Even with the best preventative measures, cyber incidents can still occur. An effective incident response plan, regularly tested and updated, is essential to minimise the impact of a breach. This plan should clarify roles, responsibilities, communication strategies, and recovery processes.

Boards and CEOs should partake in incident response drills, ensuring they are ready to lead in times of crisis.

7. Form Partnerships with External Partners
Cyber resilience extends beyond internal measures to include collaboration with external partners, such as cybersecurity firms, industry groups, and governmental bodies. These partnerships can offer valuable insights, assistance, and intelligence-sharing opportunities.

Boards and CEOs should promote and facilitate external collaborations to boost their organisation's cyber resilience.

8. Comply with Legal and Regulatory Obligations
Adhering to legal and regulatory mandates is a fundamental aspect of cyber resilience. This encompasses data protection laws, industry standards, and various cybersecurity regulations.

Boards and CEOs must ensure their organisations comply with these stipulations and stay abreast of changing regulations to avoid legal and financial repercussions. A firm's legal counsel should be advised immediately in the event of a cyber breach, so they can provide timely legal advice.

9. Embrace Continuous Improvement
As the cyber threat landscape continually evolves, so should an organisation's efforts towards cyber resilience. This means regularly revising and updating cybersecurity policies, practices, and technologies.

Boards and CEOs should champion a culture of ongoing improvement, drawing on lessons from cyber incidents and industry advancements.

10. Utilise Cybersecurity Reporting and Metrics
Effective cybersecurity reporting and metrics are vital for boards and CEOs to understand their organisation's cybersecurity stance and make informed choices. This includes routine reports on cyber risks, incidents, and the efficacy of cybersecurity measures.

Boards and CEOs should identify key cybersecurity metrics that align with their strategic goals, allowing them to track progress and adapt strategies accordingly.

APPENDIX SEVEN
CREATIVITY

When resources are scarce or a firm is losing market share, the imperative to be creative kicks in.

In general, three killers of creativity must be remedied:

1. Inertia – an inability to adapt to change.
2. Entropy – in isolated systems, disorder increases.
3. Bias – a repeating preference to always think the same way.

Inertia - CEOs need to ask better questions, think differently, and patiently seek insight to combat inertia. Gaining insight takes time, as depicted in Figure A7.1.

Entropy - to regain order and avoid entropy, CEOs need to embrace diversity, share ideas openly and make superior decisions.

Bias - CEOs must lose their rose-coloured glasses and raise their consciousness to overcome bias. Bias can only be successfully addressed using a higher level of consciousness than the consciousness that created it.

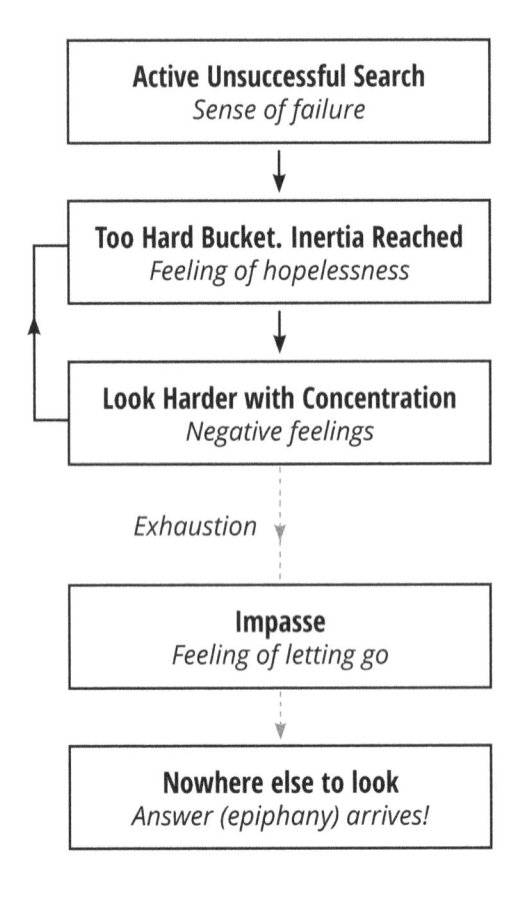

```
┌─────────────────────────────┐
│  Active Unsuccessful Search │
│      Sense of failure       │
└─────────────────────────────┘
              ↓
┌─────────────────────────────┐
│ Too Hard Bucket. Inertia Reached │
│    Feeling of hopelessness  │
└─────────────────────────────┘
              ↓
┌─────────────────────────────┐
│ Look Harder with Concentration │
│      Negative feelings      │
└─────────────────────────────┘
         Exhaustion ↓
┌─────────────────────────────┐
│           Impasse           │
│     Feeling of letting go   │
└─────────────────────────────┘
              ↓
┌─────────────────────────────┐
│      Nowhere else to look   │
│    Answer (epiphany) arrives! │
└─────────────────────────────┘
```

Figure A7.1 Insight Process

The consciousness of cultures and countries influences creativity. Rigid hierarchical nations, like China and Russia, prefer to copy. In egalitarian societies like Sweden, Germany and California, inclusive idea-sharing propels creativity.

On a blank page, jot down a list of the **Innovative Ideas** that make up your product, service or business model. Try combining what you do with seemingly unrelated things, perhaps inspired by nature, to

APPENDIX SEVEN: CREATIVITY

create creative and outrageous ideas and options for product, service or business model extensions.

Write down three new ideas that apply something that works in one area to another area. Suspend all judgment. Try finding new value and untapped synergies in the intersection of two opposites.

Pair mutually exclusive ideas in a new context.

Try reversing direction whenever a direction is implied.

Q1. What other ideas can you jot down?

List some widely held **Assumptions** about your industry, consumer behaviour and society in general. For example, banks are safe places to deposit savings, married people are happy, governments will care for the elderly, prescription drugs make life better, prisons reform criminals, fresh food markets are safer than supermarkets, and public and household Wi-Fi zones are harmless. Upon reflection, some of our assumptions may be irrational despite being commonplace and taken for granted by most people.

Q2. Can you push the boundaries of these assumptions so they break, bend or blend into new forms?

Q3. What new value could you add if innovative thinking successfully challenged and defeated these assumptions?

Write down areas where you may always have a competitive weakness. As an exercise, accept that you will never be the biggest, fastest, prettiest or most affordable.

Q4. What constraints could you use on yourself to narrow your firm's innovation focus to create something new in a rare and uniquely valuable way?

Jot down the innovative ideas from placing this constraint on your future design activities.

Reflect on your list of innovative ideas.

Keep imagining.

1. Schedule four one-hour meetings to share ideas with four other people from unrelated industries.
2. Take plenty of paper and 2B or 4B pencils and leave all judgements and preconceptions at the door.
3. Don't be lazy. Don't fear failure.
4. Remember, it is always easier to be a critic than a creator!
5. **Sharing and Brainstorming** with a diverse range of people who are removed from your business can enhance the value of the future you are creating.
6. Finally, when you brainstorm, make sure you spend most of your time brainstorming for better questions.
7. Better questions lead to better ideas.

APPENDIX SEVEN: CREATIVITY

INDEX OF ILLUSTRATIONS

Figure 1.1 Leadership Theory Matrix. 20
  Douglas McGregor.

Figure 1.2 Global Leadership Approaches 23
  Hale Consulting Group.

Figure 1.3 Conflict-Trust Moves 28
  Hale Consulting Group.

Figure 2.1 United Nations Gender Inequality Index 42
  Hale Consulting Group.

Figure 2.2 Dunning-Kruger Effect. 47
  David Dunning and Justin Kruger.

Figure 2.3 Estée Lauder Portfolio Map. 53
  The Estée Lauder Companies Inc.

Figure 3.1 Going beyond sympathy and empathy 70
  Rowan Hooper.

Figure 3.2 Empathy and Presence 72
  Hale Consulting Group.

Figure 3.3 CEO as Coach 76
  Adapted from Rasmus Hougaard.

Figure 3.4 Caring CEO Matrix 79
  Hale Consulting Group.

Figure 3.5 Spectrum of Human Emotions. 82
  Robert Plutchik.

Figure 4.1 Reed Hastings' streaming prediction was right. 93
  Netflix.

Figure 4.2 Netflix Pro Sports Team Slide 95
  Netflix.

Figure 4.3 Netflix Severance Package Slide 96
   Netflix.
Figure 4.4 Netflix Keeper Test Slide 97
   Netflix.
Figure 4.5 Netflix Hard Work Slide 108
   Netflix.
Figure 5.1 World Behaviour Map (1850 to 1950) 122
   James De Meo.
Figure 5.2 VUCA World View 126
   U.S. Army War College.
Figure 5.3 BANI World View 130
   Jamais Cascio.
Figure 5.4 Strategic Planning Cone 135
   Amy Webb.
Figure 6.1 CEO Game Gauge 155
   Hale Consulting Group.
Figure 6.2 Eisenhower Matrix 158
   Dwight D. Eisenhower.
Figure 6.3 Tesla Confidence-Performance Curve 162
   The Economist.
Figure 7.1 Opportunity-Win Matrix 174
   Pragmatic Institute.
Figure 7.2 BCG Marketing Matrix 177
   Boston Consulting Group.
Figure 7.3 Combat Tactics Table 181
   Hale Consulting Group.
Figure 8.1 Five Pillars Life Quality 206
   Peter Attia.
Figure 8.2 Brain Energy 208
   Adapted from Christopher Palmer.
Figure 8.3 Support Matrix 212
   Hale Consulting Group.

INDEX OF ILLUSTRATIONS: CREATIVITY

Figure 9.1 Apple Product Strategy Matrix 228
  Apple Inc.

Figure 9.2 The Apple Way 230
  Adapted from Stephen Covey.

Figure 9.3 Countries for iPhone Sourcing 233
  Adapted Geert Hofstede.

Figure 9.4 Herd Mentality Process 238
  Gustave Le Bon.

Figure 10.1 Investment Decision Matrix 257
  Lynn Elgert.

Figure 10.2 Growing Digital Wings 262
  Hale Consulting Group.

Figure 10.3 Corporate Digital Strategy 264
  Woerner, Weill et al., MIT.

Figure 11.1 Picking SEAL TEAM SIX 281
  US Navy SEALs.

Figure 11.2 The Five Temptations 287
  The Table Group.

Figure 11.3 After Action Review 290
  Dave Cooper.

Figure 12.1 Co-Designing with Country 311
  Adapted Jack Gillmer.

Figure 12.2 Consequential Decision Matrix 314
  Adapted Stuart Pugh.

Figure 12.3 McKinsey 7S Model 317
  McKinsey & Co.

Figure A7.1 Insight Process 378
  Adapted Jonah Lehrer.

GLOSSARY OF TERMS

ACE Survey: Adverse Childhood Experiences Survey is a research study that assesses the correlation between childhood trauma and well-being later in life.

AdSense: A program run by Google that allows publishers in the Google Network of content sites to serve automatic text, image, video or interactive media advertisements targeted to site content and audience.

AdWords: Now known as Google Ads, AdWords is Google's online advertising platform. It allows businesses to display ads on Google's search engine and other Google properties.

Affordable Care Act: Often referred to as "Obamacare," a comprehensive healthcare reform law enacted in March 2010 (as amended) aimed at expanding health insurance coverage, controlling healthcare costs, and improving healthcare delivery systems.

African American: An ethnic group of Americans with total or partial ancestry from any of the black racial groups of Africa.

After-Action Reviews (AAR): A structured review or debrief process for analysing what happened, why it happened, and how it can be done better by the participants and those responsible for the project or event.

Agile: A set of principles for software development under which requirements and solutions evolve through the collaborative effort of self-organising cross-functional teams. It advocates adaptive planning, evolutionary development, early delivery and continual improvement. It encourages rapid and flexible responses to change.

Anti-Trust: Laws and regulations designed to promote competition and prevent monopolies in the marketplace, typically to protect consumers from predatory business practices.

Apple Vision Pro: Apple's spatial computer that merges digital and physical realms, offering a boundless app canvas and a 3D interface navigated through eye, hand and voice inputs.

Aridification: The process of a region becoming increasingly dry and desert-like, often as a result of climate change, deforestation or improper land management.

Armoured Society: A term that refers to a society that is defensive and protective in nature.

ARPANET: The Advanced Research Projects Agency Network is an early packet-switching network and the first to implement the TCP/IP protocol suite. It is widely regarded as the predecessor to the modern Internet.

Artificial General Intelligence (AGI): Machine intelligence that has the ability to understand, learn, and apply knowledge in a comprehensive way that is not limited to specific tasks, essentially mirroring human cognitive abilities.

GLOSSARY OF TERMS

Artificial Intelligence (AI): Machines that are programmed to think like humans and mimic their actions. AI can refer to any machine that exhibits traits associated with a human mind such as learning and problem-solving.

Asleep State: The illusionary and unaware state of being in spiritual contexts.

Atlassian: An Australian enterprise software company that develops products for software developers, project managers and content management.

Authoritative Leadership: A leadership style characterised by individual control over all decisions and little input from group members, often leading with a clear vision and direction.

Authority Bias: A cognitive bias that causes people to attribute greater accuracy to the opinion of an authority figure and be more influenced by that opinion.

BANI: An acronym for Brittle, Anxious, Non-linear and Incomprehensible, describing a world that is less predictable and more fragmented.

BCG (Boston Consulting Group): A global management consulting firm known for its business strategy expertise and the BCG matrix, a tool for portfolio analysis.

Big Pharma: A term used to refer to the world's largest pharmaceutical companies, often with an implication of their having significant political and economic influence.

Bitcoin: A digital currency, also known as a cryptocurrency, that operates on a decentralised network of computers where transactions are recorded on a public ledger called a blockchain.

Blockbuster: The former video rental chain that was prominent before the rise of digital streaming services.

Board-Level Synergies: Collaborations and strategic alignments at the Board of Directors level in a company, aimed at creating value greater than the sum of individual efforts.

Brahmin: A member of the highest Hindu caste traditionally assigned to the priesthood and teaching.

Bricks and Mortar: A traditional street-side business that deals with customers face-to-face.

Buddha: Siddhartha Gautama, the founder of Buddhism, who achieved enlightenment and taught the principles of Buddhism.

Burj Khalifa: The second tallest structure and building in the world, in Dubai, United Arab Emirates.

Canva: An online graphic design platform used to create visual content such as presentations, posters, documents and other visual products.

GLOSSARY OF TERMS

Capacity to Carry: In finance, it refers to the maximum amount of financial burden a company or an economy can carry.

Captain Richard Phillips: The captain of the MV Maersk Alabama during its hijacking by Somali pirates in 2009, later portrayed by Tom Hanks in the movie "Captain Phillips".

Carbon Dioxide Emissions Per Capita: A measure of the amount of carbon dioxide emissions produced by an individual over a certain period, typically calculated on an annual basis.

Carrying Charges: In finance, these are costs associated with holding a financial position or physical commodities over some time, including storage costs, insurance, and interest on invested funds.

Cash Rate: The overnight interest rate that banks charge to lend money to each other; central banks often use it to control inflation and money supply.

Climate Change: The long-term alteration of temperature and typical weather patterns in a place caused by natural factors and human activities.

Climate Crisis: A term that emphasises the urgent nature of the impact of climate change, indicating a more immediate, serious, and threatening phase of climate change effects.

CNBC: A leading business news channel in the United States, providing real-time financial market coverage and business information.

Company Culture: The collection of values, expectations and practices that guide and inform the actions of all team members within a company.

Compaq: Formerly a sizeable American computer company that merged with Hewlett-Packard (HP) in 2002, known for its PCs and services.

Compassion: The emotional response when perceiving suffering and involves an authentic desire to help alleviate that suffering.

Consciousness: The state of being awake and aware of one's surroundings and having an understanding of oneself within the wider environment.

Cost of Capital: A company's cost of funding, whether through debt, equity or both, representing the rate of return that a company must earn on its investment projects to maintain its market value and attract funds.

CRM Systems: Customer Relationship Management systems are a category of software that covers a broad set of applications and software designed to help businesses manage customer data and interactions, access business information, automate sales, and facilitate customer support.

CSR (Corporate Social Responsibility): A self-regulating business model that helps a company be socially accountable - to itself, its stakeholders and the public.

GLOSSARY OF TERMS

'Culture Eats Strategy for Breakfast': A phrase attributed to Peter Drucker that suggests that a strong organisational culture is more influential than any strategic plan.

Data Science: An interdisciplinary field that uses scientific methods, processes, algorithms and systems to extract knowledge and insights from structured and unstructured data.

Debt-to-Equity Ratio: A financial ratio indicating the relative proportion of shareholders' equity and debt used to finance a company's assets.

Departmental Silos: A metaphor for when departments or management groups do not share information, goals, tools, priorities and processes with other departments.

Design Thinking: A non-linear, iterative process teams use to understand users, challenge assumptions, redefine problems and create innovative solutions to prototype and test.

Distribution Channel: The chain of businesses or intermediaries through which a good or service passes until it reaches the end consumer.

Domino Effect: The cumulative effect produced when one event sets off a chain of similar events, like a falling row of dominos.

'Dumb Money': Investments that do not return enough to cover the firm's Cost of Capital.

Dunning-Kruger Effect: A cognitive bias in which people with low ability at a task overestimate their ability.

Early Childhood Conditioning: The process of shaping a child's behaviours and attitudes during the early years of life, which are critical in developing personality.

Emotionally Safe: An environment where one feels secure to express emotions and be themselves without fear of judgment or harm.

Emotionally Unavailable Bosses: Refers to executives or managers who are not open to, or able to, engage with their employees' emotional needs or concerns.

Empathy: The ability to understand and share the feelings of another.

Empathy Fatigue: Emotional exhaustion resulting from the prolonged and intense emotional labour involved in caring for others.

Enlightenment: The realisation of one's true natural, beyond space and time.

Enneagram: A model of the human psyche that is principally understood and taught as a typology of nine interconnected personality types.

EQ (Emotional Quotient): A measure of a person's ability to recognise, understand and manage their own emotions and the emotions of others.

ERP System (Enterprise Resource Planning System): Organisations use software systems to manage day-to-day business activities such as accounting, procurement, project management and manufacturing.

ESG (Environmental, Social and Governance): Criteria used to evaluate a company's ethical impact and sustainable practices in its operations.

ESG Commitments: The obligations or pledges a company makes to operate sustainably and ethically in areas related to environmental, social and governance factors.

Executive Military Command: The highest level of command in the military, usually held by a senior-ranking officer who is responsible for making strategic decisions and managing military operations.

Fair Trade: A trading partnership based on dialogue, transparency and respect that seeks more significant equity in international trade. It contributes to sustainable development by offering better trading conditions and securing the rights of marginalised producers and workers.

Familial Homicide: Homicide in which the victim is related by blood or marriage to the offender.

FBI (Federal Bureau of Investigation): The domestic intelligence and security service of the United States, which also serves as its principal federal law enforcement agency.

First-Order Effects: The immediate consequences of an action or decision, as opposed to the longer-term second-order (and beyond) effects.

Five Digital Wings: Digital strategy framework created by Hale Consulting Group (HCG) to assist business owners and CEOs maximise the business value from in investment in technology.

Five Temptations of Leaders: A concept from a leadership fable by Patrick Lencioni that discusses common pitfalls leaders face that can undermine their organisations.

FLA (Fair Labour Association): A collaborative effort of universities, civil society organisations, and businesses committed to improving the health, safety and treatment of workers in global supply chains.

Foreign Exchange Cover: Financial protection tools against the risks associated with movements in the foreign exchange market, including hedging strategies like options and forward contracts.

Free-Throw Percentage: A statistical measure in basketball reflecting the ratio of free throws made to the total number attempted.

Frontline Employees: Workers who are directly involved with customers or the production of goods, often considered the face of a company to its customers.

Game Theory: A mathematical framework designed for analysing competitive situations where the outcomes depend on the actions of multiple agents.

Gen Z: The demographic cohort following the Millennials, typically defined as people born from the mid-to-late 1990s to the early 2010s.

Genital Mutilation: The partial or total removal of external genitalia or other injury to the genital organs.

'Get the Right People on the Bus': A concept from Jim Collins' book "Good to Great" emphasises hiring the right people for a team or organisation before deciding on a direction or strategy.

Gigafactory: Term popularised by Tesla, Inc. to describe its large-scale battery and electric vehicle component factories.

GII (Gender Inequality Index by the United Nations): A composite measure reflecting inequality in achievement between women and men in three dimensions: reproductive health, empowerment and the labour market.

Glass Ceiling: A metaphor for the invisible barrier that prevents specific individuals, often women and minorities, from rising beyond a certain level in a hierarchy.

Glassdoor: A website where employees and former employees anonymously review companies and their management.

Google Analytics: Google Analytics is a web analytics service offered by Google that tracks and reports website traffic. Currently, it is a platform inside the Google Marketing Platform brand.

GPT: Refers to the Generative Pre-trained Transformer, an autoregressive language model that uses deep learning to produce human-like text.

Greenwashing: A form of marketing spin in which green PR or green marketing is deceptively used to persuade the public that an organisation's products, aims and policies are environmentally friendly.

HIIT (High-Intensity Interval Training): A form of cardiovascular exercise strategy alternating short periods of intense anaerobic exercise with less intense recovery.

Hyper-object: A concept from philosophy that refers to objects massively distributed in time and space relative to humans.

IBM: International Business Machines Corporation, an American multinational technology company known for its computer hardware, software and IT services.

ICT (Information and Communications Technology): An extensional term for information technology (IT) that stresses the role of unified communications and the integration of telecommunications and computers, as well as necessary enterprise software, middleware, storage and audio visual systems.

GLOSSARY OF TERMS

Indulgence is a behaviour or attitude that allows oneself to enjoy pleasures; in a cultural context, it may refer to societies prioritising leisure and enjoyment.

Infinite Game: A concept from game theory where the game has no finite endpoint and the goal is to continue play and iteration, often applied to business strategies and life philosophy.

Intellectual Property (IP): Legal rights that result from intellectual activity in the industrial, scientific, literary and artistic fields.

IPO (Initial Public Offering): The process through which a private company can go public by selling its stocks to the general public.

IQ (Intelligence Quotient): A score derived from standardised tests designed to assess human intelligence.

Jeddah Tower: A skyscraper in Jeddah, Saudi Arabia, is the world's first 1-kilometer-high building.

'Jumping Ship': Colloquially, leaving a job or organisation suddenly, often to work for another, typically without warning.

'Just Money': Investments that return just enough to cover the firm's Cost of Capital.

Kaizen: A Japanese business philosophy of continuous improvement of working practices and personal efficiency.

Keeper Test: A concept used in business, particularly by Netflix, asking managers which of their employees they would fight to keep, helping to assess their value to the organisation.

KPI (Key Performance Indicator): An organisation's performance measurement to evaluate success in reaching targets.

Left Hemisphere of the Brain: The side of the brain associated with logical thinking, analytical skills and language processing.

LGBTQIA+: An acronym for lesbian, gay, bisexual, transgender, queer or questioning, intersex and asexual or allied individuals, with the "+" representing other sexual identities.

Limited Liability Companies (LLCs): Business structures where owners are not personally liable for the company's debts or liabilities.

Luxe Brands: High-end brands typically associated with superior quality, exclusivity and luxury.

Magical Feedback: A highly effective and surprisingly straightforward phrase that gives no information about how to improve but delivers a powerful cultural signal.

Marines: A branch of the military specialised in support for naval and army operations, both at sea and on land.

Market Capitalisation: The total market value of a company's outstanding shares of stock.

Massive Fleet Learning: A concept in AI and machine learning where a large number of devices or entities (such as cars in Tesla's fleet) learn from shared data, improving the system as a whole.

MBA (Master of Business Administration): A graduate degree focused on business management, covering various aspects of business such as accounting, finance, marketing, human resources and operations.

MCC (Model Coach Care Framework): A framework used in management and HR to structure the way managers interact with their team members, focusing on modelling behaviour, coaching employees and showing care for their well-being and development.

Meditation: A practice where an individual uses a technique – such as mindfulness, or focusing the mind on a particular object, thought, or activity – to train attention and awareness, and achieve a mentally clear and emotionally calm and stable state.

Meta: The new name for Facebook's parent company, reflecting its broadened scope beyond social media into areas like virtual reality.

Microeconomics: The branch of economics that studies the behavior of individuals and firms in making decisions regarding the allocation of limited resources.

Military Intelligence (as an oxymoron): This phrase is often used humorously to suggest that military intelligence is contradictory or incongruent, although, in practice, it refers to gathering information for a nation's defence.

Millennials (Generation Y): The demographic cohort following Generation X, typically said to be born from the early 1980s to the mid-1990s to early 2000s.

Mirror Neurons: Neurons that fire when an individual acts and when the individual observes the same action performed by another, thought to be related to the understanding of intention and empathy.

Mission Statement: A formal summary of the aims and values of a company, organisation or individual.

MIT: The Massachusetts Institute of Technology, a private research university in Cambridge, Massachusetts, is known for its strong emphasis on scientific, engineering and technological education and research.

'Mongrel': Commonly refers to a dog of mixed origin but can also be used metaphorically to describe a person who is uncharacteristically aggressive towards others.

Moral Compass: An internalised set of values and objectives that guide a person's behaviour with regard to ethical questions and decision-making.

Naval Special Warfare Development: A component of the United States Navy responsible for developing and testing special warfare capabilities and tactics.

GLOSSARY OF TERMS

NDA (Non-Disclosure Agreement): A legally binding contract establishing a confidential relationship between parties to protect confidential and proprietary information or trade secrets.

NEOM: A new cross-border city in the Tabuk Province of northwestern Saudi Arabia, that incorporates smart city technologies and functions as a networked tourist destination.

Net Zero: Refers to achieving an overall balance between emissions produced and emissions taken out of the atmosphere, typically in the context of carbon dioxide.

Neuralink: A neurotechnology company founded by Elon Musk and others, developing implantable brain–machine interfaces (BMIs).

OpenAI: An AI research lab consisting of the for-profit OpenAI LP and its parent company, the non-profit OpenAI Inc., focused on developing and promoting friendly AI to benefit humanity.

Operational Security (OPSEC): The protection of information critical to an organisation's mission is typically categorised under Operations Security (OPSEC), a practice refined by adept military commanders, CEOs, managers and other leaders in decision-making roles.

Osama Bin Laden: The founder of the pan-Islamic militant organisation al-Qaeda, known for the September 11 attacks on the United States and other mass-casualty attacks against civilian and military targets.

Outsourcing: The business practice of hiring a party outside a company to perform services and create goods that traditionally were performed in-house by the company's own employees and staff.

Pacemakers: Medical devices implanted in the chest to help control abnormal heart rhythms with electrical pulses.

Paid Maternity Leave: The period of time that a new mother is allowed away from work, with pay, after the birth of her child.

Paris Agreement: An agreement within the United Nations Framework Convention on Climate Change (UNFCCC) dealing with greenhouse gas emissions mitigation, adaptation and finance, signed in 2016.

Participatory Leadership: A leadership style that involves all team members in identifying essential goals and developing procedures or strategies to reach those goals.

Patent Cliffs: Refers to the expiration of a pharmaceutical company's patents on essential drugs, which may lead to a sharp decline in sales as generic competitors enter the market.

Patents: Legal documents that grant exclusive rights to inventors or their assignees to make, use and sell an invention for a specified number of years.

Patriarchal: Describe a system or society controlled by men or where men hold power and women are largely excluded.

Peter Attia: A contemporary physician focusing on the applied science of longevity, emphasising diet, exercise, sleep and emotional health.

'Pity Party': Informal phrase referring to an overly self-indulgent focus on one's problems and a self-pitying attitude.

Power Distance: A term used in social sciences to describe the extent to which less powerful members of organisations accept and expect that power is distributed unequally.

Predictive AI: Artificial intelligence systems that can predict future events or trends based on data analysis.

Presidents' Manufacturing Council: An advisory committee consisting of representatives from various manufacturing industry sectors to advise the US president on matters related to manufacturing and industry.

Price War: A competitive situation where rival companies continuously lower their products or services prices to gain market share and outdo their competition.

Prime Delivery: A service offered by Amazon that provides fast, free delivery for eligible items to its Amazon Prime members.

Prime Wardrobe: A try-before-you-buy service offered by Amazon that allows Prime members to try on clothing, shoes and accessories before purchasing.

Pro Bono: Professional work undertaken voluntarily and without payment or at a reduced fee as a public service.

Probability Trees: Diagrams used to represent and calculate the probabilities of multiple related events, particularly when sequential decisions are involved.

Queensland Law Society: The professional association for legal practitioners in Queensland, Australia.

Receivership: A type of corporate bankruptcy in which a receiver is appointed by bankruptcy courts or creditors to run the company.

Relationship-Based Trust: Trust arises from the personal relationships developed over time between individuals.

Renewable Energy: Energy from sources that are not depleted when used, such as wind or solar power

Reverse Mentoring Program: A program where junior employees mentor senior employees, typically on topics like technology, social media and current trends.

ROI (Return on Investment): A financial metric used to evaluate the likelihood of gaining a return from an investment. It is a ratio that compares the gain or loss from an investment relative to its cost.

GLOSSARY OF TERMS

San Bernardino Terrorist Attack: Refers to a terrorist attack that occurred in December 2015, when a married couple killed 14 people and seriously injured 22 others in San Bernardino, California.

SDGs (Sustainable Development Goals), United Nations: A collection of 17 interlinked global goals designed to be a "blueprint to achieve a better and more sustainable future for all" by 2030.

SEALs: Members of the United States Navy's Sea, Air and Land Teams, a special operations force known for their elite military capabilities.

SEC (Securities and Exchange Commission): A US federal agency that oversees securities transactions, activities of financial professionals and mutual fund trading to prevent fraud and intentional deception.

Second-Order Effects: Consequences of the consequences of actions, such as the indirect impact of events, may not be immediately apparent.

Sensitivity Analysis: A technique used to determine how different values of an independent variable affect a particular dependent variable under a given set of assumptions.

SEO (Search Engine Optimisation): Increasing the quantity and quality of traffic to your website through organic search engine results.

Severance Payout: A sum of money usually given to employees upon termination of employment, which is above and beyond any earned wages.

Shadow Self: A psychological concept introduced by Carl Jung refers to an unconscious aspect of the personality that the conscious ego does not recognise.

Shop Your Looks: Likely a reference to a service or feature offered by fashion retailers where customers can browse and purchase clothing and accessories that match a particular style or look.

Siren Song: A metaphorical phrase that refers to an appeal that is hard to resist but that, if heeded, will lead to a bad outcome.

Six Stages of Business Growth: A model developed by Hale Consulting Group (HCG) outlines the six phases a successful business typically goes through as it expands.

'Skin in the Game': A term used to describe a situation in which someone allocates their own time or money towards a prospective venture.

Smart Money: Investments that return more than the firm's Cost of Capital.

SMTP (Simple Mail Transfer Protocol): An Internet standard for email transmission across Internet Protocol (IP) networks.

Social Justice: A concept of fair and just relations between the individual and society, measured by the distribution of wealth, opportunities for personal activity and social privileges.

GLOSSARY OF TERMS

Solar City: A subsidiary of Tesla, Inc. specialises in solar energy services and is known for its solar panel installation.

Space Shuttle Challenger: The NASA space shuttle orbiter that tragically broke apart on January 28, 1986, shortly after lift-off, leading to the death of all seven crew members.

SpaceX: An American aerospace manufacturer and space transportation company founded by Elon Musk to reduce space transportation costs and enable the colonisation of Mars.

Stakeholderism: A system in which corporations are oriented to serve the interests of all their stakeholders, including employees, customers and the community, not just the shareholders.

Stakeholders: Individuals or groups that have an interest in any decision or activity of an organisation.

Starlink Satellite Network: A satellite internet constellation being constructed by SpaceX to provide satellite Internet access.

Stents: Small tubes inserted into the lumen of an anatomic vessel or duct to keep the passageway open, commonly used in managing coronary artery disease.

Stoic: This philosophy of Stoicism teaches the development of self-control and fortitude to overcome destructive emotions.

Strategic Mindset Process: A six-step process that helps boards, CEOs, and business leaders to future-proof their organisations, which is explained in The Strategy Book by John Hale.

Style Shuffle Feature: A feature typically found in online retail platforms allows users to indicate preferences on a series of images for a more personalised shopping experience.

Sun Tzu: An ancient Chinese military strategist, philosopher and author of "The Art of War," an influential work on military strategy and tactics.

Surrogates: Individuals who act on behalf of others.

Sustainable Capitalism: An economic system that maximises long-term economic value creation by reforming markets to address real needs while integrating environmental, social, and governance (ESG) metrics.

SUV (Sport Utility Vehicle): A motor vehicle category that combines elements of road-going passenger cars with features from off-road vehicles, such as raised ground clearance and four-wheel drive.

Talent Density: The concept of having a high concentration of talented individuals within a team or organisation, which drives superior performance.

Task-Based Trust: Trust built upon the consistent performance and completion of tasks.

GLOSSARY OF TERMS

Tesla Autopilot System: An advanced driver-assistance system feature offered by Tesla that provides a range of autonomous driving capabilities.

Tesla Roadster: An all-electric sports car produced by Tesla, Inc., known for its high performance.

The 7S Model: A management model developed by McKinsey consultants that identifies seven factors to organise a company effectively: strategy, structure, systems, shared values, style, staff and skills.

The Art of War: An ancient Chinese military treatise attributed to Sun Tzu, a military strategist and philosopher, highly regarded for its strategic thinking and applied in various fields beyond the military.

The Boring Company: An infrastructure and tunnel construction services company founded by Elon Musk to reduce traffic congestion through an extensive network of underground tunnels.

The Harvard Study of Adult Development: One of the world's longest studies of adult life, which tracked the health of over 700 men for decades, aiming to identify predictors of healthy aging.

The Peter Principle: A concept in management theory formulated by Dr. Laurence J. Peter, which observes that people in a hierarchy tend to rise to their "level of incompetence."

Theory X and Theory Y: Two theories of human work motivation and management proposed by Douglas McGregor. Theory X emphasises authoritarian management styles, whereas Theory Y highlights a participative style.

Third-Order Effects: In systems thinking, these are the impacts that result from the second-order effects, representing an even broader scope of consequences of a decision or event.

TikTok: A social media platform for creating, sharing and discovering short music videos.

Trusted Influencers: Individuals who have built a reputation for their expertise and integrity in a specific area, and who can affect the purchasing decisions of others because of their authority, knowledge, position or relationship with their audience.

UNIX: A family of multitasking, multiuser computer operating systems derived from the original AT&T UNIX.

Unlimited Vacation Policy: A workplace policy that allows employees to take as much time off as they choose as long as they meet their performance standards.

US Senate Permanent Subcommittee on Investigations: A subcommittee of the US Senate Committee on Homeland Security and Governmental Affairs responsible for investigating government and private sector inefficiencies, fraud and abuse.

Verge Consulting: Dave Cooper's consulting agency aims to transform organisational complexity into capability by recognising the diverse and interconnected nature of modern business dynamics to empower individuals, teams, and organisations to reach their full potential.

Vision Statement: A declaration of an organisation's objectives to guide its internal decision-making.

Vitamin D: A group of fat-soluble secosteroids responsible for increasing intestinal absorption of calcium, magnesium, phosphate, and many other biological effects.

VUCA: An acronym for volatility, uncertainty, complexity and ambiguity, describing the nature of some difficult conditions and situations.

Vulnerability Loop: A psychological concept where mutual vulnerability fosters closeness and trust between people, leading to deeper relationships.

Warren Buffett, The Oracle of Omaha: Renowned American investor, business tycoon, philanthropist and the chairman and CEO of Berkshire Hathaway, known for his wisdom in investing and for being one of the richest individuals in the world.

Wicked Problems: Complex problems that are difficult or impossible to solve because of incomplete, contradictory and changing requirements that are often difficult to recognise.

Xià Dāntián: In traditional Chinese medicine and martial arts, the lower dāntián located below the navel where one's qi (vital energy) resides.

Youth Dew: A famous fragrance for women that was launched by Estée Lauder in 1953. It is known for its rich, spicy and balsamic notes.

BIBLIOGRAPHY

Introduction

1. Johnson, M. *Family Village Tribe – The Evolution of Flight Centre*. William Heinemann 2005.
2. Bruce, R. *The Way of the Enneagram*. Enneagram Academy 2023.
3. www.loveoutloud.io

Habit One

4. Edmondson, A. *Psychological Safety and Learning Behaviour in Work Teams*. Administrative Science Quarterly, 44, Sage 1999.
5. Economist. *How to manage teams in a world designed for individuals*. Economist, 6 Nov 2023.
6. McGregor, D. *The Human Side of Enterprise*. McGraw-Hill 2006.
7. '*Culture eats strategy for breakfast*' is a popular quote attributed to Peter Drucker. To clarify, Drucker did not mean that strategy was unimportant. Implementing strategy in a robust and empowered culture is preferable to attempting the same in a weakened and divided one.
8. Kerin, P. *How long should CEOs stay?* AICD 2015.
9. Tversky, A., and Kahneman, D. *Judgment under Uncertainty*. American Association for the Advancement of Science, 1974.
10. Raffaella, S. Fuller, J. Hansen, S. Neal, P. *The C-Suite Skills That Matter Most*. HBR 2022.
11. McGregor, D. *The Human Side of Enterp*rise. McGraw Hill 2006.
12. Economist. *How not to motivate your employees*. Economist 20 Nov 2023.
13. Simmons, B. *The Book of Basketball: The NBA According to The Sports Guy*. Ballantine Books 2014.
14. Eisenberg, J. *How Gregg Popovich became the greatest coach in NBA history*. Forbes 2019.

15 Windhorst, B. *Popovich's approach to player rest and health has turned San Antonio into an NBA model*. ESPN 2018.
16 Coyle, D. *The Culture Code: The Secrets of Highly Successful Groups*. Random House 2018.
17 Simmons, B. *The Book of Basketball: The NBA According to The Sports Guy*. New York: Ballantine Books 2014.
18 Eisenberg, J. *How Gregg Popovich became the greatest coach in NBA history*. Forbes 2019.
19 Coyle, D. *The Culture Code: The Secrets of Highly Successful Groups*. Random House 2018.
20 Ibid.
21 Ibid.
22 Scott, K. *Radical Candor - How to Get What You Want by Saying What You Mean*. Macmillan 2017.
23 Meyer, E. *The Culture Map: Breaking Through the Invisible Boundaries of Global Business*. Public Affairs 2015.
24 Ibid.
25 Popovich finds foreign players to be less of a headache than their American counterparts.
26 Mills is of Torres Strait Islander and Aboriginal Australian descent. A culture that relies on a mix of relationship-based and authoritative leadership.
27 Yeager, D. S. et al. *Breaking the Cycle of Mistrust*. Journal of Experimental Psychology 2014.
28 Finette, P. *Expectations and Trust*. The Heretic 2014.
29 Yeager, D. S. et al. *Breaking the Cycle of Mistrust*. Journal of Experimental Psychology 2014.
30 Coyle, D. *Gregg Popovich Uses 'Magical Feedback' to Inspire the San Antonio Spurs*. TIME Magazine 2018.
31 Ibid.
32 Edinger, D. *Always Be Consistent and Always Innovate*. Coach Ed Science 2018.
33 Krippendorff, K. *Hide a Dagger Behind a Smile*. Platinum Press 2008.
34 Coyle, D. *The Culture Code: The Secrets of Highly Successful Groups*. Random House 2018.

BIBLIOGRAPHY

Habit Two

35. Lauder, L. *The Company I Keep: My Life in Beauty*. Harper Collins 2021.
36. Zaleznik, A. *Managers and Leaders: Are They Different?* HBR Jan 2004.
37. Kanter, R. M. *Men and Women of the Corporation*. Basic Books 1977.
38. Peter, L. J., & Hull, R. *The Peter Principle: Why Things Always Go Wrong*. William Morrow and Co. 1969.
39. *The Makings of a Beauty Tycoon: Estee Lauder is Born*. Evan Carmichael. com 2015.
40. Lauder, L. *The Company I Keep: My Life in Beauty*. Harper Collins 2021.
41. Turban, S. Wu, D. Zhang, L. *When Gender Diversity Makes Firms More Productive*. HBR 2019.
42. Bilimoria, D. van Esch, C. *Managing Cultural Diversity*. HBSP 2021.
43. www.worldpopulationreview.com/country-rankings/gender-equality-by-country
44. Ibid.
45. Dixon-Fyle, S. *Diversity wins: How inclusion matters*. McKinsey & Co 2020.
46. Lauder, L. *The Company I Keep: My Life in Beauty*. Harper Collins 2021.
47. Mc Meel, R. *Leonard Lauder Shares Eight Secrets to Leading the Estée Lauder Empire*. The CEO Magazine May 2021.
48. UNFPA. *Impact of the COVID-19 Pandemic on Family Planning and Ending Gender-based Violence*. UNFPA 2020.
49. UN Women. *What does gender equality look like today?* UN Women Headquarters 2021.
50. Our Watch. *The link between gender inequality and violence against women*. Our Watch Mar 2024.
51. United Nations. *United Nations Human Development Report* 2022-2023.
52. Sander, P. *An HR Lesson From Steve Jobs: If You Want Change Agents, Hire Pirates*. Fast Company 2012.
53. Lauder, L. *The Company I Keep: My Life in Beauty*. Harper Collins 2021.
54. Ibid.
55. The Economist. *The magic formula*. The Economist 8 Oct 2022.
56. Ibid.
57. McMeel, R. *Leonard Lauder Shares Eight Secrets to Leading the Estée Lauder Empire*. The CEO Magazine May 2021.
58. Israel, L. Estee Lauder - Beyond the Magic. Macmillan Publishers 1985.
59. McMeel, R. *Leonard Lauder Shares Eight Secrets to Leading the Estée Lauder Empire*. The CEO Magazine May 2021.

60 Bloomberg Television. How Estée Lauder Is Building on a History of Diversity. Bloomberg L.P. 2019.
61 Freda, F. Christensen, K. *CEO Spotlight: Staying Relevant in an Age of Transformation*. HBSP 2017.

Habit Three

62 Nadella, S. *Hit Refresh: A Memoir by Microsoft's CEO*. William Collins 2018.
63 Iqbal, M. *Time to Hit Refresh on Customer and Employee Experience Design Efforts?* Customer Think November 2017.
64 Nadella, S. *Hit Refresh: A Memoir by Microsoft's CEO*. William Collins 2018.
65 Gates, W. *Satya Nadella's Guide to the Future*. Gates Notes September 2017.
66 Gangaji. *The Diamond in Your Pocket: Discovering Your True Radiance*. Sounds True, 2005.
67 Poggi, I. *Enthusiasm, and its Contagion*. International Conference on Affective Computing. Rome 2007.
68 Hougaard, R. Carter, J. *The Mind of the Leader*. HBSP 2018.
69 Hougaard, R. Carter, J. *Compassionate Leadership: How to Do Hard Things in a Human Way*. HBSP 2022.
70 Dalai Lama XIV. *The Art of Happiness - A Handbook for Living*. Hodder & Stoughton 1999.
71 Griffiths, C. *The Creative Thinking Handbook*. HBR 2023.
72 Walker, S. *Negotiate Like a Pro*. HBR 2024.
73 Nadella, S. *Hit Refresh: A Memoir by Microsoft's CEO*. William Collins 2018.
74 Koutsoupaki, M. *Navigating the New Normal: COVID-19 Pandemic and the Rise of Generative AI*. International Curriculum Association August 2023.
75 Sharby, T. *People Don't Leave Companies: They Leave Managers*. Granite State College 2019.
76 Economist. *The Impossible Job*. Economist 28 Oct 2023.

Habit Four

77 Dey, A. *When Hiring CEOs, Focus on Character*. HBR 2022.
78 Gulati, R. *Netflix: A Creative Approach to Culture and Agility*. HBR Sep 2019.
79 www.ted.com/talks/reed_hastings_3_secrets_to_netflix_s_success
80 www.statista.com/statistics/1209552/average-time-spent-with-one-employer-in-europe
81 Ibid.

BIBLIOGRAPHY

[82] Stack ranking is a system used by some companies to evaluate their employees. In this system, employees are compared against each other and ranked based on their performance. Those at the top of the rankings typically receive more rewards, such as bonuses or promotions, while those at the bottom may receive less compensation or even face termination. It's intended to foster competitiveness and identify high and low performers within the organisation.

[83] Fleming, C., Parker, M. Ms SB [2014] The Fair Work Commission's first substantive ruling within its new bullying jurisdiction.

[84] Giang, V. *She created Netflix's Culture, and it ultimately got her fired.* Fast Company Feb 2016.

[85] www.jobs.netflix.com/culture

[86] Hastings, R. Meyer, E. *No Rules Rules: Netflix and the Culture of Reinvention.* Penguin Books 2020.

[87] Dusterhoff, C. Cunningham, J. *Getting rid of performance ratings: Genius or folly?* Cambridge Press 2014.

[88] Adler, A. "The chief danger in life is that you may take too many precautions."

Habit Five

[89] DeMeo, J. *Saharasia: The 4000 BCE Origins of Child Abuse, Sex-Repression, Warfare and Social Violence.* Natural Energy Works 2011.

[90] Ibid.

[91] Hale, J. *The Strategy Book – Cultivate a Strategic Mindset and Future-Proof your Business.* Ingram 2022.

[92] Taleb, N. *Antifragile: Things That Gain from Disorder.* Random House 2012.

[93] Economist. *A New Year's message from the CEO.* The Economist, 1 Jan 2024.

[94] Bruce, R. *Creating your Strategic Future.* Harper Business, 2000.

[95] Henderson, J. *BT Al-Saudia – driving digital transformations in the Kingdom.* BizClik Media Group Technology Magazine June 2020.

Habit Six

[96] Isaacson, W. *Elon Musk.* Simon & Schuster 2023.

[97] Golding, W. *Lord of the Flies.* Faber and Faber 1954.

[98] Collins, J. Porras, J. *Built to Last – Successful Habits of Visionary Companies.* Random House 1998.

99 Tesla official website - www.tesla.com
100 Ibid.
101 Bødker, S. *Effective CEO Communication: The Role of Speeches and Presentations*. HBR 2020.
102 Kurtzman, J. *Thought Leaders: Insights on the Future of Business*. Jossey Bass 1997.
103 Lencioni, P. *The Advantage: Why Organizational Health Trumps Everything Else in Business*. Jossey-Bass, 2012.
104 McGonigal, K. *The Upside of Stress - Why Stress Is Good for You, and How to Get Good at It*. Avery Publishing 2016.
105 Kahneman, D. *Thinking, fast and slow*. Farrar, Straus and Giroux 2013.
106 Riggio, R.E. *Listening to the Voice of the Employee*. Routledge 2016.
107 Bazerman, M. *Judgment in managerial decision making*. Wiley 2017.
108 Tannenbaum, S. Schmidt, W. *How to choose a leadership pattern*. HBR 2017.
109 Hackman, J.R. *Leading teams: Setting the stage for great performances*. HBSP 2015.
110 Adler, R.B. *Effective Communication*. McGraw-Hill 2017.
111 Kotter, J. *Leading Change*. HBSP 2017.
112 Kennedy, R. *The Power of Social Media for CEO Communication*. HBR 2016.

Habit Seven

113 Sinek, S. *The Infinite Game*. Portfolio Books 2019.
114 Krippendorf, K. Hide a *Dagger Behind a Smile*. Platinum Press 2008.

Habit Eight

115 Attia, P. *Science of Aging*. The Peter Attia Drive Podcast #248 2023.
116 World Economic Forum. *Women are more productive than men at work these days*. WEF 2018.
117 Parker, K. *Gender Pay Gap Facts*. Pew Research Centre, 2023.
118 United Nations Dept of Economic and Social Affairs. *World's Women 2020: Trends and Statistics*. UN 2020.
119 Lake, K. *Why Self-Care is Critical for Leaders*, HBSP 2020.
120 Kwik, J. *Limitless: Upgrade Your Brain, Learn Anything Faster, and Unlock Your Exceptional Life*. Hay House 2020.
121 Ibid.
122 Ibid.
123 Ibid.

BIBLIOGRAPHY

[124] Vaillant, G. *The Harvard Study of Adult Development*. American Journal of Psychiatry 2012.
[125] Waldinger, R. Schulz, M. *The Good Life: Lessons from the World's Longest Scientific Study of Happiness*. Simon & Schuster 2023.
[126] Attia, P. *Outlive: The Science and Art of Longevity*. Penguin 2023.
[127] Mental Health First Aid International. *Mental Health is a Global Priority*. MHFA International, 1 April 2024.
[128] Palmer, C. M. *Brain Energy: A Revolutionary Breakthrough in Understanding Mental Health*. BenBella Books 2022.
[129] The fifth edition of the Diagnostic and Statistical Manual of Mental Disorders (DSM-5) is a comprehensive handbook published by the American Psychiatric Association. It encompasses 20 broad categories such as Neurodevelopmental Disorders, Anxiety Disorders and Depressive Disorders. Each category on average comprises 10 to 15 primary diagnoses. On any given day, patients with fluctuating energy levels and persistent emotions may exhibit a variety of symptoms that could qualify them for not just one but typically many out of 200 to 300 unique diagnoses.
[130] Dr. Chris Campbell. www.drchriscampbell.com
[131] Lake, K. *How I Get It Done: Stitch Fix CEO Katrina Lake*. The Cut, NY Magazine 2019.
[132] Economist. *Executive coaching is useful therapy that you can expense*. Economist, 13 July 2023.

Habit Nine

[133] Kahney, L. *Tim Cook: The Genius Who Took Apple to the Next Level*. Penguin 2018.
[134] Frei, F. Morriss, A. *Storytelling That Drives Bold Change*. HBR, Nov-Dec 2023.
[135] Kahney, L. *Tim Cook: The Genius Who Took Apple to the Next Level*. Penguin 2018.
[136] Gallo, C. *The Presentation Secrets of Steve Jobs: How to Be Insanely Great in Front of Any Audience*. McGraw-Hill 2009.
[137] Gallo, C. *The Apple Experience: Secrets to Building Insanely Great Customer Loyalty*. McGraw-Hill 2010.
[138] Kahney, L. *Tim Cook: The Genius Who Took Apple to the Next Level*. Penguin 2018.

139 Merchant, B. *The One Device: The Secret History of the iPhone*. Brown and Company 2017.
140 VanHemert, M. *Apple Gets Roasted by Ricky Gervais During the Golden Globe Awards Show*. MacTrast 2020.
141 Mickle, T. *How Tim Cook Made Apple His Own*. WSJ 2020.
142 Maharani, D. *Implementing Ethical 'Code of Work Ethics': A Case Study of Apple*. Bina Nusantara University 2022.
143 Novet, J. *Inside Apple iPhone: Where parts and materials come from*. CNBC 2018.
144 Hofstede, G. *Dimensionalising cultures: The Hofstede model in context*. Psychology and Culture 2011.
145 Maali, Bassam, and Ali Al-Attar. *Corporate Disclosure and Cultural Values*. The Journal of Developing Areas 2017.
146 Hofstede, G. *Dimensionalising cultures: The Hofstede model in context*. Psychology and Culture 2011.
147 Meyer, E. *The Culture Map: Breaking Through the Invisible Boundaries of Global Business*. Public Affairs 2015.
148 Geradin, D. Katsifis, D. *The Antitrust Case Against the Apple App Store*. Journal of Competition Law & Economics 2021.
149 Voelcker, S. Baker, D. *Why There Is No Antitrust Case against Apple's App Store*. Latham & Watkins LLP Goettingen 2020.
150 Apple has instituted environmental report cards for all its devices in 2008.
151 Trindade, R. *Data Privacy as Strategic Competitive Advantage*. San Paulo Business School 202.
152 Jung, C. J. Hull, R. *The Archetypes and the Collective Unconscious Collected Works of C.G. Jung*. Taylor & Francis 1991.
153 'Social Media is the toilet of the internet.' - Lady Gaga on Jimmy Kimmel 2019.
154 Roni, S. Wilk, V. Jie, F. *Supply chain insights from social media users' responses to panic buying*. Edith Cowan 2022.
155 Warnock, A. *Copy and Paste: How Social Media has Intensified Mob Mentality*. Linfield 2019.
156 Gallo, C. *The Apple Experience: Secrets to Building Insanely Great Customer Loyalty*. McGraw-Hill Education 2010.
157 iPhone in Canada. Apple Ireland Tax Prompted by US Senate Tip-Off. iPhone in Canada 2016.
158 Isaacson, W. *Tim Cook: The Innovative Leader of Apple*. Simon & Schuster 2019.

BIBLIOGRAPHY

Habit Ten

[159] Neeley, T. *Merck CEO Ken Frazier discusses a COVID Cure, Racism and why Leaders need to walk the talk*. HBSP 2020.
[160] Ibid.
[161] Atsmon, Y. *How Nimble Resource Allocation Can Double Your Company's Value*. McKinsey & Co 2016.
[162] Bruce, R. McKern, B. Pollard, I. Skully, M. *Handbook of Australian Corporate Finance – Fifth Edition*. Butterworths 1997.
[163] Hale, J. *The Strategy Note*. Ingram 2022.
[164] Dunbar, R. *Neocortex size as a constraint on group size in primates*. Journal of Human Evolution 1992.
[165] Adapted from Woerner, S. Weill, P. Sebastian, I. *Future Ready: The Four Pathways to Capturing Digital Value.* HBSP 2022.
[166] Woerner, S. et al. *Future Ready: The Four Pathways to Capturing Digital Value*. HBSP 2022.
[167] Merck. *Merck Publishes Impact Report 2022-2023*. Merck & Co. 2024.
[168] Merck. *Innovation in the Fast Lane*. Merck & Co. 2024.
[169] www.merckgroup.com/en/news/two-ai-partnerships-in-healthcare-20-09-2023.html
[170] Merck. *Merck Announces the Launch of the Merck Digital Sciences Studio*. Merck & Co. 2024.
[171] Global Data. *Merck & Co., Inc. - Enterprise Tech Analysis*. Global Data 2024.
[172] ARC. *Merck & Company Drives New Product Development for Better Customer Outcomes*. ARC Advisory Group 2024.

Habit Eleven

[173] Coyle, D. *The Culture Code: The Secrets of Highly Successful Groups*. Random House 2018.
[174] University of Connecticut. *"David M. Cooper."* Office of External Engagement. Accessed Apr 2024.
[175] Ibid.
[176] McRaven, W. *Make Your Bed*. Penguin Random House 2017.
[177] Ibid.
[178] Navy SEALs. *SEALFIT – An Education from Admiral McRaven*. NavySeals.com 2024.
[179] Coyle, D. *The Culture Code: The Secrets of Highly Successful Groups*. Random House 2018.
[180] Ibid.

181 Ibid.
182 Ibid.
183 Quinn, C. *The Voice of Value with Chad Quinn: Speaking to Authority with Dave Cooper.* YouTube 2022.
184 Cooper, D. *Professional Biography of David M. Cooper.* Verge Consulting 2024.

Habit Twelve

185 Nooyi, I. *My Life in Full: Work, Family and Our Future.* Portfolio 2021.
186 Ibid.
187 Wikipedia. *Indra Nooyi.* Wikipedia retrieved Apr 2024.
188 Apumone. *Indra Nooyi Net Worth 2022, Age, Height, Family, Husband, Children, Leadership.* www.apumone.com/indra-nooyi-net-worth
189 Strategy Punk. *Indra Nooyi's Leadership Style: Key Insights and Impact.* Strategy Punk Retrieved Apr 2024.
190 Wikipedia. *Indra Nooyi.* Wikipedia Retrieved Apr 2024.
191 Ignatius, A. *Indra Nooyi, Former CEO of PepsiCo, on Nurturing Talent in Turbulent Times.* HBR November 2021.
192 Business Insider. *Here's how Indra Nooyi changed PepsiCo in her 12 years as CEO.* Business Insider India 2018.
193 World Finance Staff. *How Indra Nooyi changed the face of PepsiCo.* World Finance 2021.
194 Nooyi, I. *My Life in Full: Work, Family and Our Future.* Portfolio 2021.
195 Ibid.
196 Ibid.
197 Wiersema, M. Mors, M. *How Women Improve Decision-Making on Boards.* HBR November 2023.
198 Moon, E. *Firms with Diverse Boards Achieve Higher ESG Ratings.* HBR October 2023.
199 Pearlson, K. *Tool to Help Boards Measure Cyber Resilience.* HBR October 2023.
200 Peterson, R.Falcão, P. *Six Kinds of Board Members - and How to Influence Them.* HBR December 2023.
201 Yunkaporta, T. *Sand Talk - How Indigenous Thinking Can Save the World.* Text Publishing 2019.
202 Legends of America. *Native American Tribes List.* www.legendsofamerica.com/na-tribelist. Retrieved April 2024.

BIBLIOGRAPHY

[203] Emeneau, M. *The Brahman and the Mongoose*. Proceedings of the American Philosophical Society 1940. JSTOR 985117., p.507
[204] McKinsey & Company. *Enduring ideas: The 7-S Framework*. www.mckinsey.com/capabilities/strategy-and-corporate-finance/our-insights/enduring-ideas-the-7-s-framework. Retrieved April 3, 2024.
[205] Mootee, I. *How Indra Nooyi Turned Design Thinking into Strategy*. Harvard Business Review 2015.
[206] The Chair of the Board is often considered the penultimate stakeholder in the business hierarchy as the ultimate stakeholder is invariably the customer, whose needs and satisfaction are paramount to the company's success.

Conclusion

[207] Dolores Cummins. www.dolorescummins.com
[208] Dr. Chris Campbell. www.drchriscampbell.com
[209] Economist. *America's bosses just won't quit: That could spell trouble*. Economist 4 Sept 2023.
[210] Luecke, R. *Scuttle Your Ships Before Advancing*. Oxford University Press 1994.

Appendix One

[211] Dobson, T. Miller, V. *Aikido in Everyday Life - Giving in to Get Your Way*. North Atlantic Books 1973.

Appendix Six

[212] Cybergymiec. *Platforms Overview*. www.cybergymiec.com/platforms-overview. Enquiries: ohauptman@yahoo.com

ACKNOWLEDGEMENTS

I have learned a great deal about the art of leadership from many players on the world stage. The substance of this book includes empirical and anecdotal accounts of the leadership journeys of inspiring people who, through their dedication, make our world a brighter place. Thank you to Gregg Popovich, The Lauder Family, Satya Nadella, Reed Hastings, Mohammed bin Salman, Elon Musk, Susan Wojcicki, Katrina Lake, Tim Cook, Kenneth Frazier, Dave Cooper and Indra Nooyi.

Much of the inspiration for The CEO Book comes from the thought leadership of Harvard Business School, MIT Sloan CISR and the wonderful work of Daniel Coyle, the *New York Times* bestselling author of *The Culture Code*.

I am thankful to colleagues, mentors, friends and family for their willingness to read early drafts of The CEO Book and offer generous feedback: Rowan Gilmore, Marcus Van Vugt, Tony Ryan, Nash Campbell, Rob Bruer, Dolores Cummins, Claire Hale, Oscar Hauptman, Jane Oliver, Brad Reece, Hamish Cain, Shaun Conroy, Robert Bruce, Rebecca Hale, Joshua Lewis, Vicky Mills, Tom Smith, Ariana Doolan, Mario van Eck and Bryan Worn.

Finally, I would like to acknowledge my precious wife, Johanna Hale, for her love and patience during the creation of The CEO Book.

ABOUT THE AUTHOR

John Hale is the founder of Hale Consulting Group (HCG), a globally focused management consulting firm specialising in strategy, leadership and change. As a motivational speaker, John has delivered over a thousand talks in twelve countries across four continents, to leaders from Fortune 500 and mid-sized companies to start-ups and public sector organisations.

John has also worked as an early-stage investor and advisor. He is a Visiting and Adjunct Professor and has taught in five business schools, including Singapore Management University, Bond University and Melbourne Business School.

As a young child, John grew up in the developed and developing world. Living in both patriarchal and matrilineal cultures grounded him in the need for truth and justice as well as the ethics of care and co-operation. John brings a balance of sense and sensibility to his work. He currently resides in Australia.

HALE CONSULTING GROUP
VALUE DRIVEN STRATEGIES

Hale Consulting Group is dedicated to helping organisations of all kinds drive value through better strategy, leadership and corporate wellbeing.

Please visit our website and explore

Motivational Speaking: John Hale shares value-driven ideas and strategies with thousands of leaders each year at global forums, national conferences and company events.

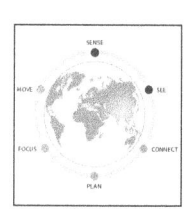

Consulting: HCG Consultants deliver strategy and organisational assignments for corporate, industry and professional groups, across a variety of industries in various parts of the globe.

Leadership Mentoring: HCG Consultants provide expert mentoring programs and executive coaching that empowers leaders and helps organisations advance in healthy ways.

www.halecg.com +61 407 301 200

www.ingramcontent.com/pod-product-compliance
Ingram Content Group UK Ltd.
Pitfield, Milton Keynes, MK11 3LW, UK
UKHW051902030625
6213UKWH00031B/728